High praise for

Type Talk at Work

Please turn the page for more extraordinary acclaim....

"*Type Talk at Work* takes the rich and sometimes complicated concepts of psychological type and turns them into easy-to-understand, practical applications for the workplace. Real-life stories are combined with the authors' extensive knowledge of type to offer the reader a realistic and intriguing guide to solving problems that arise between people at work every day." —BETSY STYRON, PRESIDENT & CEO, CENTER FOR APPLICATIONS OF PSYCHOLOGICAL TYPE (CAPT)

"Applying the chapter on Time Management alone has already made me money."
—ROBERT ANDERSON, CEO, MIDWEST HEALTH SYSTEMS

"Otto Kroeger Associates' work with our organization helped us see conflict in a more neutral light and *Type Talk at Work* helped walk us through that process."
—MARGARET GINNUS, HUMAN RESOURCES MANAGER, TECHSOLUTIONS.COM

"I had a fear of being boxed in by this theory, but the authors have shown great talent in explaining and transforming complex ideas into a simple, easy-to-use format. I will use this with my clients."
—KEISHA JACKSON, M.S., INDEPENDENT CONSULTANT

"I bought one copy [of *Type Talk at Work*] for the office, but we started fighting over it (until we re-read the chapter on Conflict Resolution). It is now a reference book for every desk—and a funny one at that!"
—BRADLEY J. ROTHING, CHIEF FINANCIAL OFFICER, COMPUTER DYNAMICS INSTITUTE, INC.

Dell Books by Otto Kroeger and Janet M. Thuesen

Type Talk
Type Talk at Work

Type Talk at Work

How the 16 Personality Types Determine Your Success on the Job

OTTO KROEGER
with
JANET M. THUESEN
and
HILE RUTLEDGE

A DELL TRADE PAPERBACK
A TILDEN PRESS BOOK

A DELL TRADE PAPERBACK
Published by
Dell Publishing
a division of
Random House, Inc.
1540 Broadway
New York, New York 10036

ISBN: 0-440-50928-9

Manufactured in the United States of America
Published simultaneously in Canada

August 2002
Previous edition published July 1993
RRH 10 9 8 7 6 5

CONTENTS

I: INTRODUCTION TO TYPEWATCHING

II: PUTTING TYPEWATCHING TO WORK

III: THE SIXTEEN PROFILES AT WORK

ACKNOWLEDGMENTS

Because this book involves people and their organizations, the list of those to whom we are indebted for their contributions could be endless, comprising hundreds of companies and thousands of individuals. We will refrain, however, and acknowledge only those individuals and organizations that deserve special recognition and thanks.

Susan Scanlon gave us license to borrow freely from her fine newsletter, *The Type Reporter*, the results of which appear among the boxes throughout this book. Her generosity has been a valuable contribution.

This book, like its predecessor, *Type Talk*, would not have happened without the efforts of Joel Makower. He is an unending resource who has a talent for crafting our rambling thoughts into the readable and intelligible work that follows. Sometimes encouraging, sometimes confronting and directing, but always pursuing excellence, Joel has been the driving force behind this project.

The people at Dell Publishing have been very supportive and insightful. Initially Bob Miller, then Jody Rein and Isabel Geffner, provided necessary guidance. Thanks to Andrea Nicolay for her guidance and support for this revised edition.

Two other clusters of people deserve special note. The first provided personal vignettes, which served as useful illustrations. Included in this group are W. Brendan Reddy; Chum Robert, an associate; Cline Frasier; John Orr; George R. McAleer, Jr.; and Tom Kaney.

The second group involves those who have read and commented on the manuscript, or some part of it. John D. Adams provided great help in the chapter on stress. Cal Voss, Chaplain Vincent Guss, and Marjorie Kelly, editor of *Business Ethics* magazine, offered their insights on the ethics chapter. John Clemons, of Hartwick College, along with James H. Johnson, James Sebolka, Andrew Ackerman, Janne Albertsen, Edvard Borbye, Vibeke Bruhn, and Mike Esnard, all read and reacted to the manuscript, providing valuable feedback.

So many of our clients have supplied data as well as the illustrative material. Over the years they have willingly allowed us to use them as "guinea pigs" as we together developed various interpersonal configurations aimed at growth, development, and increased organizational awareness. Among those organizations are American Telephone & Telegraph, Alza Corporation, Beatrice Hunt-Wesson, Bell Atlantic, AT&T Bell Laboratories, Cigna Corporation, Charles Stark Draper Laboratory, Equitable, Hoechst Celanese, General Electric, Hughes Aircraft, ManuLife Financial, McDonnell Douglas, SmithKline Beecham, Sovran Bank, Westinghouse Corporation, Martin Marietta, and the war colleges of the United States Army, Navy, Air Force, and Department of Defense.

Chances are, if you and your company have been involved with us over the past years, some part of you is reflected in the pages that follow. For that we are eternally grateful.

—O.K. and J.M.T.
Falls Church, Virginia

FOREWORD

It is so refreshing to look at our personalities in a way that helps us to understand one another with a credible and appreciative approach to our differences—to focus not on the right or wrong ways of being or behaving, but rather on understanding how our individual preferences impact ourselves and others.

The Myers-Briggs Type Indicator® approach has brought such insights to millions of people. It has enhanced our personal awareness and greatly improved our understanding of family, friends, and workplace colleagues. In fact, I attribute the salvation and success of my forty-year marriage in large part to the use of type. It has helped us reframe our differences—from difficulty into delight.

Over the years, Otto Kroeger and Janet M. Thuesen's Typewatching books have harnessed the power of the MBTI® to make an enormous impact on managers and leaders around the world. At hundreds of companies, *Type Talk at Work* has become a critical resource for understanding and managing people. This updated edition brings the authors' insights to bear on the overwhelming challenges that face organizations in the twenty-first century, in part through its significant new chapter on Typewatching and leadership.

More and more, the leaders of organizations are expected to understand today's complex working world in order to provide vision, motivate employees, and serve as the coaches for future leaders. Typewatching promotes the kind of awareness that greatly enhances our leaders' effectiveness when making choices that will impact a global workforce.

Translated effectively across cultures and into more than two dozen languages, the Myers-Briggs Type Indicator assessment has become a global tool. I have used the MBTI in working with organization leaders and managers in Asia, Europe, Canada, and, most recently, Cuba. In Havana I introduced the MBTI® for the first time, to much acclaim. Around the world, type proves itself a great gift to managers and leaders of countless organizations.

Otto, Janet, and the rest of us owe a profound debt of gratitude to Isabel Briggs Myers for bringing us this marvelous way of understanding people and ourselves. Only recently has she received the recognition due her. In September 2001, she was granted a posthumous honorary doctorate degree by Hartwick College. Isabel, who died in 1980, had once been sponsored for an honorary doctorate, but the ceremony was canceled at the last minute because it was deemed that her work wasn't rigorous enough to merit this recognition. On the occasion at which she was finally honored, Otto invited me to speak at a symposium entitled "A Celebration of Women by Women." To reflect the fact that Isabel, much like the tool she created, had finally risen above society's stereotyping, I titled my talk "Duped by Society—Up Until Now."

Isabel invented an instrument that has helped us create a better world. Thank goodness she used her energy, creativity, and intelligence in that remarkable way.

We owe Otto, Janet, Hile Rutledge, and their supporting cast at Otto Kroeger Associates our utmost appreciation for continuing and building on Isabel's legacy through Typewatching in general and through this book in particular. This updated edition of *Type Talk at Work* will continue to provide us and our organizations with new opportunities to understand ourselves better in today's increasingly complex world.

—Edith Whitfield Seashore
Organization Consultant
October 2001

HOW TO READ THIS BOOK

As you'll see throughout this book, different personalities can accomplish everyday tasks in very different ways. That's certainly true when it comes to reading books.

This book is divided into three main sections. Part One introduces the basics of Typewatching and can help you determine your personality preferences and explain how this self-awareness can help you in every aspect of your work. In Part Two we show you how to apply that knowledge and insight in the ten most significant parts of any business. Finally, in Part Three, we offer in-depth profiles of the sixteen personality types, revealing their strengths and weaknesses on the job.

Here are some suggestions on how to take advantage of all this information in a way that will satisfy your individual style and needs:

- If you're the kind of person who likes to share what you read with others and learns best by talking things through, we encourage you to do so. In fact, we recommend sharing some of the boxed material immediately with your co-workers. It will make for some lively discussions.

- However, if you're the kind of person who likes to reflect and contemplate on what you've read, that's perfectly legitimate. We encourage you to find some quiet, reflective place and time in which you can contemplate parts of the book and integrate them into your thinking.

- If you're the kind of person who likes to take things from beginning to end, with as few detours as possible, read on. We have presented this material in a format whose orderly progression should be to your liking.

- However, if you're the kind of person who enjoys scanning, occasionally jumping in when something catches your eye, then letting your imagination run wild, you will find plenty of possibilities on almost any page. Your scanning will be most effective if you lay a foundation by reading the first three chapters of Part One.

- If you're a natural skeptic, particularly when it comes to psychology and management theory, rest easy. This book is not going to "psych you out," and the theory upon which it is based has nearly fifty years of research behind it. As you'll see, the theory even encourages healthy skepticism.

- However, if you're the kind of person who likes psychology or other motivational materials that help people feel good about themselves and their accomplishments, you will find much to your liking here. But don't get carried away with the notion that happiness is its own reward. There's hard work to be done, and the principal goal of this book is to harness personality differences to get the job done.

- If you're the kind of person who likes things to be organized and to go according to a rigid plan, we recommend that you schedule a fixed time each day to read a section of the book. You will find that we have organized this book into bite-size chunks so that even ten minutes' reading will offer a complete thought.

- However, if you're the kind of person who resists plans and prefers to do things on the spur of the moment, don't worry if you're not able to read the entire book in a few sittings. Even if you put the book down for a few weeks or even months, you can apply what you've already read to your everyday work. But it is our sincere hope that you eventually get through the entire book.

As you can see, there are very different ways of doing something as simple as reading a book. And yet each way is valid. The process may be different, but the result is the same.

That's a central theme of this book: Our individual differences, when understood and appreciated, make everyone's contribution more effective and the organization as a whole more productive and profitable.

So read on—however you choose to do it.

I

Introduction to Typewatching

The Importance of People

"Would you mind doing this *our* way?"

We are so well intentioned. Nearly everyone, it seems, talks a good game when it comes to being open, accepting others' differences, and staying on top of our fast-changing world. If we were to ask you, "Will you be open with us?" or "Would you do this our way?" you'd probably respond, "Of course!" And you'd most likely mean it.

But life, as we know all too well, just isn't that simple.

Accepting others' differences is a difficult thing to do for even the most open-minded individual. One way that we deal with differences—in looks, behavior, attitudes, or anything else—is through name-calling: "He's such an *eager beaver.*" "She's kind of a *motor mouth.*" "He's as skinny as a *bean pole.*" And on and on. Name-calling is a convenient way of cataloging or labeling an individual's characteristics. It's one of the most natural things we do.

Nowhere does name-calling have more impact than at work. Our co-workers, bosses, subordinates, and customers provide a wealth of material for name-calling, whether we think these things or actually say them. That colleague down the hall who insists on bursting into your office every time he's got something to say, regardless of how little you may welcome the intrusion, is dubbed a *chatterbox.* That customer who insists on reading every word of every document—twice—is known as a *nitpicker*. The employee who always wants to do things her own way is called a *rebel*. And the superior who never gives you praise no matter how hard you work is referred to as a *coldhearted jerk*. And it isn't even time for your morning coffee break!

The fact is each of us has his own style, his own preferences, and his own ways of facing life's challenges. One person's *laid-back style* is another person's *lack of motivation*. Your thinking out loud is our *annoying distraction*. Someone's need to keep up with change is someone else's conviction to *not fix what ain't broken*. Those differences in style can lead to a great deal of misunderstanding, miscommunication, and resentment. And in the process feelings get hurt, communication channels break down, and a host of organizational illnesses proliferate, from absenteeism to alcoholism. Left unchecked, productivity and profits, to say nothing of morale, will inevitably plummet.

At work our good intentions are further tested by the increasingly diverse nature of our jobs and workplaces. Almost every imaginable culture and gender truth is being challenged. It's rare these days that someone stays with a company for more than a few years; we're almost expected to jump from job to job, and even career to career, over the course of our work lives. Everything about the workplace seems to be in flux: the technology, the language, our job descriptions, our ethics, and sometimes our very selves. Wherever you sit in your organization—at the top, middle, or bottom—the challenges are greater, the pace is quicker, and "the future" is closer than ever before.

The ability of some companies to survive and even thrive amid all this turmoil is directly linked to the degree with which employees and management communicate effectively with one another. We're not talking necessarily about an open and frank exchange of views, or about becoming best friends with your bosses, colleagues, and subordinates. We're talking about turning the many differences among us into powerful tools instead of divisive intrusions. We're talking about putting our good intentions to work in a way in which everybody wins.

We're talking about *Typewatching*.

Typewatching is a constructive response to the inevitability of name-calling. Labels are perfectly natural; that's how we distinguish one thing or person from another. Typewatching is based on the notion that as long as we're going to label one another, we might as well do it as skillfully, objectively, and constructively as possible. It is an organized, scientifically validated system that has been used for more than forty years by individuals and organizations that want to communicate better. It can be used in any workplace of any size and can be applied to a wide range of organizational activities, from hiring and firing to marketing and sales. With only moderate practice it can help bosses boss, workers work, managers manage, and salespeople sell. Best of all, Typewatching can be fun.

The more you learn about Typewatching, the more you will see that its application by no means ends when you leave work. Indeed Typewatching can be as varied and as useful as the people you encounter every day: friends, lovers, spouses, parents, children, neighbors, and veritable strangers. (Our previous book, *Type Talk*, an introduction to Typewatching, offers a broad range of everyday situations in which Typewatching can increase understanding and communication.) In our counseling, training, and seminars we have helped people make career changes, settle old scores with their parents (or children), straighten out their finances, even gain control of their eating habits. We apply Typewatching to everything, including friends, associates, children, pets, and the plans for our own wedding.

You needn't do that, of course, but there is a reasonable possibility that the more you Typewatch, the more ways you will find to use it. In fact, some people find it mildly addicting, although such an addiction isn't something to be concerned about. One of the great advantages of Typewatching, as we've learned over the years, is that it is a judgment-free psychological system, a way of explaining "normal" rather than abnormal behavior. There are no good or bad "types" in Typewatching; there are only differences. Typewatching celebrates those differences, using them constructively rather than to create strife. It enables us to view objectively actions that we might otherwise take personally. With Typewatching, the tendency for someone to be constantly late to meetings or appointments, for example, might

A BRIEF HISTORY OF THE THEORY OF TYPE

Typewatching's roots date back more than sixty years, when the Swiss-born psychiatrist C. G. Jung suggested that human behavior was not random but was in fact predictable and therefore classifiable. At the start Jung was out of step with many of his colleagues because he suggested that the categories he proposed, for which he coined some new words, were not based on psychological sickness, abnormalities, or disproportionate drives. Instead, Jung said, differences in behavior, which seem so obvious to the eye, are a result of *preferences* related to the basic functions our personalities perform throughout life. These preferences emerge early in life, forming the foundation of our personalities. Such preferences, said Jung, become the core of our attractions and aversions to people, tasks, and events all life long. (Jung's 1923 work *Psychological Types* brilliantly outlines his classifications. However, unless he or she is either a very serious student of psychological typology or a masochist, this book is not likely to appeal to the lay reader.)

Fortunately for Jung's work, two women, neither of them psychologists, became very interested in classifying people's observable behavior. One of them, Katharine Briggs, had begun as early as the turn of the twentieth century, independently of Jung, to classify people based on their differences in living styles. Simply put, she came to the conclusion that different people approached life differently. When Jung's works appeared in English in 1923, Briggs set aside her own work and became an exhaustive student of Jung's. With her exceptionally gifted daughter, Isabel Briggs Myers, she spent the 1930s observing and developing better ways to measure these differences. Spurred by the onslaught of World War II and the observation that many people in the war effort were working in tasks unsuited to their abilities, the two women set out to design a psychological instrument that would explain, in scientifically rigorous and reliable terms, differences according to Jung's theory of personality preferences. And so was born the Myers-Briggs Type Indicator® instrument. The idea behind the MBTI® instrument was that it could be used to establish individual preferences and then to promote a more constructive use of the differences between people. Jung's theory has become increasingly popular since the 1980s largely due to the landmark accomplishments of this mother-daughter team.

Today the MBTI is one of the most widely used psychological instruments. According to Consulting Psychologists Press, publisher of the instrument, more than two million people took it in 1990. The test has been translated into Japanese, Spanish, French, German, and many other languages.

be viewed as a typological characteristic rather than a personal affront or a character defect. Someone for whom following detailed instructions doesn't come naturally can be viewed in a more positive, constructive light. In short, Typewatching elevates name-calling from a negative, "put-down" tactic that mainly produces distance and distrust to a positive, healthy exercise with the potential for producing not just harmony but synergy at work as well as at home.

The Importance of People

The positive, people-oriented nature of Typewatching makes it an especially appropriate technique for the workplace of the 1990s and beyond, an environment in which human capital—people—is being increasingly recognized as one of the key ingredients for organizational success. Harnessing the power of that human-capital investment means relying more than ever before on relationships with customers, suppliers, employees, and oneself. These relationships are the building blocks of today's successful companies.

Take a look around your organization. Chances are it relies more than ever on manipulating information and providing personal services. To do these things effectively requires good work relations, teamwork, and employees who are motivated and cooperative. This relationship-centered workplace requires that you understand those around you—those above and below you as well as your colleagues, customers, and suppliers—so that you may connect quickly and intensely with them to solve the problems at hand. Success at any level requires that you must rely heavily on others and be tuned in to each individual's needs, preferences, and styles. Simply put, you must become a people expert.

Our failure to do this in the past can be directly linked to what has become a litany of discouraging statistics about the American workplace. It's difficult to read the business press without hearing, for example, that nearly half the workforce expends only the minimum effort needed to get by, according to the National Commission on Productivity, or that fewer than half of American workers think their bosses properly motivate them, as a survey by Wyatt Co. found out in 1987. Even worse news came from a national survey released in 1989 that found that fully 43 percent of American workers believe that "lying, putting on a false face, and doing whatever it takes to make a buck" are part of our basic human nature. And it isn't just the rank and file that is at issue here. A survey of four hundred managers' attitudes about trust and loyalty conducted by Carnegie Mellon found that fully one third of them distrust their own direct bosses and over half don't believe top management.

Is it any wonder that stress-related problems are costing American companies $150 billion a year in reduced productivity and increased absenteeism?

We aren't about to suggest that Typewatching will eliminate all of these problems, but we can assure you that it can go a long way toward helping you find solutions to your organization's present and future challenges. By dramatically improving communication and understanding, Typewatching will allow you to draw on your own organizational and individual strengths. It's truly amazing: With relatively little effort Typewatching permits intractable people problems to get resolved, longtime squabbles between departments to get ironed out, work-flow logjams to unclog, and chronically missed deadlines to get met. We've seen it happen time after time with our clients, which include Fortune 500 companies such as HSBC, AT&T, IBM, Ford Motor

Company, and Bell Atlantic; government agencies, including all four branches of the U.S. armed forces; and many smaller entrepreneurial firms.

What Typewatching Can Do

In some ways we're in the business of teaching people the obvious, of helping them to experience at a new level what they already know. As you'll see in the chapters that follow, there is practically no limit to the applications of Typewatching at work, from individual problem solving to restructuring entire companies. Here are just a few of the types of problems for which we've found it useful:

- There are some individuals who, by virtue of their personality preferences, are natural at engaging people and making them feel at ease and affirmed. But others of a different type, especially those of the opposite sex, can interpret that behavior as a sexual come-on. The result can be a flurry of miscommunication that can lead to anything from bruised feelings to mistrust to charges of sexual harassment. Similarly, other individuals' natural behavior to be cool and aloof can be misinterpreted as anything from simple disinterest to outright sexual or racial discrimination. By understanding others' behavior in typological terms, we can often avoid misreading their behavior by recognizing that, though different than ours, theirs is a natural way of relating.

- Some individuals are natural at responding to constantly changing situations. Their energy for completing tasks can come in last-minute surges. (These are the midnight-oil burners.) Unfortunately these individuals tend to start more projects than they finish, and it's not uncommon for them, if they make a list, to have more items on it by the end of the day than they started with. The result can be perceived by others (the list and PERT chart makers) as missed and stretched deadlines, lack of follow-through, and a general sense of chaos. Typewatching helps us to understand that this type's productivity is maximized when they're allowed to work in their own style. To try to "shape them up" will almost always create a no-win situation.

■ Another type of individual, one whose natural style is to generate ideas and inspire big-picture thinking, often rises to the top of organizations, or these people find themselves heading their own company or division. But such positions of responsibility also require a discipline and attention to details that they find not only unappealing but also extremely stressful. Their distaste for such specifics often leads to their avoiding dealing with them. In the long run these rising stars can burn themselves out. By understanding Typewatching, they might learn to delegate more freely or otherwise find some way of coping with something they know is not their forte.

These are admittedly brief scenarios, albeit everyday ones, and are only a taste of the rich variety of daily problems that Typewatching can address. But before we can offer more specific applications, it's first necessary to explain the basic principles behind Typewatching.

How Typewatching Works

Do you prefer people who are the same as you or people who are different? If you're like most people, you are initially attracted to people who are different, but over time you find that those differences don't wear well. In fact, whether with a boss, employee, or customer, after the initial attraction has subsided, you may find yourself quite intolerant of the differences. If you are in a position to do so, you might even demand that these differences simply be eliminated: "Shape up or ship out." If you are not in a position to make such demands, you may simply become distant and alienated.

It is interesting that we think we prefer differences yet in reality few of us make much allowance for them. Though we may say, and truly believe, "different strokes for different folks," we are nonetheless resistant to those who choose to "do their own thing." In an organizational setting, such nonconformity may be viewed as disloyal at best, dangerous or destructive at worst. But with Typewatching you will gain enough insight to understand the attractiveness of some of those differences and will develop the patience to allow them to exist for the benefit of the individuals—as well as the entire organization.

The whole process starts with understanding yourself. Typewatching allows you to identify your personal preferences and how you are similar to and different from those with whom you work. You can identify where those similarities and differences make for harmony and where they cause discord.

With that in mind, let's take a look at how your preferences are formed and what they mean for your life. Such self-insight is the key to Typewatching.

The Birth of a Type

According to typological theory, each of us is born with a predisposition for certain personality preferences. There are four pairs of preference alternatives:

Extraverted*	(E)	or	Introverted	(I)
Sensing	(S)	or	iNtuitive**	(N)
Thinking	(T)	or	Feeling	(F)
Judging	(J)	or	Perceiving	(P)

Keep in mind that these eight labels reflect *preferences*. By way of analogy, think of left- versus right-handedness. If you are

---

* While the preferred dictionary spelling of this word is *extroversion*, Jung preferred *extraversion*, which is the way it is spelled throughout his writings—and throughout type literature, including this book.

** The letter *N* is used to designate iNtuition because the letter *I* is already used for Introversion.

PUTTING TYPEWATCHING TO WORK

The applications of Typewatching at work are almost as unlim-
ited as the variety of people and situations you encounter every
day. By improving your understanding of the needs and behavioral
preferences of people in your work life, you can harness the rich differences of the people within your organization. Here are just a few
of the things we will cover in this book that Typewatching can help
you do better:

- **Conduct meetings more effectively** by allowing various points
  of view to be heard and differing needs to be met
- **Match individual potential with job requirements** by understanding individual strengths and weaknesses
- **Further your career** by similarly understanding and accepting
  your own strengths and weaknesses at work
- **Resolve conflicts more quickly and effectively** by defining
  problems in typological terms rather than interpersonal ones
- **Improve your interviewing skills**—whether giving one or getting one—by cutting through the hype to reach the real issues
- **Negotiate ethical differences** by understanding that each type
  views an ethical situation in a different way—and is convinced
  that his or her way is the only pure one
- **Break work-flow bottlenecks** by allowing each person to work
  according to his or her own style and everyone to know what
  everyone else is doing
- **Set more realistic and more widely accepted organizational
  goals** by including a broader range of different perspectives,
  needs, and ideas
- **Reduce stress levels** by understanding that what can excite and
  energize one person can stress and drain another
- **Meet deadlines better** by realizing that different types deal
  with time in different ways

right-handed, it doesn't mean that you never use your left hand. It simply means you *prefer* the right. And you may prefer it strongly, in which case you make relatively little use of your left hand, or you may prefer it barely at all, in which case you border on being ambidextrous. The same is true for the preferences listed above. You may prefer one characteristic a great deal and another only slightly. As we further examine the preferences, describing the two sides of each pair, you may find that you identify with both. Within each pair, however, there is one that you prefer—that you rely upon and to which you more naturally gravitate.

According to typological theory, each of us develops a preference early in life and sticks with it. And the more we practice those preferences—intentionally or unintentionally—the more we rely on them with confidence and strength. That doesn't mean we're incapable of using our nonpreferences from time to time. In fact, the more we mature, the more our nonpreferences add richness and dimension to our lives. However, they never take the place of our original preferences. So, Extraverts never become Introverts, and vice versa. (Back to the left-hand, right-hand analogy. Right-handers do not become left-handers, and vice versa. The longer they live, the more they may learn to use their nonpreferred hand effectively. But no matter how long a right-hander lives, he or she will never become a left-hander.)

Perhaps another way to view this is to liken an individual's type development to a house. Your type is like the foundation of a house: It doesn't really experience many radical changes through life. The rest of the house, and especially that part readily seen by others, can be likened to your behavior, the outward appearances of your type. Over time the house experiences many changes—an added room, a coat of paint, landscaping, interior renovations, and all the rest. The house, after twenty years of living, is changed significantly from what it was when it was built—but the foundation is still intact. So, too, with our personalities and behavior. Over the years we experience many changes and may appear to be considerably different to a friend we haven't seen in years. But like the house's foundation, our personalities remain pretty much intact, and the changes are, for the most part, merely behavioral.

This is not to rule out real change, growth, and development or to imply that we are all hopelessly rigid. But it does mean that change comes slowly to our more basic selves and that to effect change and growth in the malleable parts of our lives is a full-time job, day in, day out. Just to manage yourself and your own growth constitutes a busy day, never mind trying to "psych out" the rest of the world.

In fact, we maintain that the key to managing others effectively is to manage yourself first. The more you know about yourself, the more you can relate to others from a position of confidence, self-assurance, and strength. Hence, it is our intention in this book to direct your energy primarily toward yourself—where Typewatching skills can best be used to maximize every waking hour.

2

What's Your Type?

"Doesn't anyone care about what *I* want?"

The most effective way to determine your type is to take the Myers-Briggs Type Indicator. The material in this chapter will give you a good working framework that will enable you to obtain an informal determination of your own and other people's preferences. (If you already know your four-letter type, you may want to skip this chapter and move on to subsequent chapters.)

As this book unfolds, you will gradually develop an increasing understanding of your own preferences, as well as those of others. But to start out, we're going to give you some shortcuts to help you translate your everyday behavior in typological terms. By counting how many of the statements in each section you agree with, you will see your own preferences beginning to emerge.

As you read the statements below, you will find that you agree with some strongly, some a little, and some not at all. You'll also find that you may agree strongly with some of the statements attributed to, say, Extraverts, as well as some of those attributed to Introverts; the same will probably be true for each of the other three pairs of preferences. This is quite natural. Remember, what we're dealing with are *preferences*.

Each of us has some Extraversion and some Introversion (as well as some of each of the other six characteristics). What Typewatching is all about is determining which alternatives you *prefer* to use.

As we stated earlier, we'll be looking at four pairs of preference alternatives, the meaning of which we'll explain more thoroughly in Chapter Three.

Extraversion	vs.	Introversion
Sensing	vs.	iNtuition
Thinking	vs.	Feeling
Judging	vs.	Perceiving

First we'll deal with the way people prefer to interact with the world and the way they prefer to receive stimulation and energy: as Extraverts (E) or as Introverts (I).

IF YOU ARE AN EXTRAVERT (E), YOU PROBABLY:

- Tend to talk first, think later, and don't know what you'll say until you hear yourself say it; it's not uncommon for you to berate yourself with something like, "Will I *ever* learn to keep my mouth shut?"

- Know a lot of people and count many of them among your "close friends"; you like to include as many people as possible in your activities.

- Don't mind reading or having a conversation while there is other activity going on (including conversation or television or radio) in the background; in fact, you may well be oblivious to this "distraction."

- Are approachable and easily engaged by friends, co-workers, and strangers, though perhaps somewhat dominating in a conversation.

- Find telephone calls to be welcome interruptions; you don't hesitate to pick up the phone (or drop in on someone) whenever you have something to say.

- Enjoy going to meetings and tend to let your opinion be heard; in fact, you feel frustrated if not given the opportunity to state your point of view.

- Prefer generating ideas with a group to doing it by yourself; you become drained if you spend too much time in reflective thinking without being able to bounce your thoughts off others.

- Find listening more difficult than talking; you don't like to give up the limelight and often get bored when you can't participate actively in a conversation.

- "Look" with your mouth instead of your eyes—"I lost my glasses. Has anyone seen my glasses? They were here a minute ago"—and when you lose your train of thought, verbally "find" your way back—"Now, what was I saying? I think it had something to do with this morning's meeting. Oh, yes, it was about what Harriet said."

- Need affirmation from colleagues, superiors, and subordinates about who you are, what you do, how you look, and just about everything else; you may think you're doing a good job, but until you hear someone tell you, you don't truly believe it.

IF YOU ARE AN INTROVERT (I), YOU PROBABLY:

- Rehearse things before saying them and prefer that others would do the same; you often respond with "I'll have to think about that" or "Let me tell you later."

- Enjoy the peace and quiet of having time to yourself; you find your private time too easily invaded and tend to adapt by developing a high power of concentration that can shut out nearby conversations, ringing telephones, and the like.

- Are perceived as "a great listener" but feel that others take advantage of and run over you.

- Have been called "shy" from time to time; whether or not you agree, you may come across to others as somewhat reserved and reflective.

- Like to share special occasions with just one other person or perhaps a few close friends.

- Wish that you could get your ideas out more forcefully; you resent those who blurt out things you were just about to say.

- Like stating your thoughts or feelings without interruptions; you allow others to do the same in the hope that they will reciprocate when it comes time for you to speak.

- Need to "recharge" alone after you've spent time in meetings, on the phone, or socializing; the more intense the encounter, the greater the chance you'll feel drained afterward.

- Were told by your parents to "go outside and play with your friends" when you were a child; your parents probably worried about you because you liked to be by yourself.

- Believe that "talk is cheap"; you get suspicious if people are too complimentary or irritated if they repeat something that's already been said by someone else. The phrase "reinventing the wheel" may occur to you as you hear others chattering away.

Again, keep in mind that these are preferences. It is likely that you've agreed with some statements under each preference.

That's to be expected. Remember, also, that everything is relative. Some people may agree with every Extraverted statement and none of the Introverted ones. They are probably strong Extraverts. Others may agree with half the Extraverted statements and half the Introverted ones; their preference for one over the other is not as clear, although they probably do have a preference, if only a very slight one. There's nothing at all wrong with having a very strong or a very weak preference, or entertaining strong but inconsistent preferences. In fact, that's perfectly natural.

We can't emphasize enough that there are no right or wrong choices. The beauty of Typewatching, as we've already said, is that there are no good or bad types; there are only differences.

Now we'll take a look at the two ways people prefer to gather data: as Sensors (S) or as iNtuitives (N).

IF YOU ARE A SENSOR (S), YOU PROBABLY:

- Prefer specific answers to specific questions; when you ask someone the time, you prefer "three fifty-two" and get irritated if the answer is "a little before four" or "almost time to go."

- Like to concentrate on what you're doing at the moment and generally don't wonder about what's next; moreover you would rather *do* something than *think* about it.

- Find most satisfying those jobs that yield some tangible result; as much as you hate doing housekeeping, you would rather clean your desk than think about where your career is headed.

- Believe that "if it ain't broke, don't fix it"; you don't understand why some people have to try to improve *everything*.

- Would rather work with facts and figures than ideas and theories; you like to hear things sequentially instead of randomly.

- Think that *fantasy* is a dirty word; you wonder about people who seem to spend too much time indulging their imagination.

- Read magazines and reports from front to back; you don't understand why some people prefer to dive into them anywhere they please.

- Get frustrated when people don't give you clear instructions or when someone says, "Here's the overall plan—we'll take care of the details later"; or worse, when you've heard clear instructions and others treat them as vague guidelines.

- Are very literal in your use of words; you also take things literally and often find yourself asking, and being asked, "Are you serious or is that a joke?"

- Find it easier to see the individual trees than the forest; at work you are happy to focus in on your own job or department and aren't as concerned about how it fits into the larger scheme of things.

- Subscribe to the notion that "seeing is believing"; if someone tells you "the mail is here," you know it really isn't "here" until it lands on your desk.

IF YOU ARE AN INTUITIVE (N), YOU PROBABLY:

- Tend to think about several things at once; you are often accused by friends and colleagues of being absentminded.

- Find the future and its possibilities more intriguing than frightening; you are usually more excited about where you're going than where you are.

- Believe that "boring details" is a redundancy.

- Believe that time is relative; no matter what the hour, you aren't late unless the meeting/meal/event has started without you.

- Like figuring out how things work just for the sheer pleasure of doing so.

- Are prone to puns and word games (you may even do these things standing up).

- Find yourself seeking the connections and interrelatedness behind most things rather than accepting them at face value; you're always asking, "What does that *mean*?"

- Tend to give general answers to questions; you don't understand why so many people can't follow your directions, and you get irritated when people push you for specifics.

- Would rather fantasize about spending your next paycheck than sit and balance your checkbook.

Again, you probably see yourself as having some of both preferences. Everyone has some Sensing characteristics and some iNtuitive ones. Besides, it is quite natural for the same person to perceive things differently at different times. Every April 15, for example, even the most iNtuitive individual must deal with the specific hard facts and figures of income taxes.

As you read these statements and try to identify your preferences, you'll probably find some preferences emerging more clearly than others. This, too, is natural. You might, for example, be a very clear Extravert, a slight iNtuitive, a moderate Thinker, and a very clear Judger. In such a case, you'd identify with a lot of the Extravert and Judger statements and with fewer of the other two.

Next we'll look at how people prefer to make decisions: as Thinkers (T) or as Feelers (F).

IF YOU ARE A THINKER (T), YOU PROBABLY:

- Are able to stay cool, calm, and objective in situations when everyone else is upset.

- Would rather settle a dispute based on what is fair and truthful than on what will make people happy.

- Enjoy proving a point for the sake of clarity; it's not beyond you to argue both sides in a discussion simply to expand your intellectual horizons.

- Are more firm-minded than gentle-hearted; if you disagree with people, you would rather tell them than say nothing and let them think they're right.

- Pride yourself on your objectivity despite the fact that some people accuse you of being cold and uncaring; you know this couldn't be further from the truth.

- Don't mind making difficult decisions and can't understand why so many people get upset about things that aren't relevant to the issue at hand.

- Think it's more important to be right than liked; you don't believe it is necessary to like people in order to be able to work with them and do a good job.

- Are impressed with and lend more credence to things that are logical and scientific; until you receive more information to justify Typewatching's benefits, for example, you are skeptical about what it can do.

- Remember numbers and figures more readily than faces and names.

IF YOU ARE A FEELER (F), YOU PROBABLY:

- Consider a "good decision" one that takes others' feelings into account.

- Feel that "love" cannot be defined; you take great offense at those who try to do so.

- Will overextend yourself meeting other people's needs; you'll do almost anything to accommodate others, even at the expense of your own comfort.

- Put yourself in other people's moccasins; you are likely to be the one in a meeting who asks, "How will this affect the people involved?"

- Enjoy providing needed services to people although you find that some people take advantage of you.

- Find yourself wondering, "Doesn't anyone care about what *I* want?" although you may have difficulty actually saying this to anyone.

- Won't hesitate to take back something you've said that you perceive has offended someone; as a result you're accused of being wishy-washy.

- Prefer harmony over clarity; you are embarrassed by conflict and will try to either avoid it ("Let's change the subject") or smother it ("Let's all shake hands and be friends").

Interestingly enough, Thinking and Feeling are the only two preferences that have gender-related issues. About two thirds of all males are Thinkers, and about the same proportion of females are Feelers. Again, this is neither good nor bad, right nor wrong. And not conforming to your sex's preference is also neither good nor bad (though it may be inconvenient at times). We'll get into this much more in subsequent chapters.

As you continue reading through these statements, you should consider checking your self-perceptions against a mate's or colleague's perception of you. Sometimes others see us in ways we can't see ourselves.

Now on to the last set of preferences, which pertain to how people prefer to orient their lives—as structured and organized Judgers (J) or as spontaneous and adaptive Perceivers (P). Among other things, this preference determines what you most naturally share when you first open your mouth.

IF YOU ARE A JUDGER (J), YOU PROBABLY:

- Are always waiting for others, who never seem to be on time.

- Have a place for everything and aren't satisfied until everything is in its place.

- "Know" that if everyone would simply do what they're supposed to do (and when they're supposed to do it), the world would be a better place.

- Wake up in the morning and know fairly well what your day is going to be like; you have a schedule and follow it and can become unraveled if things don't go as planned.

- Don't like surprises, and make this well known to everyone.

- Keep lists and use them; if you do something that's not on your list, you may even add it to the list just so you can cross it off.

- Thrive on order; you have a special system for keeping things on your desk, in your files, and on your walls.

- Are accused of being angry when you're not; you're only stating your opinion.

■ Like to work things through to completion and get them out of the way, even if you know you're going to have to do something over again later to get it right.

IF YOU ARE A PERCEIVER (P), YOU PROBABLY:

■ Are easily distracted; you can get "lost" between the front door and the car.

■ Love to explore the unknown, even if it's something as simple as a new route home from work.

■ Don't plan a task but wait and see what it demands; people accuse you of being disorganized, although you know better.

■ Have to depend on last-minute spurts of energy to meet deadlines; you usually make the deadline, although you may drive everyone else crazy in the process.

■ Don't believe that "neatness counts," even though you would prefer to have things in order; what's important is creativity, spontaneity, and responsiveness.

■ Turn most work into play; if it can't be made into fun, it probably isn't worth doing.

■ Change the subject often in conversations; the new topic can be anything that enters your mind or walks into the room.

■ Don't like to be pinned down about most things; you'd rather keep your options open.

■ Tend usually to make things less than definite from time to time, but not always—it depends.

Did you agree with more of the Extraverted statements than the Introverted ones? If so, enter *E* on the first line below; if you agreed with more Introverted statements, enter *I*. Then do the same with each of the other three pairs of preferences.

E or I   S or N   T or F   J or P

_____   _____   _____   _____

These letters shouldn't be carved in stone—or even written in ink. You may want to verify your results by turning to the profiles in Part Three and reading your four-letter profile. As you read through the rest of the book and hone your Typewatching skills, you may find yourself erasing one or more of these letters, because you'll be increasing your knowledge of how each of the eight preferences comes into play in a variety of situations, as well as gaining a fuller understanding of your own preferences—and how to use them constructively through Typewatching.

3

The ABCs of Type

"Would you please look with your *eyes* instead of your *mouth*?"

To the uninitiated the alphabet soup of type can be confusing, to say the least. But with a little time and patience, it can become second nature. As with most other new skills—from speed-reading to speaking French—practice makes perfect.

What do all these letters mean? To understand the basic components of typology requires a brief understanding of some basic principles.

In the world of psychological type there are four basic preferences:

■ The first has to do with where you get your energy—from outside yourself (Extraversion) or from within yourself (Introversion).

■ The second has to do with how you gather information about your world—in a literal, sequential way (Sensing) or in a more figurative, random way (iNtuition).

■ The third relates to the way you prefer to make decisions—objectively and impersonally (Thinking) or subjectively and interpersonally (Feeling).

- The last has to do with your day-to-day lifestyle—do you prefer to be decisive and planned (Judging) or flexible and spontaneous (Perceiving).

Let's take a look at each pair of preferences.

Where You Get Your Energy: Extraverts vs. Introverts

This first preference determines how and where you perform some of your most basic personality functions. According to type theory, each of us prefers to do this in one of the following ways:

- As you observe and make decisions about your world, do you *verbalize* much of what you are observing and deciding—that is, do you prefer to do these things in the outer world of other people? Do you tend to open mouth and then engage brain? Are you energized by *people* and *action*? Do you become drained if you spend too much time by yourself? Would you rather *talk* than listen? Do you tend to leave meetings saying, "Will I ever learn to keep my mouth shut?" If so, you are probably an Extravert, designated by the letter *E*. You are an Extravert if words like *lively* or *popular* are more to your liking than *calm* and *private*.

- Or would you rather keep your observations and decisions inside? Are you energized by *thoughts* and *ideas* but drained by intense discussions? Would you rather *listen* than talk? Do you often leave a meeting thinking, "Why didn't I say . . ."? If so, you likely have a preference for Introversion, designated by the letter *I*. You are an Introvert if you find it necessary to "recharge"—to be alone with yourself and your thoughts—after spending a few hours with one or several people.

In American society Introverts are outnumbered about three to one by Extraverts. As a result Introverts must develop extra coping skills early in life because there will be an inordinate amount of pressure on them to "shape up," to act like the rest of the world. Classroom teachers unwittingly pressure Introverts by announcing that "one third of your grade will be based on classroom participation." Such statements automatically tilt an otherwise level playing field in the Extravert's favor. At work Extraverts monopolize meetings, wow the opposition with their social skills, and otherwise gain far more attention than they often deserve. Of course this does not mean they are more successful at what they do, as we shall repeatedly see throughout this book.

The fact is, Extraverts can be a problem even to other Extraverts. For example, those who lose something—be it the storeroom keys or their train of thought—want to "talk their way back" until they find it. ("Now, what was I saying? Let's see, I was talking about that meeting I had with Stanley last week in which he told me about Harry and Alice. By the way, did you hear that Denise is pregnant? That means Don will probably get her job, which means—Oh, yes. I was talking about Don's assistant, Steve, who wants to meet with us about the new contract.") In doing so, the Extravert not only invades everyone's space but often fills the air with seemingly empty words. It's at this point that the Introvert, with some sense of righteousness, jumps in with something like "Would you please look with your *eyes* instead of your *mouth*?"

Extraverts can be particularly difficult for Introverts to put up with. Consider what happens when an Introvert needs time alone. Typically Extraverts not only invade that time, they may actually try to take it away. It's not uncommon, for example, for an Extravert parent to force an Introverted child to play with others ("What are you *doing* up there alone in your room?") or for an Extraverted boss to force Introverted employees to engage in group discussion or some other Extraverted activity. In management circles we see such things as Introverts working in "bullpens" divided at most by short partitions, no floor-to-ceiling walls. Ironically such environments, designed to facilitate worker productivity, facilitate mostly headaches for the Introverts, who

ANOTHER MEANINGFUL DIALOGUE

Introvert to Extravert: "Excuse me for talking while you were interrupting."

need space to themselves to reflect on things and sift through information. Such "alone time" is essential to Introverts for making good, clear decisions. They don't want someone else's phone calls or conversations to be an invasion of their space.

Not that Introverts do all the suffering. The opposite problem occurs when an Extraverted manager who had made it to the top is rewarded with a private office and a door that closes, shutting him or her off from all the other workers who have provided the inspiration and energy for the rise to the top! This is the manager who establishes an "open-door policy," who makes employees feel guilty for not "stopping in," and manages by walking around; often, he or she may be found running down the hall glad-handing whoever is within arm's length, finding out "what's going on," often minding everyone's business but you-know-who's.

What's important to remember is that both kinds of behavior are perfectly normal, depending on who's doing the behaving. It is from their respective behaviors that Introverts and Extraverts draw their energies and strength. And for anyone of either type to operate for too long a period outside their preferred attitude, regardless of how successful one becomes at it, is ultimately bad news.

The litany of Introvert-Extravert problems is unending. Extraverts, for example, typically need a great many more overt "strokes" than Introverts. Introverts, in contrast, tend to be suspicious of those same overt "strokes." True, both need affirmation, but too much affirmation makes the Introvert wonder why so much is needed, while to the Extravert "too much affirmation" is a contradiction in terms. As a result Extraverted managers tend to overpraise employees; the other Extravert recipients of the praise love it, but the Introverts begin to wonder if such praise isn't superficial, unnecessary, or maybe even phony. This can in turn make praisers feel uneasy and wonder "whether it's worth it" to proffer such praise, though their natural tendency would be to pile it on. Conversely, Introverted managers often refrain from stroking, even when they know that their employees would like it, because they feel like phonies doing it. This in turn makes the Extravert feel rejected or at best unappreciated. Both are being true to their respective types while sending the wrong signals to each other.

It's simply amazing to watch a true-blue Extravert at work. Witness it for yourself: An Extravert will walk into a room, present a situation, ask for an opinion, arrive at his own conclusion, thank anyone who happens to be in the room, and walk out, while never interrupting his own thought process. Introverts are not only amazed (and sometimes amused) by such behavior, they often wonder whether the Extravert ever really wanted an answer in the first place. An Introvert reverses the process: He works inwardly, explores a number of possible scenarios,

Here are some key words that describe how Extraverts and Introverts differ:

Extraverts (E)	vs.	Introverts (I)
Sociability		Territoriality
Interaction		Concentration
External		Internal
Breadth		Depth
Extensive		Intensive
Multiple relationships		Limited relationships
Energy expenditure		Energy conservation
External events		Internal reactions
Gregarious		Reflective
Speak, then think		Think, then speak

THE COMPLEXITY OF THE INTROVERT

At work and in life there is something important to understand about Introverts. Unlike Extraverts, who wear their personalities on their sleeves, Introverts often keep their best to themselves. With Extraverts, what you see is what you get. With Introverts, what you see is only a portion of what is really driving their personality. The richest and most trusted parts of an Introvert's personality are not necessarily shared with the outside world. It takes time, trust, and special circumstances for them to begin to open up.

What makes this difficult is that our society rewards Extraversion, and the external world rules. Consequently we tend to overlook and undervalue the Introvert's contribution: depending upon his or her other three preferences, the ability to contribute precision, vision, objectivity, or insight.

The most important thing to remember is that if you are an Introvert, you must demand reflective, contemplative time alone. If you are an Extravert, you must respect others' demands for such "quiet time" and make this an integral part of the workday.

reaches some kind of conclusion about them, and never says a word to anyone. Moreover, if confronted, he may even *swear*—in all good faith—he told the others what he decided. The Introvert does this because, having rehearsed the issues so thoroughly inside his head, including imagining what the other person might have said in return, it seems clear to him that he has communicated his thoughts—without his actually ever having spoken a word on the subject. Needless to say, arguments result from

HELP!

Typewatching the NF way: Better to help the wrong person and feel guilty than to help no one at all.

such communication gaps. The sad part is that in both situations—the Extravert letting it all out and the Introvert keeping it all in—each party would likely have benefited from the other's perspective, if only they had been able to communicate.

It's very important to keep in mind that in most real-life situations, we are not dealing with extremes. That is, Extraverts need to introvert and Introverts need to extravert. And we all do both. As we've stated repeatedly, typology deals with *preferences*.

Gathering Information and Making Decisions

According to C. G. Jung, upon whose work all type theories are based, everything that lives and breathes—plants, animals, and of course people—engage in two basic functions every waking moment: *gathering information* about the world and *making decisions* based on that information. Those two functions make up the next two letters of one's psychological type. We'll call the first the information-gathering function and the second the decision-making function. (Jung hypothesized these theories in his landmark work *Psychological Types*, which first appeared in English in 1923.)

We believe that these functions are essential to the very processes of life. An animal in the wild hears a sound (gathers information) and runs away (makes a decision). A plant receives sunlight or rain (information) and either grows or wilts (decision). Obviously not all these "decisions" are conscious ones. So, too, with people: The "decisions" we make based on the "information" we obtain are often done without thinking. A strong wind comes up (information) and we grab our hat (decision). We didn't even have to think about whether or not to do it; we just did it. The many, many decisions we make every hour extend deep into our personalities, helping to govern how we think, act, and relate to others.

How You Gather Information:
Sensors vs. iNtuitives

Let's start with information gathering. According to type theory, there are two basic ways we take in information about the world around us:

- As you observe the world and collect data about it, do you prefer to be quite *literal* about it all? Do you prefer to be *practical* and *realistic* and enjoy the *tactile* side of life? Are you more interested in the *experience*, in the *hands-on, tangible, here-and-now* parts of a situation? If so, your information-gathering preference is toward Sensing, designated by the letter *S*. You are a Sensor if you like things presented to you in a *specific* manner and if you have come to rely primarily on your five senses as a means of gathering information—you rely only on those things you can see, hear, touch, taste, or smell. Sensors prefer to focus on the *facts* and *details* of something and have less need to interpret what they mean. About 70 percent of the U.S. population prefers to gather information about the world this way.

- Instead of preferring the above ways of gathering information, it is possible that you would rather be *figurative* about it all. As you gather information from your five senses, do you immediately translate it through your intuition, looking for *possibilities, meanings*, and *relationships* between and among various things? Do you prefer to look at the *grand scheme*, the *holistic* aspect of things, and try to put things into some *theoretical framework*? Are words like *approximate* ("close enough for government work") and *random* to your liking? If so, then you have come to rely on your intuition as a means of information gathering. About 30 percent of the U.S. population prefers to gather information this way. They are iNtuitives, designated by the letter *N*. (As we said before, this is done because the letter *I* is used to describe Introversion.)

"WHERE IS THE COPIER ON THIS FLOOR?"

Sensor: "Go to the end of the hall and turn left, through the revolving door. You'll pass a set of red doors marked Electrical Closet No. 3. Go another twenty-five feet and you'll see a fire extinguisher. The copy room is right next to that. Go in, the copier's on the left."

iNtuitive: "Follow the hall around to the left. It's down there on the right. You can't miss it."

The way we gather information is the starting point for almost all human interactions. If two people gather information differently, it becomes readily apparent that all further communication is at risk. For example:

Sensor: "What time is it?"
iNtuitive: "It's late!"
Sensor (somewhat surprised): "What *time* is it?"
iNtuitive (insistent): "It's time to go!"
Sensor (getting impatient): "Hey, read my lips! *What time is it?*"
iNtuitive (equally impatient): "It's a little past three."
Sensor (exasperated): "Close, but no cigar! I asked a specific question and expect a specific answer."
iNtuitive (self-righteously): "You shouldn't be so picky."

And things go downhill from there. Remember, Sensors are literal; they want specific information. The iNtuitive, in contrast, may find a hundred ways to answer a question, none of which may be specific enough for the Sensor.

For iNtuitives everything is relational: It must have meaning. If an iNtuitive is looking for something in particular, he or she may walk right by it, never recognizing its existence. Sensors find that very difficult to comprehend. For them something is real, it exists, it is there—how can you not see it?

There's a classic S-N dilemma in the Book of Exodus. You probably remember the story: Moses sent twelve spies to check out the Holy Land. It is clear from their responses that ten members of the group were Sensors and two were iNtuitives. The Sensors, according to the biblical account, reported with astounding accuracy the number of people, what they did, and where they spent their time, among other details. The iNtuitives, on the other hand, surveyed the same scene and concluded that it was "a land flowing with milk and honey"—which must have been laughable to the Sensors, who couldn't even perceive that the land was flowing with *water.*

Sensor-iNtuitive communication gaffes have been the stuff of comedy for decades. You know the old vaudevillian lines: Question: "What was the book about?" Answer: "About three hundred pages." Or, question: "Will you love me always?" Answer: "Sure, which way would you like to try first?"

We're also reminded of a "Peanuts" cartoon a few years back. Lucy, a true-blue Sensor, is reminding Snoopy, a hard-core iNtuitive, "You get out of life *exactly* what you put into it—nothing more, nothing less." Snoopy walks away reflecting, "Somehow I'd like a little more room for error."

Here are some key words that describe how Sensors and iNtuitives differ:

Sensors (S)	vs.	iNtuitives (N)
Direct		Random
Present		Future
Realistic		Conceptual
Perspiration		Inspiration
Actual		Theoretical
Down-to-earth		Head-in-clouds
Fact		Fantasy
Practicality		Ingenuity
Specific		General

But S-N dilemmas can be far from laughing matters. So many of our communication difficulties begin with S-N misperceptions: One person sees a forest, the other sees trees. The differences have a lot to do with the way we learn, particularly in school or professional training. Sensors prefer to learn through facts, which they prefer be given sequentially. ("There are three simple steps to closing a sale. The first is . . .") In contrast, iNtuitives gather things in a more random fashion, making "leaps" along the way. ("In closing a sale it's important to understand the overall picture about what the customer wants to get out of the purchase.") Even seemingly simple instructions—"Please sort through these applications to find the most qualified people"—can mean something completely different to a Sensor than to an iNtuitive.

How You Make Decisions: Thinking vs. Feeling

Once you've taken in information, whether as a Sensor or as an iNtuitive, it usually leads to some kind of decision or action. Unlike the information-gathering function, which is open-ended and nondirected (because it is the process of taking in information before doing something with it), the decision-making function seeks closure and is very focused. Its purpose is to make judgments and decisions, which are usually finite and closed-ended, even if those decisions are changed in a matter of seconds. When you bite into a steak, for example, you may *perceive* that it is big or tender or juicy or whatever; your *judgment* is that the steak was (or wasn't) prepared exactly how you like it.

As with information gathering, we make decisions in one of two ways:

▪ You may be among those who, in the decision-making process, prefer to be very *logical*, *detached*, *analytical*, and driven by *objective* values as you come to your conclusions. As a group such individuals tend not to get *personally involved* in a decision and would prefer that the *consequences of the action* be the driving factor wherever possible. This group

MEMBERSHIP HAS ITS PRIVILEGES

Typewatching the SJ way: Better to belong and bitch than not to belong at all.

strives for *justice* and *clarity*; they are also often called *firm-minded*. In typological terms these individuals have a preference for Thinking decisions, designated by the letter *T*.

■ For others the decision-making process is driven by an interpersonal involvement that comes from subjective values. Words like *harmony*, *mercy*, and *tenderhearted* come to mind with this group. The impact of the decision on people is extremely important to this group's final action. These people have a tendency to *identify with* and *assume others' emotional pain*. In typological terms such individuals prefer to make Feeling decisions, designated by the letter *F*.

It's a bit unfortunate that Jung used the terms *Thinking*, which usually refers to intellect, and *Feeling*, which refers to emotion, to describe the decision-making process. As a result, there are often misunderstandings about the meanings of these preferences. It is important to remember that Thinkers feel and that Feelers think. Both types can be equally intellectual and emotional. What we're talking about is the process one *prefers* in making a decision. At their worst Thinkers *think* that Feelers are fuzzy-headed, and Feelers *feel* that Thinkers have ice for blood. At their best Thinkers bring objectivity to any decision-making situation, and Feelers bring an awareness of how that decision will ultimately affect others.

Let's look at a typical workplace situation to see how the T-F difference plays itself out. Jim approaches his manager with a simple request: to take Friday off so that he can take his two children to visit their grandmother a few hundred miles away; the grandmother hasn't been well, Jim explains, and this is his kids' only grandparent. Unfortunately the manager has been

Here are some key words that describe how Thinkers and Feelers differ:

Thinkers (T)	vs.	Feelers (F)
Objective		Subjective
Firm-minded		Tenderhearted
Laws		Circumstances
Firmness		Persuasion
Just		Humane
Clarity		Harmony
Analytical		Appreciative
Policy		Social values
Detached		Involved

frustrated with a high level of absenteeism in his department lately and is not wild about encouraging another employee to miss a day's work.

Let's examine the thought process of both the *T* manager and the *F* manager and note that it's possible for Ts and Fs to arrive at the same conclusions through entirely different paths. It's the route to the decision, not the decision itself, that characterizes the person. We've italicized key words in each rumination that typify Thinkers and Feelers.

Arguments for Giving Him the Day Off

THINKER: If I deny Jim the day off, I'll keep him here, but how much work will he really get done? Knowing he'd rather be somewhere else, his productivity probably won't be very high. Furthermore he's been up front about why he wants the day off; he could have told me something else or just called in sick. If others can see that such forthcoming behavior is rewarded, it may encourage more esprit de corps on everyone's part. On a time-cost analysis the department is in pretty good shape right now, and we could spare Jim for a day. That makes it a win-win for both the company and Jim.

FEELER: How would I feel if I were in Jim's shoes? I can really relate to his situation. He's being open and honest and expressing his need very directly. Clearly this is one way to build loyalty and keep motivation high. This is a chance to show how much we value Jim and how much we want to keep everyone happy.

Arguments Against Giving Him the Day Off

THINKER: It's lonely at the top. As the boss I'm not here to be liked; I'm here to make decisions in the best interests of the company. I know that while Jim will sulk for a bit, he'll get over his sulking. In the meantime productivity won't be interrupted. If I give him a day off, everyone will want a day off. You simply can't run a business that way. It's not right to give one person the day off when everyone else has to come to work.

FEELER: I remember once when I was at the bottom of the ladder and my boss didn't respond to a personal request. I was angry and felt like nobody cared about me at work. But when I sorted it all out, I realized the boss was handling it the best way he could under the circumstances and his action was ultimately quite protective of me. So Jim will have to realize that while it hurts me to say no to him, it's in everyone's best interests.

Don't let the above "debates" make you think that individual Thinkers or Feelers can't make decisions. Like everyone, they can be very decisive—or very indecisive. The answer to the quandary could come in a matter of seconds, or it could rage on. The issue here is the process, and in this example note that the Thinker is objective and removed while the Feeler is totally involved. Both care, both think, and both feel, but the routes by which each arrives at the final conclusion are so very different. More often than not, one doesn't understand the other, and both can fall into the common trap of resentment and frustration.

As we stated in Chapter Two, this is the only preference pair that conforms to a gender bias. Over the short term, men and women may be charmed by this difference between them: Opposites usually do attract—for a while. But over the long haul, this factor becomes a major source of interpersonal problems, whether in personal relationships or in working relationships. At work, as in life, when a female who prefers to make Thinking decisions behaves in ways for which similar behavior in a male would be lauded, she is called a variety of bad names, as is a male who prefers to make Feeling decisions. "Real men," as conventional wisdom has it, don't show feelings. Real women, it would follow, can't make "tough" decisions, those that require that personal feelings be put aside. Both statements of course are simply untrue.

This Thinking-Feeling, male-female dilemma haunts the world of work. The Thinking woman swims upstream against a rather swift negative current in most aspects of her life, and nowhere is this more true than at work. If she is objective and decisive, she is viewed as "hard" and "unfeminine," among the more printable terms. The Feeling male is similarly called a wimp simply for his caring nature. As is frequently the case, however, being male does have its advantages: While he still must swim upstream, the current against which the Feeling male must swim is not as swift as that opposing the Thinking female.

How You Orient Your Life: Judgers vs. Perceivers

The fourth letter of your psychological "type" is, we believe, the most significant source of interpersonal tension at work. It deals with which function—information gathering or decision making—you most naturally use as you relate to the outer world, verbally and behaviorally.

Once again there are two preferences:

- If the environment you have created around you is *structured*, *scheduled*, *ordered*, *planned*, and *controlled*, and if you are *decisive*, *deliberate*, and able to make *decisions* with a minimum of stress, chances are you prefer to use the decision-making function as you relate to life; you are a Judger, designated by the letter *J*. Judgers *plan their work* and *work their plan*. Even playtime is organized. For Js there's usually a "right way" and a "wrong way" to do anything.

- If, however, you have created an environment that allows you to be *flexible*, *spontaneous*, *adaptive*, and *responsive* to a variety of situations, if making and sticking to decisions causes anxiety, if other people often have trouble understanding where you stand on a particular issue, you are more likely to use the information-gathering function as you relate to life. That makes you a Perceiver, designated by the letter *P*. Perceivers prefer to take a *wait-and-see* attitude on most things—what work needs to be done, how to solve a particular problem, what to do today.

Put another way, Perceivers have a tendency to perceive—to keep collecting new information—rather than to draw conclusions (judgments) on any subject. Judgers, in contrast, have a tendency to judge—to make decisions—rather than to respond

SWEET REVENGE

A Typewatching trainer divided her group into Judgers and Perceivers. She asked each group to "design a new library wing" while the other group watched. The Js went first. Someone had a bag of jelly beans, and in five minutes the group had laid out a floor plan in jelly beans.

Then it was the Ps' turn. They complained about the assignment briefly, then they ate the jelly beans.

Here are some key words that describe how Judgers and Perceivers differ:

Judgers (J)	vs.	Perceivers (P)
Resolved		Pending
Decided		Wait and see
Fixed		Flexible
Control		Adapt
Closure		Openness
Planned		Open-ended
Structure		Flow
Definite		Tentative
Scheduled		Spontaneous
Deadline		What deadline?

to new information, even (or perhaps especially) if that information might change their decision. At their respective extremes, Perceivers are virtually incapable of making decisions, whereas Judgers find it almost impossible to change theirs. Such extremes, however, are not usually the rule.

It's hard to describe the extent of the problems resulting from J-P conflicts. For example, Judgers run Perceivers up the wall with their continued need for closure—to have an opinion, a plan, and a schedule for nearly everything. Perceivers, meanwhile, drive Judgers to drink with their ability to be spontaneous and easygoing about everything short of life-and-death issues, and

A PLACE FOR EVERYTHING

Nothing is ever lost: Either a Perceiver has it and can't find it, or a Judger has filed it and forgotten it.

sometimes even about those. Js, we're fond of saying, aren't beyond making great time going in the wrong direction. And thanks to constantly changing information, some Ps can have no direction at all. Neither preference, Perceiving or Judging, is right or wrong or more desirable. Indeed, we need both types in our world. Js need Ps to inspire them to relax, not make a major issue out of everything; and Ps need Js to help them become reasonably organized and to follow through on things.

What's needed is a balancing act. A preference for too much J or P without the other is dangerous, a strength maximized into a liability. Judgers need Perceivers because they provide alternatives and excitement and the playful or childlike part of life. And Perceivers need Judgers because they provide the necessary follow-through to any project, from making breakfast to making a business work. In Transactional Analysis terms—a theory of psychological behavior popular in the 1970s, based on Eric Berne's best-selling book *Games People Play*—the J in each of us is the critical parent and the P is the natural child, and within any given person it is healthy to be able to activate both parent and child.

Everything Is Relative

You have now made a tentative approximation of your type in Chapter Two, which gave you some indication of your four preferences; and you've read the above descriptions, which either confirmed your feelings or helped you make adjustments. You should therefore have a good idea of your four letters, which, combined, constitute your "type." It's important to keep in mind that there are no "good" or "bad" types. Each has its own strengths and weaknesses. It literally takes all types to make a world. You can see all sixteen types on the table on the following page.

It is also important to remember that in Typewatching there are no absolutes and that everything is relative. If your two best friends are both Extraverts, but one is socially gregarious while the other is a bit more reflective, the tentative friend may seem to be an Introvert by comparison. So it is perfectly possible to have accurate Typewatching skills and still be uncertain about

		SENSORS		INTUITIVES			
		WITH THINKING	WITH FEELING	WITH FEELING	WITH THINKING		
INTROVERTS	JUDGING	ISTJ	ISFJ	INFJ	INTJ	JUDGING	INTROVERTS
INTROVERTS	PERCEIVING	ISTP	ISFP	INFP	INTP	PERCEIVING	INTROVERTS
EXTRAVERTS	PERCEIVING	ESTP	ESFP	ENFP	ENTP	PERCEIVING	EXTRAVERTS
EXTRAVERTS	JUDGING	ESTJ	ESFJ	ENFJ	ENTJ	JUDGING	EXTRAVERTS

The Type Table is used with the written permission of the Publisher, Consulting Psychologists Press, Inc., Palo Alto, CA 94303.

a particular call. One Typewatching expert has put it this way: "An Extravert is like every other Extravert, like some other Extraverts, and like no other Extraverts." Which is to say that while Extraverts are fairly predictable in their behavior, every now and then you'll meet someone who doesn't fit the mold. The same is true for Introverts and all the other preferences.

It is important not to feel boxed in by your type. Despite the relative pigeonholing, each of the sixteen types still encompasses a wide range of behavior, styles, values, and tastes. Still, you will find that understanding your type and that of others provides some valuable insights on how to interact with those whose preferences are different—or even the same.

4

The Ten Commandments
of Typewatching

Typewatching, like any good value system, has its own Ten Commandments. These are guiding principles that can help you use Typewatching most effectively. They can also prevent you from using Typewatching recklessly, inappropriately, and unethically.

1. **Life tends to support our preferences, making us even more distrustful of our nonpreferences.** Whatever your type, you will find that the day's events seem to take place according to your preferences. So if you are a Judger, you will be glad at day's end that you had a structured plan, for it likely saved your hindquarters more than once. And if you're a Perceiver, you'll sigh at day's end that you were able to hang loose and cope with the many surprises you encountered. This will be true with each of the eight preferences. In a stressful situation Thinkers will be glad their objectivity helped to keep them cool under fire whereas in the same situation Feelers will be equally glad that they were able to be supportive to the people who needed them. And so on.

2. **Your strength maximized becomes a liability.** It is perfectly natural for us to rely on that part of us with which we feel

most comfortable. But by doing so, we can further neglect other parts of ourselves, which eventually become uncomfortable, underdeveloped, and unskilled. So, while Extraverts, for example, can bring excitement to any situation, they can become poor listeners or can overpower others. Introverts, on the other hand, have good listening skills and the power of concentration, but when maximized these strengths can lead to isolation and avoidance of controversial issues in the external world. Thinkers, for their part, bring objectivity and rationality to any situation, but when these qualities are maximized, they can lead Thinkers to disregard others' likes and dislikes. Feelers, meanwhile, bring subjectivity and people concerns to a situation, but when these qualities are maximized, Feelers can overpersonalize and can carry grudges for years.

3. **Typewatching is only a theory; it takes real life to validate it.** Once you have a sense of your type preferences—or those of others—it still must be validated against actual behavior, experience, and self-awareness. For many reasons, we often see ourselves or others differently from how we really are. For example, if you are expected by others in your organization to be objective, analytical, and organized, you may behave that way. Over time you may come to believe that these are your preferences. In fact, you may simply be adapting to the environment. Or you may assume that someone will be outgoing and assertive in a situation because you know him to be an Extravert. However, if, for whatever reasons, his behavior doesn't match his preference, you have either mistyped the person or there is some other extenuating circumstance that is causing him to behave differently from his preferences. In any case it is essential to validate one's observations with one's experience before leaping to conclusions or making false assumptions.

4. **Typewatching is only an explanation: it's never an excuse.** There's nothing more offensive in Typewatching than the neophyte's readiness to excuse all bad behaviors as the result

of his or her personality preferences. For example, "I meant to return your call, but I'm an Introvert, and we don't return phone calls." Or, "I meant to be on time today, but I'm a Perceiver, and we're always late." Such excuse making may be acceptable in small doses or in special circumstances, but in the day-to-day workplace, it's an unacceptable cop-out. Seasoned Typewatchers will use such occasions as the basis for genuine negotiations about differences.

5. **The whole is greater than the sum of its parts.** No doubt you've heard this before, but nowhere is this more true than in Typewatching. This is both good news and bad news. The good news is that the "parts" of Typewatching—the four pairs of preferences—make Typewatching easy to apply instantly. You may not easily be able to distinguish whether someone is an ENTJ or ESTJ, for example, but you may readily spot their Extraversion (their constantly thinking out loud) or even their preference for Extraverted-Judging (their constantly complaining about everything). On the other hand, the complexities of putting all four preferences together are immense. The ENTJ, to use the example above, is a big-picture person who wants to improve the whole world; the ESTJ, in contrast, is a hands-on person who prefers to establish an administrative procedure for the world's good. So, two people who look so similar can end up with severe differences.

6. **Typewatching is only one lens through which to view human personality.** While facilitating, affirming, and dramatically insightful, the four-letter descriptions of Typewatching are only door openers to understanding the people behind the letters. Gender, ethnicity, values, socioeconomic factors, and many other things combine to make us who we are. One of the dangers of Typewatching is that there's a tendency to take the four letters as gospel. That not only violates some basic ideals of Typewatching but, in the business world, often causes more harm than good. There's nothing

that can turn off any level of employee more quickly than being put into a four-letter box as the sum and substance of his or her humanity.

7. **To be effective, Typewatching must begin with yourself before you can apply it to others.** The more you know about yourself, the more you will be in a position to collaborate and negotiate with those who are different. The process must begin with self-understanding and self-awareness before it can become a frame of reference for collaboration.

8. **Typewatching is easier said (or thought about) than done**. We'll admit that Typewatching can present some difficult challenges. There's a natural tendency for people to want to stick with what works. If your preference is always to be in control, for example, it will likely be difficult for you to cede that control to others, even when such an action might be in everybody's best interest. To make the most constructive use of differences involves commitment, personal skill, and an underlying trust that the process will lead to a better end result.

9. **Don't blame everything on your opposite type.** This is a natural thing to do. It's easy to believe that everyone who doesn't agree with you is your typological opposite. For one thing, some types naturally disagree or are prone to arguing. That doesn't necessarily mean they are against an idea; arguing is sometimes a means of sorting things out. Moreover some types need to see a bottom line—where a discussion is leading, for example. In their quest for direction, they may continually raise questions that sound like disagreements. When something doesn't go as expected, don't leap to assume that it was sabotaged by someone of another type.

10. **Typewatching can't solve everything.** Because Typewatching is very positive and because it explains many parts of everyday behavior, there is a tendency on the part of enthusiasts to use it as an explanation for everything. Such a tendency

moves beyond Typewatching's original intent and may add meanings to behavior that cannot be explained by type. Sometimes, for example, people have physical or psychological problems that are outside the realm of "normal" behavior. Some people have personalities that are so complex—or so simple—as to defy easy analysis. Typewatching doesn't have all the answers. It is legitimate and even professional for a Typewatcher to declare occasionally, "I can't explain that," or simply, "I don't know."

5

A Typewatching Shortcut: The Four Temperaments

"Hi, I'm an NF, and I'm here to help."

In Typewatching, understanding Extraversion, Introversion, Sensing, iNtuition, and all the other preferences is only the beginning of understanding your or someone else's type. When you put preferences together—Extraversion with Judging, for example, or Sensing with Thinking—the combination of the two preferences results in behavior that is richer and more complex than any of the individual preferences. When you add a third, or fourth, preference, things get even more complex. So, while you may understand Extraversion, iNtuition, Thinking, and Judging, you still may not fully comprehend what it means for someone to be an ENTJ, for example.

One shortcut we believe to be helpful in making Typewatching easier to learn and use has to do with what are called Temperaments. They are four special two-letter combinations, the creation of David Keirsey and Marilyn Bates, authors of *Please Understand Me*, another book on type. Temperaments are useful because they allow you to know just two letters of someone's type and still make some pretty accurate predictions about his or her behavior. So, even if we don't understand how all four letters fit together, the two-letter Temperament helps us predict such things as how people teach, learn, lead others, socialize, manage money, and relate to others.

The Sensing-iNtuitive difference is the first key to determining Temperament. The reason is that differences in how people gather information about the world are the starting point for most human interactions. Without some understanding of how someone gathers information, communication is extremely difficult, since each individual believes his or her own data are *the* data. If we see a tree and you see a forest, each of us believes we're right—and we are—and distrusts the other's information-gathering process. A tree is a tree to a Sensor; for an iNtuitive a tree is part of a system, an organic whole called a "forest." The tree therefore prompts images of the forest—when viewed by an iNtuitive. Is a cup half empty or half full? Sensors and iNtuitives each see it differently: iNtuitives, who see possibilities in everything, will be more optimistic about the glass's contents; Sensors, who focus only on what's actually there, not on what could be there, are less inclined to see the potential. Before either type begins to make a decision (Thinking or Feeling), and regardless of whether it's expressed internally or externally (Introversion or Extraversion), the data must first be gathered.

So, the first letter of a Temperament is either *S* or *N*. The second letter of a Temperament is determined by what the first letter is.

If you're an iNtuitive: Your preference for gathering data is abstract and conceptual. The second most important preference in reading your Temperament is *how you prefer to evaluate the data you have gathered:* objectively (Thinking) or subjectively (Feeling). For iNtuitives, then, the two basic Temperament groups are NF and NT.

If you're a Sensor: Your preference for gathering information is concrete and tactile. The second most important preference is not how you evaluate the data but *what you do with them*: Do you organize them (Judging) or continue to take them in, perhaps even seeking more (Perceiving)? So, for Sensors, the two Temperament groups are SJ and SP.

Don't worry about the theory behind these. Even Keirsey recognizes that the theory may not be logical. But we believe it to be behaviorally sound, and our longtime Typewatching experiences bear this out.

Accordingly, each of the sixteen types falls into one of the four Temperaments:

NF	*NT*
ENFJ	ENTJ
INFJ	INTJ
ENFP	ENTP
INFP	INTP

SJ	*SP*
ESTJ	ESFP
ISTJ	ISFP
ESFJ	ESTP
ISFJ	ISTP

We're not saying that when you've seen one NT—or NF, SJ, or SP—you've seen 'em all. There still are sixteen distinct types, each with differences we discuss throughout this book. Temperaments, however, do provide us with some genuine insights and useful tools for developing Typewatching skills.

Styles of the Four Temperaments

Let's take a look at the different styles of each of the four Temperaments.

The NF Temperament

NFs look at the world and see possibilities (iNtuition) and translate those possibilities inter- and intrapersonally (Feeling). They eat, sleep, think, breathe, move, and love people. Representing about 12 percent of the U.S. population, according to Keirsey and Bates, they are the idealists of life and tend to serve causes that advance human interests: teaching, humanities, counseling, religion, and family medicine, for example. As idealistic do-gooders, NFs articulate and champion various causes:

They create anti–drunk-driving campaigns and peace movements and collect money to protect endangered species. But
their sensitivity leads them to personalize any form of criticism,
often resulting in their needlessly feeling hurt. Overall, NFs feel
that the most important thing is to be in harmony with themselves and with others. Everything else will naturally fall into
place.

The NF's strengths—which, when maximized, become liabilities—include

■ A phenomenal capacity for working with people and drawing
  out their best
■ Being articulate and persuasive
■ A strong desire to help others
■ The ability to affirm others freely and easily

At work NFs are positive, affirming idealists whom others may
like, but their warm style can make it difficult for others to disagree with them. NFs often have difficulty being supervisors
and tend to give workers too much leeway. In their idealism NFs
tend to make heroes and heroines of authority figures and, as
such, can become fiercely loyal when things are going well;
when they learn that these heroes are "only human," their loyalty can give way to disillusionment, even dissatisfaction, and

TEMPERAMENT WORK STYLES

NF   Searches for meaning and authenticity
        Empathetic
        Sees possibilities of institutions and people
        Communicates appreciation, enthusiasm, approval
        Highly responsive to interpersonal transactions
        Keeps in close contact with others
        Highly personalized
        Gives and needs strokes freely

NT   Hungers for competency and knowledge
         Works well with ideas and concepts
         Intrigued and challenged by riddles
         Sees life as a system to be designed and redesigned
         Focuses on possibilities through nonpersonal analysis
         Likes to start projects, but not good with follow-through
         Not always aware of others' feelings
         Responsive to new ideas

SJ   Strives to belong and contribute
         Prizes harmony and service
         Orderly, dependable, realistic
         Understands and conserves institutional values
         Expects others to be realistic
         Supplies stability and structure
         More likely to reward institutionally than personally
            (trophies, letters, etc.)
         Can be critical of mistakes more easily than rewarding
            expected duties

SP   Hungers for freedom and action
         Deals with realistic problems
         Flexible, open-minded
         Willing to take risks
         Highly negotiable
         Can be perceived as indecisive
         Challenged by "trouble spots" but not over the long term
         Best at verbal planning and short-range projects

work can lose its meaning. In conducting business NFs are less concerned with others' credentials than they are with how much they like them. While that dynamic can add valuable enthusiasm to any transaction, it also risks that genuine contributions may be overlooked if personality differences get in the way.

The NF's slogan is "Hi, I'm an NF, and I'm here to help."

The NT Temperament

NTs gather data consisting largely of abstractions and possibilities (iNtuition), which they filter through their objective decision-making process (Thinking). Their driving force, in their never-ending quest for competence, is to theorize and intellectualize everything. Driven to try to understand the universe, they ask "Why?" (or "Why not?") of everything: *Why* does this rule exist? *Why* can't we do things differently? NTs are enthusiastic pursuers of adventures who, in their enthusiasm, may take risks that unintentionally imperil people close to them.

NTs—who, according to Keirsey, represent about 12 percent of the population—learn by challenging any authority or source. They have their own standards and benchmarks for what is "competent," against which they measure themselves and everybody else. They are always testing the system. Relentless in their pursuit of excellence, they can be very critical of their own and others' shortcomings, and impatient when confronted with them. They are frequently perceived by others—often incorrectly— as aloof, intellectual snobs.

The NT's strengths—which, when maximized, become liabilities—include

- A ready ability to see the big picture
- A talent for conceptualizing and systems planning
- Insight into the internal logic and underlying principles of systems and organizations
- The ability to speak and write clearly and precisely

At work NTs are the strategic planners and researchers, although they can get lost in their strategies and overlook day-to-day business. An NT's loyalty is directly related to an individual's competencies. If the NT discerns an individual is competent, credentials are totally unimportant; conversely if the NT deems an individual to be incompetent by NT standards, all the credentials in the world are of little use. Even when an NT does judge someone as competent, the judging process continues. In fact, "competence" is merely an invitation to further testing, challenging, and intellectual stretching.

The NT's slogan is "Change for the sake of change produces learning, even if the only thing we learned is that we shouldn't have changed."

The SJ Temperament

SJs' information-gathering process is practical and realistic (Sensing), to which they prefer to give organization and structure (Judging). SJs' purpose in life is to belong to meaningful institutions. They are the foundations and backbone of society—America, Motherhood, and a Hot Lunch for Orphans. They are trustworthy, loyal, helpful, brave, clean, and reverent. They are stabilizing traditionalists who represent about 38 percent of the population. As Judgers their tendency is to organize— people, furniture, projects, schedules, and entire companies. Just as people are integral to NFs and *conceptualization* is integral to NTs, SJs thrive on procedure. They have a procedure for everything, from making breakfast to making love.

The SJ's strengths—which, when maximized, become liabilities—include

- Administration
- Dependability
- The ability to take charge
- Always knowing who's in charge

At work SJs make phenomenal administrators of systems that require precision and organization. They have a tendency to do what needs to be done today, often to the neglect of what must be done tomorrow. For the SJ, authority is in the system; credentials are important. One of the beautiful qualities of the SJ is that he or she gives the benefit of the doubt to a credentialed appointed person. Even if the SJ thinks the person is incompetent,

WOULD YOU LIKE TO HAVE A CUP OF COFFEE?

SPs ask themselves: "Do I need a change of pace?"
SJs ask themselves: "Is it time for a coffee break?"
NTs ask themselves: "Is everything else under control?"
NFs ask themselves: "Will it make me feel good?"

he starts with the assumption that if the system has appointed this person, he or she must have some credentials. So, one must trust the system and give this person the benefit of the doubt. Generally Js, and SJs in particular, are not a very patient type, yet they have an abundance of patience with "the system." The downside of this is that when things go wrong, SJs tend to blame the system, saying, "I was only following orders."

The SJ's slogan is "Don't fix what ain't broke."

The SP Temperament

SPs' data collection is practical and realistic (Sensing), to which they bring spontaneity and flexibility (Perceiving). This combination makes them the original "now" generation. Their Sensing grounds them in the reality of the moment, and their Perceiving keeps them open for other ways of dealing with that reality. The only thing an SP can be sure of is the moment; a "long-range plan" is a contradiction in terms. Their quest is for action, leading them to "act now, pay later." Representing about 38 percent of the population, SPs are attracted to careers that have immediate, tangible rewards: firefighting, emergency medicine, mechanics, farming, carpentry, and anything involving technical skills. Although they are frequently misunderstood because of their somewhat hedonistic, live-for-now nature, they make excellent negotiators and troubleshooters.

The SP's strengths—which, when maximized, become liabilities—include

- Practicality
- Adept problem-solving skills, particularly at hands-on tasks
- Resourcefulness
- A special sense of immediate needs

At work SPs are good at resolving crises and are geniuses at generating solutions to problems. But they are not above intentionally creating crises to solve, just to give themselves a sense of purpose. For SPs, "authority" isn't necessarily in an individual or institution; it's accomplishing whatever needs to be done in a given moment. SPs operate under the assumption that "it's easier to get forgiveness than permission." Rather than go through channels, they would rather take their marching orders from the sneaker company that once advertised, "Just do it."

The SP's slogan is "When all else fails, read the directions."

As we said at the outset, Temperaments are a shortcut. Once you understand the basic characteristics of, say, an SP, you can then add on other preferences to get a fuller grasp of an individual's type. An Extraverted-Thinking SP (an ESTP) is very different from an Introverted-Feeling SP (an ISFP), although both share many SP traits, including the love of the immediate, hands-on experience; avoidance of theory and planning in favor of the reality of daily life; and disdain for rituals, procedures, and regulations.

As you can see, Temperaments are an easy, albeit limited, way of observing and cataloging Typewatching behavior. Now that you understand the basic concepts behind Typewatching, let's get into how it can be put to use every day at work.

HAVE A NICE DAY!

To an NT: "Have an interesting day."
To an NF: "Have an inspiring day."
To an SJ: "Have a productive day."
To an SP: "Have fun today!"

II

Putting Typewatching to Work

6

Leadership

"I must become an expert in a whole new set of skills."

Scarcely a week goes by before a new leadership tome hits the shelves of our local bookstore. Powerhouse CEOs and wise gurus take turns putting a new spin on leadership, and each has a different story, philosophy, and recipe for success. Many of these works are worthwhile and inspirational, but most are incomplete, for nearly all sum up the concept of leadership with a formula designed to suit everyone—as if it could be boiled down to a clever, one-size-fits-all mantra.

Also absent from many volumes on leadership is a focus on followers. It's been said about politics, "If the people will lead, the leaders will follow," and the same could be said for business.

The bottom line, as the business books like to say, is that human behavior and interaction are so complex that any single approach will prove insufficient. However, Typewatching can bring us closer to an understanding of leadership through its focus on how type colors, and even controls, the kind of leader you seek and the kind of leader you are hardwired to become. Our different personality types determine our various styles, motivations, and ideas of what leadership is all about.

That said, being a good leader is no simple matter of capitalizing on the strengths of one's personality type. In fact, some of the most remarkable people can get tripped up in leadership roles, often with the same set of skills and talents that got them to the top in the first place.

Consider former presidents Richard Nixon and Bill Clinton. Nixon, arguably a classic INTJ, drew strength from his inner world of vision and strategy and from his ability to grasp and analyze complex situations. He is, many historians agree, the most astute U.S. foreign policy leader of the second half of the twentieth century. But the same INTJ characteristics that took Nixon to great heights also likely helped plunge him to great depths: His need to control information and his withdrawal from personal relationships may have led him into the world of secrecy and espionage that was his downfall.

Bill Clinton, most likely an ENFP, won his following by extending broadband sympathy and empathy to everyone he met. In classic NF tradition, each new person was a potential conquest, someone he could connect with on a one-to-one level. Then, when headline-making news of his infidelity tainted his public image, it appeared that the same seductive qualities that had helped get him elected had now led him into big trouble.

You don't need to be commander in chief—or even chief executive officer—to get tripped up by your own four-letter type. Consider the story of our ESTJ client Judy, who, when we met her, had just been promoted to division manager of a major retail chain. During the decade she had already spent with the company, she'd received a great many kudos for her effective administrative and project management skills. She'd brought a painstaking attention to detail to each new project, using her ESTJ organization skills, and was expected to continue to move up the organizational ladder.

One of Judy's primary duties in her new position was to run a number of community-based services: a suicide hot line, twelve-step programs, Habitat for Humanity, and other activities that integrated company employees with community members. Her task was to set up and staff the programs and to keep them running effectively. It was a natural project for Judy.

But suddenly, the personality strengths that had worked so well for her before—her objectivity and her attention to detail—

became liabilities. They weren't appropriate in this much more subjective, feel-good arena of volunteerism and community causes. Judy applied her best ESTJ talents. She tried to micro-manage. She made unilateral decisions rather than allowing the group to work things out. She talked about accountability and wanted to know what reports would be produced and when she would see them. None of this sat well with the volunteers, who had signed on to help their neighbors and their community in a noncorporate environment. As a result, Judy's programs were flagging; volunteers weren't signing on, and those who had ei-ther weren't showing up or weren't sticking around. Even her own employees, who had given the program their enthusiastic support prior to Judy's promotion, began to lose interest. Judy was painfully aware that she had blown her new assignment.

That's where many of these stories end—with someone fail-ing on the job. To her credit, Judy engaged a variety of consul-tants, including our staff at Otto Kroeger Associates. We helped her view the situation through a typological lens, and she quickly recognized that Typewatching could help her see why things weren't working, and how they might.

As we worked together, Judy made a serious effort to change her management style and allow for her nonpreferences to shine through. For example, she began to hold open-ended meetings at which participants spent time sharing stories and focusing on their successes. Ultimately, recognizing her limited ability to stomach what to her was organizational "fluff," Judy delegated an underling to run those meetings—and in true ESTJ style, made sure that this individual was accountable for all that tran-spired. Over time, Judy turned things around, and even won a Manager of the Year award. She has since been held up as one of the company's exemplary leaders.

So, does becoming an effective leader mean changing your ty-pological stripes and toning down the natural strengths that moved you up through the organizational ranks? Of course not. But as you'll see, leaders must often learn how to access their nonpreferences—the four letters that represent the opposite of their type.

What Is Leadership?

It is difficult to define leadership in a way that all types would embrace and understand. For our purposes, we'll define it as the intentional use of power with individuals or groups toward some desired end.

Let's take a closer look at the four key components of this definition before viewing it through a Typewatching lens.

1. **Leadership is intentional.** Though not all things a leader does are deliberate—there are always mistakes, uncalculated actions, and unforeseen reactions—leadership involves the intentional use of power to influence a person or group in a chosen direction.

2. **Leadership needs people.** It might seem obvious, but leaders require followers—leadership is about how one person relates to another person or to groups of people. As a result, one's effectiveness as a leader depends not just on one's own personality type, but on that of one's followers. And, more than likely, those followers' types will range all over the typological map.

3. **Leadership is about using power.** Leaders who are able to access their individual power sources at crucial times hold a key to effectiveness and success. It is important to note that power is value-neutral—it is neither good nor bad, but simply exists. How leaders decide to use their power involves judgment.

    There are different types of power. *Personal* power is controlled by an individual, accruing by means of one's charisma, charm, knowledge, skills, and abilities. *Organizational* power is conferred upon individuals by groups and is dependent on the group's collective will or belief. Positions that bring organizational power involve authority, status, financial control, and the ability to reward and punish others. There are also hybrid power sources. For example, knowledge of a system and its bureaucracy—knowing how and by whom things actually get done and gaining that knowledge by pulling the appropriate strings—involves both organizational and personal power.

It is critical to note that authority is a type of power, but that authority—a fancy title and a corner office—does not by itself give someone the ability to achieve organizational goals. The appointed chairperson of a committee may have organizational authority, but someone else's skill set, reputation, and knowledge of the system might mean that he or she holds more real power and is in fact the more effective leader.

Conversely, sometimes people who appear to be slow to influence others can find themselves in a position of authority and can blossom into powerful, effective leaders once they have the weight and will of the organization behind them.

It is a complicated equation. Power is not authority, and neither power nor authority on its own is leadership.

4. **Leadership needs an aim.** Just as leadership cannot exist without people, it cannot exist without a direction or goal.

So, where does type fit in? Let's examine how these four components of leadership play out through the different personality types.

How Sensors and iNtuitives Lead

As stated in Chapter Three, the way we gather information is the starting point for almost all human interactions. Your preference of Sensing or iNtuition is the primary indicator of your teaching style, your learning style, and your communication style. It is also a great place to start looking at leadership style.

Sensors almost literally engage with the world around them through the five senses. Here-and-now specifics and realities—what they can touch, taste, see, smell, and feel—are the data that matter most and are most trusted; these are the things that

Sensors first notice. This makes them tactile, literal, and practical and tends to focus their work on the actual, the present, the doable. So, Sensors tend to lead by exercising their experience and their command of detail.

Among the many strengths of a Sensing leader is a natural sense of the movement of time and of how much time a project will take to complete. In addition, Sensors' attention to the practical and tangible give them an orientation toward implementation and action—in other words, toward getting stuff done. Sensing leaders tend to exercise their creativity by cleverly and effectively maneuvering within the limits of their resources and experience. What we expect of our S leaders—and as S leaders, demand from our subordinates—has a strong effect on an S's leadership style.

Criticism of Sensing leaders can be harsh and often comes from those with an iNtuitive bias. Some claim that Sensing leaders are lazy about generating new ideas, unimaginative, unwilling or unable to concentrate on the future, and prone to get lost in tending to the details of today rather than dealing with the overarching pattern or trend that the big picture brings to light.

In the end, what usually trips up Sensors is their limited perspective on things. Consider Sean, a team leader in an electronics firm we worked with. Sean was frustrated by several members of his team who he felt weren't fully engaged. Laurie would consistently come in late; Brian was often working on other, unrelated matters during team meetings; Janice's pager would seem to always go off about ten minutes into the meeting, at which point she'd leave. This lack of individual involvement was taking its toll: Sean's team had no sense of mission, urgency, or investment.

As an effective leader, Sean's first instinct was to deal with each individual—to try to make Laurie more punctual, Brian more focused, and Janice less electronically accessible. If only he could solve each of these problems, he reasoned, the whole team would be better able to move forward.

As a Sensor, Sean saw the organizational trees—the people

and their issues—but failed to see the forest. In his case, the "forest" was the pattern formed by Laurie, Brian, and Janice's behavior: The team lacked engagement, enthusiasm, and esprit de corps.

Typewatching helped Sean see the pattern. He began to realize that as a Sensor, he was a very in-basket kind of guy—he would deal with whatever was at the top of the pile, the latest thing to hit his desk. He wanted to know, "How can I make Laurie show up on time?" when the real question should have been, "How can I make Laurie more engaged?" Eventually, with this larger question in mind, Sean was able to allow the team members to restructure their roles and responsibilities without abandoning the team's mission. Laurie and her teammates soon felt reenergized and possessed of a new sense of commitment—and Laurie, as a result, started showing up on time.

People who prefer iNtuition, of course, see the world in a very different light. They see the forest quite clearly, but may fail to see the trees. They are hardwired to pick up on patterns, future possibilities, and the proverbial big picture rather than on details and specifics. The line item on a report is valuable to the iNtuitive to the extent that it suggests a trend and thus a future possibility. iNtuitives live in the future, and lead toward it by exercising their vision and drive to change and develop their colleagues and the systems around them.

Leaders preferring iNtuition tend to focus on the possibilities and the big picture first and the details later—if ever. This is a quality rewarded in senior-level and executive leaders far more than in junior and entry-level ones—leaders preferring iNtuition often find that behaviors that were liabilities early in their careers eventually enable them to reap great benefits.

Among the natural strengths of iNtuitive leaders is their ability to think systemically and strategically. iNtuitives link factual observations to form a pattern or trend, which incorporates a handful of possibilities that are connected to other ideas, possibilities, options, facts, and patterns. An effective iNtuitive leader is able to harness these perceptions into a vision of the future and to use that vision to drive creative change.

But just as Sensors can get bogged down in detail and lose the ability to see the bigger picture, iNtuitives can get seduced by the vast world of possibilities—visioning and imagining much, but doing little. When this happens, subordinates of the iNtuitive—and Sensors in particular—may regard this process as mere mental gymnastics that have nothing to do with the "real world" of life in the trenches. In the worst case, the N leader can be branded an airhead, a space cadet, or an absent-minded professor, and valuable leadership capital is lost.

How Thinkers and Feelers Lead

Leadership has a great deal to do with judgments, so the Thinking-Feeling preference, which describes how an individual prefers to make decisions, looms large.

Let's start with Thinkers. They make up only half of the population, yet they occupy the overwhelming majority of leadership ranks throughout the world. And the higher you go up the corporate ladder, the greater the concentration of Thinkers. More than twenty years of cross-cultural data we have collected show that Ts make up about 86 percent of middle managers, nearly 93 percent of senior managers, and more than 95 percent of executives.

How can this be? There are two likely explanations. First, the workplace has long been male-dominated, and two thirds of men are Thinkers. Second, it is a natural tendency for people—Thinkers and Feelers alike—to clone themselves in hiring and nurturing new personnel. This means that over time this natural tendency for Thinkers to replace and surround themselves with other Thinkers—combined with the historically male-dominated workplace—may have led to an overabundance of Thinkers in management ranks.

Thinkers strive to make decisions by standing back, removing themselves from the issue or subject at hand, and employing cause-and-effect logic to reach a conclusion. Thinkers are analytical; they work toward clarity using objectivity, logic, and analysis—all tools that depersonalize issues and situations. It's not that people and human values become unimportant, but more often than not they are trumped by the T's drive to be right, to be competent, and to remain objective. Personal issues make it into the T's decision-making equation, but they do not control or overpower the process.

Thinkers often see the world as a series of problems to be solved. T leaders, therefore, are naturally problem-oriented. Whether engaging with a person, a group, a task, or a crisis, the T leader's first reaction typically will be to ask questions like: "What is wrong here?"; "How can this issue, performance, or product be better?"; "What needs fixing?"; and perhaps, "Who screwed this up in the first place?" This orientation—especially if gone unchecked in an organization dominated by Ts—can lead to a culture of criticism between leaders and their followers. The subordinate's job then becomes delivering on or working toward a task, and the leader's job becomes criticizing the subordinate's performance. Some T leaders may even view criticism as a compliment, bestowed only upon those people they feel are worthy of their time and attention and suggestions for improvement.

Feeling leaders engage with the human element first and see it as the determining factor in any final outcome. Feelers prefer to begin their decision-making process with subjective consideration of the people involved, their circumstances, and the solution that would be in closest harmony with the F's own values. The personal and subjective nature of this process does not mean, however, that F leaders eschew tough, objective decisions. They will be factored in, but only after the personal issues have been considered and weighed.

As leaders, Feelers tend to exercise power through relationships and attention given to subjective human values. They are masters of putting themselves into other people's moccasins. Their empathy tends to make F leaders circumstantial decision makers who are more concerned with the person or people impacted by an issue than with the precedent or policy designed to deal with the issue in the first place. This tendency is another aspect of "People First," a classic F slogan, and its by-products can both help and hinder a group or organization. For example, it can create a sense of familiarity and cohesion that may be motivating and inspiring. Many people who work for effective Feeling leaders speak to us of their loyalty and personal dedication to these individuals. (How one achieves this personal connection with subordinates—or even why one would want to—is something of a mystery to Thinking leaders.) The downside to this, of course, is that subjective or circumstantial decision making can be seen as unfair when someone is left behind, or when the bar appears to keep moving to accommodate all the different human needs on a team or in an office.

Fs' sensitivity to others is not merely a feel-good exercise.

FAIR WARNING

At Org Inc., the policy is that work begins at 9:00 A.M. The employment manual says that all staff should be at their desks, engaged in their duties, by 9:00 A.M. to avoid reprimand. Today, John comes in to work twenty minutes late.

- **Thinking leader's response:** "John, I noticed you were twenty minutes late today. You know that is a violation of our policy, so in all fairness I have to give you a verbal warning that such infractions will not be tolerated." This objective approach aims to ensure fairness by maintaining—and enforcing—the same rule consistently over time.
- **Feeling leader's response:** "John, I noticed you were twenty minutes late today. Was your tardiness due to that child-care issue we spoke of last week? I know child care is a tough problem that you've been dealing with lately. Listen, we need you here on time, so let's create some backup plan so that we are not left short-staffed on mornings like this one. By the way, how is your daughter doing?" This subjective approach ensures fairness by taking into account the personal needs of all parties involved.

Which leader was more fair?

Used effectively, it can engender real power. Effective Feeling leaders use their ability to understand others' lives, to walk in their shoes, and to feel their pain as a means of strengthening a personal bond. In doing so, they often increase the amount of leverage they have with others.

There's nothing in the entire world of business that brings T-F differences to the forefront more than the awful experience of downsizing. We helped one T leader at a major defense contractor cope in a way that turned a difficult downsizing situation into . . . well, a less difficult one.

The plant being downsized was based in the Southwest U.S. and was by far the largest employer in its community. The downsizing put more than 10 percent of the entire local workforce out of a job, so it was a devastating blow to the community. Things were no less stressful at the plant, where second-generation employees also seemed doomed to lose their jobs in a region that had few reasonable employment alternatives. Moreover, the company's facility was rife with turf wars that had broken out among top managers vying to keep their groups far from the downsizing axe.

We were brought in to conduct a two-day intervention to help the plant's general manager and his sixteen direct reports through the process. One of the first things we did was study the group's typological profile, as well as that of the organization. In doing so, it became instantly clear what we were dealing with: an organization led exclusively by Thinking leaders, who had cloned themselves to the point where more than 90 percent of the company shared the Thinking preference. The impact of that T-based culture was wearing heavily on everyone.

As Thinkers, the company's managers were prone to look at things through the lens of impersonal objectivity, which can be an effective tool during a downsizing. It allows decision makers to be dispassionate, to make tough choices for the good of the company. But Ts, in their objectivity, tend to want to "fix" things—to find out what's wrong and make it right. What they lacked during this critical, turbulent time was subjectivity—the ability to deal with interpersonal dynamics.

We helped the group members to look at themselves—something Ts are generally loath to do—in order that they might come to and appreciate their organizational blind spots. This enabled them to better manage themselves and the process. Turf wars eased, stresses were reduced, and the whole sad process proceeded in a much more humane way.

Along the way, the T managers plastered the company walls with signs proclaiming their newfound commitment to one another—and did so in ultimate T fashion, with the slogan "THINK PEOPLE."

How Extraverts and Introverts Lead

Carl Jung believed the preference between Extraversion and Introversion to be the biggest discriminator among people. That's certainly the case when it comes to leadership: The behavioral differences between Extraverts and Introverts tend to be obvious and profound, and play an important role in leadership style.

Extraverts—who are energized and seduced by the outer world of people, places, and things—influence others quite naturally by engaging with them: talking, networking, and taking action. Quick to disclose plans, values, principles, and even what might seem like rather personal things about themselves, Extraverts often lead others the way they live their own lives—by putting it all out on Main Street. A good Extraverted slogan is "WHAT YOU SEE IS WHAT YOU GET." Focused on and energized by the external world, Es are generally aware of and drawn to people and groups. Therefore, as leaders, Extraverts tend to be open verbal communicators who share more than they withhold.

The potential liability for the Extraverted leader is that he or she may share, talk, and disclose regardless of whether the information being imparted has been asked for or is being listened to. More prone to talking and engaging than to listening and reflecting, Extraverts may find it difficult to get their moorings by themselves, in meditation or without the benefit of staff and team. They may also second-guess decisions or ideas that have not been discussed out loud or thrown against a sounding board first.

On the other hand, Extraverts usually have no problem making their ideas, even half-baked ones, widely known. We fondly recall Rondell, the manager of a small retail shop in our neighborhood. Rondell was the sole Extravert; his half-dozen employees were all Introverts.

Rondell loved to walk around the store Extraverting in his seemingly random way: "Did you see CNN last night? There

MANAGEMENT BY WALKING AROUND OPEN DOORS

Many of the past few years' popular management theories give an edge to Extraverts. For example, one management model that circulated a number of years ago was "Management by Walking Around." This model suggests that effective managers know their people, the world in which their people work, and the problems their people struggle with every day.

The only way a leader can know these things, so suggests the model, is to get out from behind a desk and walk around the workplace—talking, greeting, shaking hands, engaging, and observing. Clearly, this is an action-oriented, Extraverted management model. Most Introverts would be hard-pressed to sustain this style for more than a brief period.

Or consider the "Open-Door" policy, an attempt to make leaders visible and approachable by inviting just about anyone to stop by at just about any time to talk with the manager about just about anything—again, a policy only an Extravert could love. The irony is that it is pointless for Extraverted leaders to have an open-door policy because they are rarely in their offices—they are out walking around!

was a great piece on Congress. That was a crazy customer who just left. What did she want? We shouldn't waste our time with people like her. Does anyone know what the lunch special is across the street? Maybe we should move the display into the front window. I'll be in my office if anyone wants to know what I'm doing."

Rondell's dutiful staff would walk behind him, taking notes, assuming Rondell's ramblings had some weight and were leading in some significant direction or to some important conclusion. As it turned out, they rarely did.

One day, in one of his ramblings, Rondell mused, "You know, it's been a really good week and we've all worked hard. Maybe we should take Friday off." That Friday, three of his staffers failed to show up. Rondell, of course, didn't recall saying anything about taking Friday off. Others heard it as a directive.

Eventually, everyone—including Rondell—figured out that not everything Rondell said was gospel.

Introverts—energized by their inner world of ideas, thoughts, and concepts—are not often motivated to influence others. When Introverts do choose to influence others, they commonly do so by presenting ideas, plans, visions, or values—often in writing—that will be compelling and attractive. As is the case with all Introverts, an Introverted leader has a lot brewing under the surface, but only lets out or shares a small piece of it.

Sometimes the issue for Introverted leaders is the speed with which they are able to make decisions. We worked with a young man named Christopher who was clearly destined to rise up the organization. At one point, however, he found himself in a position with the company where he needed to make snap decisions; typically, because a staffer would approach him with a problem that needed to be solved on the spot.

That was a bit unfair to Christopher, who, as an Introvert, didn't have the time he needed in order to process. Often he would think about it later and come up with a different answer. In some cases, it was too late—the ship had already sailed. As a result, he was labeled indecisive.

The challenge when dealing with Extraverts and Introverts is to appreciate both what comes out of their mouths and what doesn't. With Es, it's critical to give them time to noodle things publicly, and to understand that some of this noodling will be of little value. With Is, it's critical to give them time to think about things before pressing for a final answer.

How Judgers and Perceivers Lead

Because Js are decisive and emphasize closure, structure, schedules, and order in their public lives, they usually fit the stereotype of what many believe a leader should be. Both Judgers and Perceivers, however, have unique perspectives and qualities that nurture their roles as leaders.

Evidence of the Judging orientation in the workplace exists everywhere—think about punching the clock, meeting deadlines, achieving quotas, time-tracking, and all the other minutiae of daily work life. Given these objective elements, a Judging leader is well suited to systems that are strongly oriented toward decisive action, rigid schedules, and the accomplishment of tasks. J leaders' work-now-play-later approach to life gives them a serious, no-nonsense demeanor.

Their need for control doesn't necessarily make Js better leaders than Ps. Js' strengths can easily turn into liabilities. For example, despite the Js' apparent leadership advantages, they can run into trouble when their drive for control, scheduling, and closure prevents new data from being considered. The push to complete a project may overpower the uncertainty of a given team, members of which—if given enough time to probe— might have uncovered an important reason to slow down. Judgers, in this regard, are perfectly capable of winning a battle but losing a war when their strengths are taken to an extreme.

Perceiving leaders tend to exhibit a variety of what appear to be behavioral liabilities—they're described as scattered, directionless, unscheduled, and prone to having more starts than finishes. Often overlooked, however, are the Ps' many effective leadership qualities, especially their ability to live their lives as flexible, curious, and open-minded people who can be easygoing, informal, adaptable, and fun-loving. The spontaneous nature of

ONE O'CLOCK JUMP

Two managers—a Judger and a Perceiver—each have something on their calendars for 1:00 P.M. on Tuesday. Something else has just come up that conflicts with the scheduled appointment. In both cases, the conflicting item seems attractive, even necessary.

- **The Judger's first response** is probably irritation that the day's schedule did not unfold as planned, and he will seek to control the second event to the degree that it can be made to fit the original schedule. This manager will be praised for effective task, project, and time-management skills, yet criticized for being inflexible and resistant to change.

- **The Perceiver's first response** is more than likely to be excitement that there is yet another option available at 1:00 P.M. on Tuesday, and she will readily adapt the day's schedule to accommodate the needs of the new event. This manager will be praised for being adaptable and open to last-minute changes, but roundly condemned for allowing projects to creep along and for being late to staff meetings.

Who's more effective, the controller or the adapter?

Perceiving leaders means you are never quite sure how they will respond to you, to a new challenge, or to a new opportunity.

As we've discovered with other preference pairings, the JP qualities that help people rise to the top often don't serve them well once they get there. Consider the case of Gavin, an extremely talented marketing consultant hired by a midsize business services firm to help develop new offerings. Gavin was a brilliant, visionary, and enthusiastic ENTP, usually spouting an idea a minute. Someone once likened listening to Gavin do his thing in a brainstorming session—waving arms, pacing the room, scrawling on the whiteboard, all while spewing forth an astonishing array of creative thoughts—to "trying to sip from a fire hose."

Gavin's talent served his client well. He helped the business services firm, with which he worked for several years, to increase customer retention, improve cross-selling among divisions and product lines, and generally stay ahead of the competition.

As often happens with consultants, Gavin was given a chance to work in-house permanently—the firm offered him a full-time job as marketing director. At first Gavin declined, but the client insisted and made the deal impossible to resist.

Soon after he signed on, all of the qualities that had made Gavin so valuable to the company suddenly turned against him.

For example, now that he was on board, his hit-and-run technique no longer fit the bill: He couldn't simply offer up an array of good ideas, then disappear for months while the client implemented them. Now the generating of ideas as well as all of the hands-on, nuts-and-bolts implementation fell to Gavin and his staff. It quickly became clear that he was not up to the task.

As a P, Gavin's natural abilities led him to be spontaneous, inquisitive, and open-minded—exactly what made him such a prolific idea man. As a manager, he needed to tap into his non-preferences—to work on being decisive, accountable, and, most of all, focused on results. In other words, his J side needed to emerge. That proved to be a frustrating, formidable challenge: Gavin reported that trying to cope as an insider in the company was like "pulling around a ball and chain."

Unlike Judgers, who are decisive and firm, Perceiving leaders like Gavin may choose to follow one or several courses of action as they see fit. More often than not, what you experience with Ps is openness, choice, and questions, questions, questions. Decisions and closure will come, but often not very quickly, and rarely without exploring a variety of exciting options. This does not mean that Gavin—or any Perceiver—is unable to make snap decisions or hold fast to conclusions; they simply would prefer not to do so in the open. Their public side—what they show the world—is about gathering data and staying open to new information. Conclusions are far less likely to be spoken of and shared.

In the end, both J and P stereotypes—that Judging leaders are rigid and do not listen to new data, and that Perceiving leaders are procrastinators who cannot make decisions—are off base. Both ideas fly in the face of Type theory. Judgers can be flexible and open to new data, and Perceivers can make decisions and hold to them; it's just that they prefer to do so quietly.

The critical difference between J and P leaders has less to do with decisiveness and more to do with the ability to give direction. Judgers are able to do this more easily than Perceivers, who

AN OPEN-AND-SHUT CASE

Not long ago, while Otto and Janet were co-leading a training event, the uncomfortably warm training room in which they found themselves elicited very different responses from these two experienced group leaders.

After his presentation, Otto, the Judger, said, "It's hot in here. Sue, please open up that back window." This is direction—what we count on Judgers to provide. We can reasonably assume that Otto had gathered some data about his comfort level; perhaps he'd even noticed some of the participants fanning themselves or taking off their coats. But no one really knows: With Judgers, we are usually not privy to the data gathering, only to the conclusion—in this case, that Otto wanted Sue to open the window.

After her presentation, Janet, the Perceiver, asked, "Is anyone hot in here? John, do you think it is hot?" John stated that he thought it was hot, and the group members quickly determined that most of them were hot, so three people got up to open the windows in the back of the room. This is classic Perceiver behavior: Janet didn't state a request, she only raised a point. We can assume that beneath her data gathering, Janet had concluded that it was hot and that she wanted the windows open. But the class heard neither a conclusion nor a direction—only questions. The windows were opened just the same, but it was the group's decision to do so.

are instead facilitative, and this distinction makes a big difference in their leadership styles.

It bears repeating that in the realm of leadership, the advantage frequently goes to the Judger. The ability to direct is closely associated with effective leadership, but Perceivers bring a more grassroots philosophy to leadership roles that can be equally powerful. Facilitative leadership can be an extremely effective way to build participation, ownership, and buy-in from the bottom up. Whereas highly directive leadership can often create an atmosphere of compliance—people doing the leader's bidding because they were told to do so—facilitative leadership is more apt to inspire commitment—people doing the leader's bidding because they want to.

Of course, too much of a good thing can spell trouble, and a Perceiving leader's facilitative style can be viewed, sometimes accurately, as vacillation or indecisiveness. If not careful, Ps can become overwhelmed with options, data, and interesting side roads, to the point where few time commitments are kept and few goals accomplished.

Leadership studies indicate that productivity does not depend upon a preference for Judging or Perceiving, even though the methodologies and approaches of each differ so dramatically. The real skill for an effective leader is to know when to adapt and when to control—regardless of preference or type.

What, and Where, Is Power?

Power and *authority* are loaded words, and we find in our personal coaching and group consulting that discussing someone's authority and personal power can cause anxiety and confusion. One of the principal reasons for the confusion is that the different personality types see power very differently and rooted in vastly different places. The lens of Temperament gives us tremendous insight into how each of us tends to view power itself—where it is and how we are most likely to use it.

NF Leaders—the People People

To NFs, power resides in personal relationships. Personal and interpersonal connections and values are what hold the most sway over this group: To win someone's commitment requires that a leader relate to him or her personally. This is the NF's strength, and the NF leader brings to the job an arsenal of potent power tools: a pat on the back, compliments, a warm smile, eye contact, stated feelings of warmth or appreciation, affirmation, respect, personal attention and interest, and an acknowledgment of others' values.

Effective leaders win an NF employee's commitment by making a point of caring whether the worker likes them in return. All of these efforts are for naught if insincere, for an NF highly values the genuine expression of warmth and connection but is quick to see through and resent veiled attempts at manipulation.

It's also important to understand that simple compliance with the wishes of an NF leader is not usually enough for the NF. The NF leader will continue to "sell" the idea or action until you are not only doing it, but are grateful for the opportunity and experience. NF leaders—whether in sales positions or not—never stop selling. Harmony, connection, inclusion, and group cohesion are of the utmost importance to them. Drawing on their ability to make inspirational pleas, NF leaders will be tirelessly persuasive—and take it personally if people don't follow.

NT Leaders—Competence Above All

NTs neither need nor want—and at times even actively work against—organizational or institutional structures, procedures, traditions, and hierarchy. They are not necessarily being contrary, but are merely seeking clarity and, above all else, competence. When logic, clarity, and competence—as defined by each individual NT—are not present within an organization, then the organization, its conventions, its rules, and, above all, its leaders compromise the NT's willingness to be led.

When it comes to interacting with their leaders, the NTs' scorecards are always activated and the performance bar that their leaders must clear is always on the rise. If we do a competent job leading you today, then the bar goes up overnight. Therefore, leading an NT means proving against his or her standards that you are fully competent. If you do that, you will have that NT on board—at least until the end of the day.

This drive for competence plays an important role when the NT is the leader. Because NTs are so focused on objective clarity, they tend to be quick to criticize. It is through criticism that we learn what is wrong, what could be better, and how to become more competent. One of the greatest gifts, therefore, that an NT leader can give is criticism of your performance. NT leaders, if he or she puts any stock in you, will develop you through argument and critique of your performance and ideas, eventually freeing you from their scrutiny.

SJ Leaders—the Company People

SJs see power in the structure, hierarchy, and traditions of their organizations and work teams. The power tools of an SJ are titles, salaries, tenure, official citations and commendations, managerial mandates, medals, and all of the myriad other things that make success official.

To motivate an SJ subordinate, you must first understand his or her place in the system relative to yours. SJs rely upon the system—through its leadership—to provide them with the data and structures they need to accomplish their goals. Even when SJs lose faith or confidence in a leader, they will tend to follow the proper procedures whether to transfer jobs or to file a complaint against the leader. Their faith resides in the system and its rules, not in a given individual. To SJ leaders, power is rooted in authority, and though commitment is expected, compliance is demanded.

As leaders, SJs tend to emphasize the importance of detail and practicality in order to make people efficient and capable of completing projects on time and under budget. If procedures, rules, and regulations do not exist, SJ leaders will first establish parameters and then work within them. In fact, many SJ leaders would identify this as their primary duty—to impose order over chaos. This is the SJ leader's gift.

SP Leaders—the Troubleshooters

SPs live for the moment. They are driven to stay open to new sensory data and to use action and tangible tools to produce some result with immediate impact or benefit. Unlike NFs and SJs, SPs don't put considerable weight on personal relationships or organizational procedures; both are seen as overly confining. Unlike NTs, SPs don't score competency with an abstract scorecard, but against the practical demands of the moment and the situation in which they find themselves.

SP employees look to their leaders—when they do at all—to provide them with the materials and resources needed to perform the task and with the freedom to work without managerial meddling or excessive procedural control. SPs want to be free to flex and move with the demands of the day—indeed, those of the very moment.

As leaders, SPs exercise power by solving problems and acting to address the concerns of the moment, even if so doing violates policy, procedure, organizational hierarchy, an agreed-upon project plan, or the needs of any given person or group. The needs of the moment trump all of these. This focus on the here and now tends to make SP leaders good troubleshooters, with particularly good skills at crisis management—which, in some companies, is a way of life.

Leadership and the Attitudes

Another seldom-considered combination of preference pairings has a tremendous impact on leadership and how successfully, on average, someone will rise to the challenges of a

DEFUSING THE SITUATION

OKA associate Gloria Fauth, an ENTP, tells the following true story to illustrate the personal and leadership styles of each of the four Temperaments in a crisis situation:

A meeting was taking place at a U.S. embassy in Africa. Present at the meeting were several NFs, NTs, and SJs, and a solitary SP. At one point an embassy official walked in the room and calmly notified the group that a bomb threat had been made against the embassy and that they must clear the building.

- **The NFs** dashed to the phone to call their families to let them know that everything was all right and not to worry.

- **The NTs** started debating with one another the effectiveness of embassy bombing, the practice of phoning in bomb threats, and the role each plays in the efforts of international terrorism—a discussion that continued throughout the afternoon at the café across the street.

- **The SJs** automatically went to the corner of the room and pulled out an official manual to determine the standard operating procedure for dealing with bomb threats.

- **The one SP**, within moments, was in the hallway, directing traffic, answering questions, and getting her colleagues out of harm's way.

leadership role. The Attitudes—the combination of Extraversion or Introversion and Judging or Perceiving—indicate the frequency with which people will engage in the outer world, and the way in which they will do it. The physical world of action, people, places, and things is where leaders most often have to engage, so Attitude pairings can tell us a lot about how a person's behavior will both create and inhibit leadership potential.

Extraverted-Judgers—the Natural Influencers

For the past few years, much of the energy at Otto Kroeger Associates has been focused on a dramatic research project. Among other things, we have studied the impact of type preferences on the successful completion of college. Our findings include evidence that the four Extraverted-Judging types (ESTJ, ESFJ, ENFJ, and ENTJ) tend to be the most overachieving of all types and the most successful at accomplishing anything to which they devote their energies. We have since found that Isabel Briggs Myers, creator of the Myers-Briggs Type Indicator® instrument, discovered but never published the same findings.

The college involved in our study has a competitive and highly selective professional development program designed to breed future leaders. In the program, college juniors and seniors spend one week traveling to Boston, New York, and Washington, D.C., to shadow professionals in their area of interest. The selection process involves personal interviews and candidate-written letters in which each student sells his or her ability to set and achieve goals and be successful. In the many years' worth of data we have on this program, EJs have predominated—making up more than 70 percent of the group every year.

This leadership training program attracts EJs for the same reason that EJs so frequently wind up in leadership positions wherever they go. Extraverted-Judgers seem to emit an aura of self-confidence, capability, competency, and assurance, so that even when they are uncertain or wrong, they seem decisive and right. Isabel Briggs Myers found that Extraverted-Judgers have an oversupply of what she called "stamina" that gives them an edge in life toward success. Because of this stamina, when something does go wrong for EJs, one of their first assumptions is that someone else caused it to happen. This tendency to externalize blame allows them to keep on moving and come out a winner, which gives them still more confidence and tends to leave others around them somewhere between intimidated and wanting to follow them. We hold just two preferences—Extraversion and Judging—responsible for that effect. Other preferences—Sensing or iNtuition, Thinking or Feeling—will fine-tune the effect that an EJ has on the world, but the preferences for Extraversion and Judging alone will boost an individual toward success in leadership roles and will tend to draw followers.

Introverted-Judgers—Strong, Silent Types

Introverts who prefer Judging (ISTJ, ISFJ, INFJ, and INTJ), much like their EJ brethren, lead with their judgment. Behaviorally they appear focused, decisive, closure-driven, directive, and overtly controlling. As Introverts, however, they are not drawn to the outer world of people, places, things, and action, but rather to their inner worlds of reflection, ideas, and concepts.

IJs are common leadership types, and the list of the strengths they bring to leadership roles is long. It is this type of combination that we know stereotypically as pillars of strength or strong, silent types, and their followers appreciate the focus and reflection they bring to teams and organizations. But IJs can pay for their lack of Extraversion with the criticism that they are slow to engage and frequently appear disconnected, disinterested, or even arrogant. Introverted-Judgers, unlike their Extraverted counterparts, can seem indecisive, given that upon reflection they may later revise or even reverse their decisions. Thus, although there is no doubt that Judgers have an advantage in gaining success and appearing successful in leadership roles, a preference for Introversion makes this Attitude pairing a mixed bag.

Extraverted-Perceivers—Energizing Forces

Extraverted-Perceivers (ESTP, ESFP, ENFP, and ENTP), like all Extraverts, are energized by the external world, drawn to interaction with people, things, and events. They will be verbal, engaging, action-oriented leaders, but as Perceivers, they will not place a priority on closure, schedules, or order, but rather on flexibility, curiosity, and adaptability. It is this open-endedness that tends to be EPs' biggest stumbling block to achieving or thriving in positions of leadership, and they are fairly uncommon in leadership ranks.

As leaders, Extraverted-Perceivers are seen as energizing forces for change and creativity, but conversely, they are also seen as flighty, indecisive, and chaotic. The popular explanation for why many people with this Attitude pairing do not rise within organizations, despite their many gifts, is that EPs tend to overextend themselves, with limited results.

Introverted-Perceivers—Quiet and Reflective

In terms of how successful any given person will be on average in influencing people or groups, Extraverted-Judgers have the edge, followed by Introverted-Judgers and then Extraverted-Perceivers. Introverted-Perceivers (ISTP, ISFP, INFP, and INTP) face the greatest challenges in achieving success in leadership roles.

Introverted-Perceivers tend to be quiet, reflective, and oriented toward internal values and principles that center them and compel them toward even more reflection when action is finally taken. It is rare for these principles and values to be revealed or given much voice; therefore, IPs often seem mysterious or inconsistent. Their flexibility, openness, and casual, nonhierarchical style leads to their being viewed (especially in our Extraverted-Judging–dominated systems) as weak and indecisive. Introverted-Perceivers' natural self-doubt and questioning manner may mark them as unconfident and wavering. Even when Introverted-Perceivers are confident in their conclusions, what comes out of their mouths is often open to change and frequently sounds tentative.

Where Extraverted-Judgers tend to assume that the fault lies elsewhere when they do something wrong, Introverted-Perceivers are apt to assume personal responsibility for things, events, and decisions that had nothing to do with them. All these factors contribute to a seeming lack of self-confidence and a diminished ability to influence people and groups in a world usually compelled by and drawn to the EJ's forcefulness, directiveness, and bravado.

Attitude studies reveal some troubling trends and blatant type biases, and though they do reflect reality in terms of overall trends and typological tendencies, no one's professional or personal capabilities or skill sets are determined by psychological preferences alone. Indeed, nearly everyone has the makings of an effective leader. We've known talented IPs who have risen to the top of their organizations, and EJs who have failed spectacularly as leaders. Our point is not that Extraverted-Judgers make better leaders than others; they merely tend to fit into conventional leadership roles more naturally. Conversely, Introverted-Perceivers will find more hurdles between themselves and success in most leadership positions, and there will, as a result, be far fewer of them in such spots.

We've now viewed leadership through three different lenses— the eight preferences, the four Temperaments, and the four Attitudes. That's, admittedly, a lot of data about leadership.

While we've noted the leadership advantages of each type in the business world, the real power of type in leadership derives from your ability to access your preferences as well as your nonpreferences. While lots of people can get along quite well in the world by doing what comes naturally, the truest, most effective leaders have it all: They can be verbal and gregarious, yet reflective and thoughtful; they can pay attention to the details of the moment while paying heed as well to the bigger picture; they must be fair, objective, humane, and just; and they must be focused on results while staying open to changing circumstances and new information.

When General George C. Marshall, the chief of staff of the U.S. Army during World War II, was later named secretary of state, he recognized the challenge and put it this way: "It became clear to me that at the age of fifty-eight I would have to learn new tricks that were not taught in the military manuals or on the battlefield. In this position I am a political soldier and

Leadership

IF YOU ARE AN . . .

	EXTRAVERT	INTROVERT
EXTRAVERT	• Allow Es ample time and space to talk out ideas, issues, and problems without premature closure or threat of penalty. • Remember that little of the volume generated counts for anything. • Think before you speak (count to ten). • Push and repeat what's really important.	• Talk to Is frequently and openly, engage them, and keep them active. • Remember that they tend to exercise power in a way that is vocal, visible, and active—so at times force yourself into the spotlight. • Ask for feedback and argue/discuss it on the spot. • Now and then, have a simple chat.
	EXTRAVERT	INTROVERT
INTROVERT	• Remember that silence does not mean agreement or consent. • Allow time and space for Is to assimilate and reflect. • Remember that they tend to exercise power in a way that is understated and reflective. • Ask for performance feedback, and then listen to what they have to say.	• Engage Is disclosing your ideas, intentions, and plans, and actively solicit input and feedback. • Role-model some overt actions that might facilitate communication. • Determine what issues need verbal vs. written reinforcement. • Keep reminding yourself that silence is not always golden—sometimes it's yellow!
	SENSOR	INTUITIVE
SENSOR	• Communicate how specific actions and efforts will affect the big picture. • Seek outside help to keep you aware of trends, patterns, and future possibilities. • Focus on the positive possibilities the future could bring, then communicate them to your followers, along with the specific actions.	• Remember that your focus on the big picture will irritate as much as inspire your follower(s). • Allow a focus on specifics and details, but encourage your follower(s) to discuss how microissues add up to form a bigger effort. • Remember that your vision will be realized only when details are seen to and ideas are implemented.
	SENSOR	INTUITIVE
INTUITIVE	• Remember that your focus on details and facts will frustrate as much as inspire your follower(s). • Within the context of acting on a new possibility, push your follower(s) to develop detailed plans of action. • Remember that your management of detail and specifics will manifest itself in good leadership when focused toward attaining some future state.	• Communicate what specific actions will be taken, when, and by whom. • Seek outside guidance to keep you aware of which details of your industry will impact your efforts. • There cannot be too many reality checks.

LEADING AN . . .

IF YOU ARE A . . .

	THINKER	FEELER
THINKER	• Your follower(s) will judge your effectiveness as a leader by your ability to remain objective, employ cause-and-effect logic, and make tough decisions that transcend human whim. • Focus on what the impact of your actions and decisions are on the people whom you lead. • Remind yourself that all humans have emotions and feelings.	• Your follower(s) will judge your effectiveness as a leader by your ability to remain objective, employ cause-and-effect logic. • Say what you mean, mean what you say, and let go of it. • Work hard not to personalize everything. • Be slow to compliment and to apologize.

	THINKER	FEELER
FEELER	• Your follower(s) will judge your effectiveness as a leader by your ability to connect personally and adjust your decision making to circumstances. • "Thank you" and "I'm sorry" can buy a great deal of motivation. • Try not to fix or improve everything. • Schmoozing (within limits) can be good.	• Your follower(s) will judge your effectiveness by your ability to connect personally and adjust your decision making to circumstances. • Role-model tough and impersonal behavior now and then. • The more you want to rescue and get personally involved, DO NOT!

	JUDGER	PERCEIVER
JUDGER	• Schedule a little spontaneity every so often. • Now and then, "upset the apple cart." • Role-model and show options every chance you get. • Give advance warning of impending changes.	• State your boundaries and stay within them. • Do the structure and closure thing even when you do not want to. • Limit your changes of mind to one a day or week or.... • Don't be afraid to be FINAL and STICK TO IT!

	JUDGER	PERCEIVER
PERCEIVER	• State and restate your boundaries and limits. • Let go now and then and learn from experience. • Be genuine in trying new behaviors. • Balance each criticism with a compliment or keep the criticism to yourself.	• Now and then, follow through on something. • Compete with one another in being timely. • Plan your work and work your plan. • Jointly check off, with some regularity, something on the check-off list.

LEADING A . . .

will have to put my training in rapping out orders and making snap decisions on the back burner, and have to learn the arts of persuasion and guile. I must become an expert in a whole new set of skills."

Effective leaders must know themselves typologically, but they must also be ready, willing, and able to plumb the less accessible parts of themselves for the good of the whole.

7

Team Building

"I may not be the best person to
give you advice on that subject."

No matter where you work in a company, no matter what you
do, you are part of a team. The company itself represents a team
effort to reach a goal. Each department or division represents a
team too. So do the smaller groups of people working together
within those departments. In each case a team's success is directly linked to the efforts of the individual players and how
well those players get along and work with each other.

Typewatching cuts right to the heart of building and maintaining effective teams. Success in the twenty-first century, we
believe, will result from the ability of companies to produce
more with fewer human resources and to promote collaboration
over competition within and among companies.

We see examples of this all around. Departments within a company that previously competed or worked independently find
that they must now work together. Companies that competed
bitterly unite to manufacture more cost-effectively things they
both need. And entire countries are banding together to form
powerful common marketplaces that reduce or remove barriers
to enterprise. All of this requires people to relate in new ways.

The irony is that those most likely to rise to senior management positions—the Introverted-Thinking-Judging types—are
the ones least naturally given to motivating esprit de corps. For

them you're either on the team or you're not—and there is only one team: theirs.

So, how do we build collaborative, productive teams in this complex environment? And how do we make those who are not natural team players pay more than lip service to the process?

One big stumbling block to team building is differing views of rewards and punishments. You might assume that everyone understands and accepts the need for rewards and punishments. In reality the importance placed upon rewards and punishment in business varies with individuals' types. So what seems natural or appropriate to one type can be read as ineffective and unnecessary by another. Further, the predominant type that ascends to management positions—Thinking-Judgers—is a type that overlooks rewards as a motivator of people. Ts prefer to believe that the organization itself will be motivation enough. Your job security and your regular paycheck is your reward.

We hear it all the time: "You don't need to reward what's expected." Or, "People are expendable; productivity is what's important." Or, "Why should I have to kiss someone's behind to get them to do what they're getting paid to do?" And finally, "I don't have to like you. I don't even have to give a damn about you. If you want your paycheck, do your job and check your personal life at the door when you come to work."

Different types enter the job market and stay in various positions for reasons related to their personality preferences. An Extraverted-Feeler, for example, who likes the people with whom he or she is working would often rather continue in that environment than be promoted simply for more money. A Perceiver who is given freedom and flexibility produces much more in such a work environment and might think very carefully about a promotion if it were to a more rigid situation. And a Judger would leave and go almost anywhere to get away from a workplace that is disorganized, nondirective, and in need of authoritative structure.

The management style we believe is most effective is one that endorses looking for the good in employees, rewarding their accomplishments, helping them work through failures, and valuing each person and his or her contribution to the workforce as

LET'S GET ALONG. THAT'S AN ORDER.

You can't have a team just because the boss says so. It has a lot to do with what type the boss is.

Feelers, when they make it to the top, can have a tough time building teams, largely because they place so much emphasis on the team itself and less emphasis on what the team will actually do. In other words, esprit de corps can win out over productivity.

Consider the case of an ESFJ chief executive who decided that the entire headquarters staff would be a team and would work together harmoniously and productively. All decisions were to be made by consensus, he announced, ensuring that everyone would have a contribution and feel important.

An admirable and enlightened decision, to be sure. The problem was the others in the organization simply didn't see the need for this. And ironically they felt this decision-by-consensus mandate had been imposed upon them without any input from them. This brought a great deal of stubbornness and rebelliousness to the surface. It wasn't that these folks were against the CEO's team-building effort; they just didn't think it should be forced on them when it seemed to have little relevance to their overall productivity.

We helped the boss see how imposing he was being and how his good intentions were backfiring, creating disharmony. We helped both sides see that what was going on here involved the objective Thinkers bumping against a well-meaning Feeling boss, with both sides getting stuck in their Judging rigidity.

By reducing the conflict to typological terms, we were able to show them that each side had merit but was not listening to the other side. That lone revelation allowed both parties to back off, reconsider their positions, and eventually find a common ground.

an integral part of the company and the company's product. Each individual's signature is on some part of the final product, and without the signature, the product is incomplete. Such management affirms differences and allows for them; rewards

are given according to the individual's strengths and not according to a system's rules and regulations. If products are what people make—and they are—and if productivity is the result of
what and how the people do it, then toward the people is where
the manager's attention must be directed.

The bad news is that most managers, typologically at least,
aren't "people" people and therefore are not big on team performance. They have high control needs, believe that the only way
to get the job right is to do it themselves, and think that confronting interpersonal issues is a waste of time.

So we find ourselves with a dilemma: Given that the types
most drawn to management positions are the ones least naturally inclined to be team players, how do we bring people together to do good work? The solution has to do with harnessing
the proven abilities of those in top positions and appealing to
their high sense of responsibility.

Before we get into specifics, let's look briefly at how the eight
preferences approach teamwork.

How Extraverts and Introverts Approach Teamwork

The bad news here is that Es and Is approach cooperation and
teamwork from opposite directions, which leads to all kinds of
problems, from lagging productivity to little social interaction
before, during, or after working hours.

When it comes to being a team player, Extraverts can demand more time and attention, can tire the people around
them, and can seem just plain noisy. Others see them as anything from self-centered and overbearing to spoiled brats who
never get enough attention. Clearly, such labels aren't conducive
to fostering cooperation.

In the meantime, Introverts tend to keep a great deal of information to themselves. Others may interpret such behavior
with suspicion, believing the Introvert is attempting to control
the team by withholding information—or that the Introvert just
doesn't give a damn.

Of course understanding even a little bit about Typewatching will tell you that neither of the above interpretations is accurate. Still, such pigeonholing is commonplace, leading to the daily behaviors and name-calling that block effective teamwork.

To cut through such behavior, both parties must engage in some basic and simple communication. For example, it is legitimate for an Extravert to request, or even demand, some extraverted time. But the Extravert must learn to clarify his or her needs: "Let me take a couple minutes to bounce some ideas off you." "Can I get your thoughts on this?" "I'm just thinking out loud. Don't hold me to it." Introverts, of course, should in turn be open about their state of mind: "I'd be happy to do it in a half hour when I'm finished with this paper." Or, "I may not be the best person to give you advice on that subject."

One of the big mistakes Extraverts make is to assume that if someone is not engaged with another person, that individual is simply not busy. So, it's okay to interrupt someone sitting and reading in her office because that person is probably reading only because there's no one else with whom she can talk. You can imagine what an Extravert thinks of someone who is sitting there not even reading but merely *reflecting*. Clearly that person needs to be put to some more useful task—such as listening to the Extravert's thoughts of the moment.

Introverts, for their part, must make their own requests— usually for peace and quiet so that they can think, cogitate, reflect, space out, or do whatever they need to do. While you might think that Extraverts would be better able to make such requests, given that they are more prone to express their needs verbally, in fact Introverts are very capable of stating their needs. Since Introverts are less inclined to shoot from the lip, when they do speak, their words often have more impact. The problem for both Es and Is is that because their respective needs—to verbalize or reflect—seem so obvious to *them*, both parties tend to assume that the other understands. As with so many other misunderstandings, they end up in opposite places. Instead of being a team they are competitors.

How Sensors and iNtuitives Approach Teamwork

The differing perspectives Sensors and iNtuitives have of building teams would be humorous if they weren't so troublesome. Sensors, who tend to interpret things literally, have trouble seeing what team building has to do with the business at hand. Teams, after all, appear on the playing field and want to win games. That's not the case here at work; everyone has a job to do, and that's what you get paid for. So team building becomes a boondoggle, another distraction, another excuse for not doing the real work. "If I didn't spend so much time in meetings on how to work together, I'd get my job done more quickly," a Sensor is likely to lament. It's not that Sensors can't see the value of team building at work. Give them a good metaphor—the CEO being the quarterback, who hands off an assignment to a manager (halfback), who uses a support staff (blockers) to move a project ahead to a final goal (the end zone). Once they grasp the concept, the Sensors will be the ones leading the charge down the field. But getting to this point may take more than a few huddles.

For iNtuitives the very image of a team is one that is inspiring and exciting. If everyone could catch that enthusiasm, iNtuitives believe, productivity, profits, and pride would only skyrocket. But as enthusiastic as they are about the concept, it remains only that—a concept. Turning the concept into action can involve more accountability than most iNtuitives would care to assume. So for them teamwork is something that's good for everybody but them. They're like the parents who take their kids to Sunday school but would never think of going themselves. Like the Sensors, iNtuitives, too, can become effective team members, but it may take some effort for them to move beyond the mental process into real action.

How Thinkers and Feelers Approach Teamwork

While Thinkers view teamwork as anything that accomplishes the task, Feelers view it as how well people work together in doing the task. It doesn't take much imagination to see how this difference can set up some real headaches. If a group gets the job done but the individuals involved end up not speaking, that still falls within the boundaries of a good team effort, in the Thinker's view. Accomplishment determines team effectiveness. Of course such a scenario is nothing short of a disaster to a Feeler, for whom group spirit is key. It is the Feelers who say, "If a group has cohesion, spirit, and sense of purpose, they can accomplish any task, from meeting a deadline to raising money for the United Way."

We believe that the drama of this dynamic is at the heart of the differences between the American and Japanese management models. Historically American business philosophy was of the classic T model that people were expendable: "We pay you well. If you don't want to work, we'll hire someone who does—or replace you with a machine." Personal problems, laziness, even coffee breaks were frowned upon, if not outright prohibited. (Those of you under age fifty probably can't remember that only four decades ago coffee breaks were a subject for union-management negotiation.) Akin to this philosophy was management's belief: "I don't have to like you, as long as we get the job done."

Contrast this with the F-oriented Japanese model, which places heavy emphasis on team communication, individual affirmation, and a belief that when it comes to ideas and productivity, the whole group is greater than the sum of its parts. Regardless of their personal feelings, each member of the team shows concern for everyone else, appreciates each person's contribution, and recognizes that without every member of the team doing his or her part, success—personal, organizational, and societal—would be elusive.

Unlike the other preference differences, this one is harder to overcome because it reflects opposing yet ingrained philosophies: products vs. process, head vs. heart, task vs. people. Obviously none of these philosophies is better than the others; you need both—products and services, head and heart, and so on. History has proven—and common sense would dictate—that a company that operates without esprit de corps won't fare well in the marketplace. The reverse is also true: High esprit de corps without attention to deadlines and details will create a company that is less than predictable in meeting its goals.

Typewatching is the bridge that validates the necessity for both philosophies—that a successful company is one that balances its logical task orientation (Thinking) with an awareness of the human element required to reach those tasks (Feeling). It underscores the fact that people needn't change their personality preferences in order to fit in—even if their preferences are at odds with those of the majority—but rather affirms that part of their contribution is in being themselves.

We can't stress strongly enough the need to build teams that reflect both Thinking and Feeling dynamics. American business history is filled with examples of companies that relied on the T model—that quality speaks for itself—neglecting the more subjective, emotional aspects of their markets. Companies that appeal to both Ts and Fs have succeeded even when their products were tops in their field. General Electric comes to mind as one company whose products, while not necessarily technologically superior to its competitors, have often led the field because it has successfully touched the heartstrings of the buying public—after all, it "brings good things to life."

Keep in mind that 50 percent of the working and buying public are Feelers, and the same percentage are Thinkers. That means that at least half the American population wants to feel good about their quality of life at both work and home, and about their purchases. They'll choose Product A over Product B if it makes them feel better, often regardless of cost, quality, or other key factors. That also applies to where they shop. Nordstrom, the Seattle-based department-store chain, has had phenomenal success around the country, much of it based on factors beyond the products it sells, from formally attired musicians sitting at grand pianos to clerks who make you think you're the most important customer of the day. The company has consistently outshone even its most established competitors in mall after mall.

The challenge, then, given that most companies are laden with Thinkers at the top of the management ladder, is to find ways to pay more attention to the F side of the house. We're not talking about turning Ts into Fs—that goes against Typewatching philosophy. And we're not advocating that your hiring be strictly based on type preferences. That's another no-no. The secret is

HOW TO KEEP Ts FROM TRAMPLING OTHER PEOPLE'S FEELINGS

- **Don't respond when your feelings are strong.** Tell yourself, "I'm not ready to respond to this now."

- **Prepare to respond by getting clear about what made you angry and why.** "When I read, 'I told him we'd pay him $200,' I felt resentment at being put under financial obligation without being consulted."

- **Listen to the T's side and communicate your understanding of their logic.** "Your decision not to call me was made because it was after hours and you didn't want to disturb me."

- **Explain your feelings in objective terms and show the logic in them.** "I misunderstood you. From the language in your note I could conclude you had a negative opinion of me that you didn't have in the past."

- **Suggest alternatives that can be made into a matter of policy.** "I think we should set up a policy on when we can commit funds without consulting each other."

to find the Fs within your organization and to include them on the appropriate decision-making teams.

Where do you find them? A good place to start is in your human resources development, training, and any other departments related to health and human services. Statistically these departments attract Feeling types in far greater proportions than in the rest of the company. Another place to look is to the nonmanagerial female workforce. Statistically about two thirds

HOW TO KEEP Fs FROM FAILING TO DEAL WITH THE "TOUGH STUFF"

- **Don't give feedback when you are feeling hard-nosed and critical.** "I can give you feedback tomorrow that will be more useful."

- **Prepare first by listing all the things the person did well.** "This point is well taken. This paragraph is exciting."

- **Say, in so many words: "I like you and your work, and here are ways it could be even better."** "What you are saying is important and will be heard if we can put it into a standard format."

- **Be cooperative. Tell them you want to help.** "I can show you some tricks for checking your figures if you're interested."

- **Listen to the person's feelings and show you understand by sharing a similar experience.** "I know how you feel about writing to fit a format. I feel the same way when I have to write proposals."

- **Point out the impersonal forces at work.** "We developed a standard format so that people could read reports quickly and be able to tell what's important."

of American females are Feelers. Research has shown that most women currently in high positions in the corporate world are typologically like their male counterparts—that is, Thinking-Judging. But women who have yet to rise to the upper echelons are more likely than the men in those positions to bring a subjective element to your team. Even TJ women, by virtue of their role in society as nurturers, will probably bring some subjectivity to the team.

There's no question that finding the right people is easier said than done. You can't simply invite "a couple of girls from the steno pool" to your executive team session and expect them to say what they think. Chances are you'll be dissatisfied with the answers, if you even get any. It's not that these women don't have anything to offer. It's just that there is a long history of barriers to overcome, not the least of which is trust—that the women there are more than mere window dressing. It may take some time and several meetings before these new participants feel free to contribute freely. So, this is no quick fix; what we're suggesting is an evolution, a long-term change in the way your company behaves and makes decisions.

How Judgers and Perceivers Approach Teamwork

The importance of the Thinking-Feeling dynamic notwithstanding, it is the Judging-Perceiving dimension that makes teams succeed or fail, at least on a superficial level. Often Judgers' needs for closure and control make them seem like poor team players. And the Perceivers' incessant need for alternatives and frequent fly-by-the-seat-of-their-pants style make them appear to be less than committed to the team's goals.

Picture the typical scenario for a team meeting. At nine o'clock sharp the Js are sitting in place, pencils sharpened, ready to go (having read the agenda passed out before the meeting). By 9:05 the Js are already feeling resentful that they are being punished by the latecomers. The last P straggles in at about 9:17, apologizes for being late, glances at the agenda for the first time, and suggests some changes. By 9:43 the team has already divided into several camps, among them:

- The "I'll get you for being late" camp, in which anything the latecomer says is immediately shot down
- The "I'll vote for anything to end this meeting" camp, in which commitment to the project is overshadowed by the appearance that the meeting will drag on forever
- The "Let's not make rash decisions" camp, which counters the previous two camps' need to make immediate decisions
- The "Isn't it time to take a break?" camp, which is already thinking about where the group will go for lunch because all work and no play makes for an unproductive team

So, what started out as a genuine team effort within the first hour becomes a group of competitive and conflicted individuals working their respective agendas.

How do you avoid this—or deal with it when it happens?

We'll admit that you probably can't avoid this—Ps are Ps, and they operate on their own time schedules, which means that a nine o'clock meeting doesn't really start until they show up—whatever time that is. You can't change this much, except perhaps to warn everyone about the importance of being on time. In fact, meetings ought to start at their appointed hour, no matter who's there. Let the latecomers make up for lost time, rather than having them hold everyone else up. If you're running the meeting, you might plan to start the meeting with a few less-than-critical matters, so that the latecomers don't miss crucial decisions but those who are on time feel a sense of mission and accomplishment. But don't let on that you're doing this, or no one will be there when they should.

Even if everyone shows up on time, the J-P dynamic can still wreak havoc. Js tend to make closed statements or ask questions that are really judgments—"We couldn't possibly do this, could we?" In whatever form, Js often give the impression that their mind is already made up, even if this isn't the case. Js are really hoping that you'll challenge them and thereby give them more information. But others on the team can be turned off by this apparent closed-mindedness.

Ps, on the other hand, raise many questions or make open-ended, nonspecific statements that have judgments behind them—"It sounds like the plan has a lot in it." That's a P way of saying something like, "I'm opposed to the plan because it's too complex." The Js get frustrated because the Ps don't seem to be saying what they really mean. Js often complain, "If you have an opinion, I wish you'd state it."

In both cases the issue is serious miscommunication, and the team effort gets thwarted.

The fact is you can't avoid or eliminate these problems; they're part of human nature. And amid this frustration are opportunities—for the Ps to help keep the Js from coming to decisions too quickly and for the Js to help the Ps come to closure and completion on issues. The challenge is to maximize the opportunities and minimize the potential stresses. Later on in this chapter we'll offer some specific ideas on how to increase J-P understanding and teamwork effectiveness.

Putting It All in Perspective

So far we've been talking about opposites—the team-building problems of Extraverts versus Introverts, Sensors versus iNtuitives, and so on. As we've said, the reality is that people tend to be more typologically alike than different. And that opens a whole new can of worms.

The fact is you can get by just fine with an organization that contains only Thinkers (or only Feelers or only Extraverts or whatever). But it can be stressful and less effective in the long run.

You may recall from Chapter One the analogy of left-handedness and right-handedness, that while every able-bodied person uses both hands, each person prefers one over the other and uses that one with greater skill and confidence. Imagine if you were forced to spend all day using only your preferred hand, with no help at all from your other hand. You could manage just fine. But you would be handicapped, to say the least. Using both hands will give you far greater ability, flexibility, and confidence.

So, too, with type and team building. The team may do very well in some areas and not even be aware of how poorly they are doing in others—perhaps until they're blindsided by decreasing productivity and profit. And that's exactly what happens to many successful organizations. They become too "one-handed." For big corporations that's usually Sensing, Thinking, and Judging, which can lead to conservatism, rigidity, and an inability to cope with changing demands in the marketplace. For smaller, entrepreneurial companies, the problem is usually an overdose of Sensing or iNtuitive Thinking-Perceivers, which can make an organization dynamic and risk-taking but often blind to the early danger signs that can put them under.

One reason so many companies become "one-handed" typologically is the natural tendency to surround oneself with people like oneself. A Thinking-Judging engineer executive, for example, will likely choose other engineering colleagues (who by nature tend to be TJs) to be trusted aides. Thus begins the creation of a company rooted in Thinking-Judging behavior.

But Typewatching Commandment Two ("Your strength maximized becomes your liability") will tell you that such an organization has strict limitations. Aside from the blind spots described above, another very serious issue is an inability to generate options when trouble arises. An organization full of Judgers, for example, driven by closure, will respond to a problem or crisis in a solution-oriented way, and if Judger 1 offers a solution that's different from Judger 2's, they become frozen because each party knows that he or she is right. Similarly a Perceiver-laden group can get lost in—and even distracted by—generating alternative solutions, making the incorrect and fatal assumption that someone else will carry the ideas out. An organization full of Extraverts can only shout a problem down rather than genuinely listen to alternatives. And an organization full of Introverts can face a crisis with each person internalizing it and no one communicating with anyone else about how to resolve it.

All of which makes a strong case for being very much aware of your team's overall type and where it is over- or underrepresented by a particular preference. There's no question that while a typologically diverse team may take somewhat longer to accomplish a project, the end result will always be better.

The Downside of Diversity

We said early on in this book that "type begets type" at work. When you can control the kinds of people with whom you want to work, chances are you'll pick people who are more like you than different. In our experience the people around you will likely share three out of four letters with you. Hence typological diversity, though a noble goal, will probably not happen. There may be a balance in gender, a variety of cultures and races, but odds are that the typological preferences will be similar.

This isn't fundamentally a bad thing: Studies indicate that extreme type diversity can be counterproductive to an organization's effectiveness. For example, Dr. George R. McAleer, Jr., at the Industrial College of the Armed Forces, studied the performance of small groups in relation to type and found that there was a correlation between effective group performance and type similarity. He also found that groups that had many diverse types performed worse. Concluded McAleer, "My results simply don't support the idea that diverse working groups are better producers than homogeneous ones. It leads me to question assumptions about the desirability of heterogeneous groups."

Who Become Team Leaders

In the free world most institutions are driven by two basic forces: profits and productivity. These are the fabric that binds businesses, of course, but also governments, universities, and even nonprofit businesses. All of these produce some "product," and all must be accountable to someone or something. Given this reality, there are certain personality types that will gravitate to the top levels of our profit-and-product-oriented institutions.

Yet these same "achievers" may be far less successful in other parts of the organization—sales, training, or research and development, for example.

As we said, certain types are naturally prone to rise to the top of most companies. Traits such as objectivity, punctuality, and accountability are qualities that support productivity and profit. As such, those types sharing Thinking and Judging are naturally promoted, and other types tend to be scarcer the higher up you go. Though any one of the sixteen types can and does make it to the executive level, those not sharing T and J are the exception, not the rule. It took us ten years of collecting typological data on top managers before we found executives representing all sixteen types. At the executive level upward of 90 percent are Thinking-Judgers.

As a result of all this, we can predict three things about the typological makeup of the higher echelons of the workplace:

- As long as management is predominantly TJ, women are statistically destined to be in the minority; there are simply fewer T women in the population.

- Most of the women achieving top-level positions will look typologically like their male counterparts. More than likely they will be TJs.

- The few Feeling-Perceptive types who make it to the top typically do so for one of two reasons: simply to prove to themselves that they can do it or because they have a missionary zeal to change the organization. The FPs got there not because the system accepted them so much as because of their ability to play the TJ game. While at the top the idealists do have some impact, but as soon as they leave, their programs are often obliterated with the sweep of a pen.

Therefore, diversity in the executive circles of any organization is fleeting and over the long term has low impact on organizational effectiveness.

Working with Other Teams

So much for diversity at the top. How about the rest of the organization? As we said, within each department or discipline, the individuals involved tend to be type-alike. Those in sales tend to share primarily Extraversion and Feeling. Those in accounting will most likely share Sensing and Thinking. Those in R&D will likely share iNtuition and Thinking. The training department is inevitably heavily iNtuitive-Feeling. And those in human services tend to be Sensing-Feeling.

But keep in mind that no matter what a department's type, there's a high probability that it will still have to answer to a Thinking-Judger. This can set up a right/wrong or we/they dynamic. Because so many of us (because we're type-alike) agree, how can the boss disagree? It's often because the boss is of another type. Understanding this simple dynamic is the beginning of better teamwork and communication within the office.

A second point to remember is that the other parts of the system—the other departments, which may be very different from one another—are integrally involved in the process of the company's reaching its ultimate goal. And there is little doubt in our minds that when different types communicate effectively, the end product can't help but be improved. Extraverts learn better listening skills when they work with Introverts. Introverts learn to speak more freely from Extraverts. Sensors are stretched to see the big picture from iNtuitives, and iNtuitives are better able to cover details with the collaboration of Sensors. And so on. As a result, if the largely iNtuitive-Thinking research department can communicate effectively with the mostly Sensing-Feeling human services department, the end result of the research will likely be more palatable to those for whom it is intended. When we're not aware of this, we tend only to ridicule the other departments because they are so different, rather than recognizing their potential contribution.

Given this, here are three things to understand about inter-departmental issues:

- Much of the stress between departments is often the result of personality differences. For example, 80 percent of any major organization or institution is a combination of iNtuitive-Thinkers and Sensing-Judgers. The slogans—the words that describe a type's behavioral drive—for these two groups couldn't be more different. For example, we believe the slogan for NTs could be, "Change for the sake of change produces learning. Even if the only thing we learned was that we shouldn't have changed, at least the process was exciting." For the SJs the slogan could be, "Don't fix what ain't broke." So, 80 percent of most organizations are facing fundamentally opposing behavioral stances.

- These differences are strengths if communicated effectively and used wisely. We have different departments in the first place because there are different jobs to do and they require different people to do them. We need each department to do its work, but the departments ultimately have to collaborate rather than compete. Recognizing the differences through Typewatching moves us to affirming the differences rather than looking at different types with disdain.

- If you're not a Thinking-Judger, your ceiling within a large organization is probably lower than you had originally hoped. You would be wise to stop bumping your head and resolve early on to make your contribution from within your frame of reference. In other words, if you are a Feeling-Perceiver, your contribution is to become the best Feeling-Perceiver you can be and not try to become a Thinking-Judger simply because it may move you up the ladder. In the long run it simply won't work. The rewards will not be satisfying and the stress will be considerable. It's important to realize that your own style is rich, creative, and important.

How We Unstymied Stanley:
A Case Study

We are repeatedly struck by the need for the human element at the workplace, because often those most effective at managing resources are usually lacking in "people skills."

Consider the aircraft manufacturing executive we'll call Stanley. An ENTJ, Stanley was having trouble getting his staff to work together instead of competitively. Even simple things had become power struggles among his underlings; day-to-day operations seemed to be an ongoing battle at the expense of meeting the division's goals.

Stanley approached us, wondering whether Typewatching skills could help him develop a more effective team spirit. "Nobody cares about anyone else," he said. "They're all in it for themselves. And they sure don't seem to give a damn about what we're trying to do at this company. Someone could be absent for a week before others would even notice they're gone, let alone cover for them. Can Typewatching give me the skills to whip them into shape?"

We asked to spend a day with Stanley and his group. On the appointed day he assembled the crew—a total of thirty-five people, from clerical support staff to top-level aides. It was a typical day for us: Having already administered the Myers-Briggs Type Indicator to each participant, we spent the morning introducing them to Typewatching and the afternoon applying this knowledge to their work groups.

The day was a smashing success in terms of the group's enthusiasm for their newly gained wisdom about themselves and especially their individual differences. As we do with all groups, we plotted the group members' personality types on a Type Table, which we've included below. As you can see, there is an overabundance of some types and a shortage of others. A quick glance at the table will show that the group was heavily Thinking-Judging; these preferences made up 71 percent of the group. Thinkers alone comprised 91 percent of the group, and

Stanley and His Team			
ISTJ 26%	ISFJ 3%	INFJ	INTJ 9%
ISTP	ISFP	INFP	INTP 14%
ESTP	ESFP	ENFP	ENTP 3%
ESTJ 23%	ESFJ 3%	ENFJ 3%	ENTJ 14%

Judgers alone made up 80 percent. Only three members of the group were Feelers.

We were most interested in the nature of the three Fs. As is typical of any preference that is significantly underrepresented, these three were into some unusual behaviors, and all of them were seen as ineffective and powerless. Specifically:

- One of the Feelers was a male middle manager whose wife, a psychologist, had accused him of carrying grudges and having a higher than average need for affirmation.
- Another was an upper-level manager who kept pretty much to himself and who exhibited behavior typical of alcoholics.
- The third was a female secretary.

During the day's session much of what the group talked about focused on issues of communication and interdependence. As we wrapped up the day, there was a general agreement that almost all of the issues could be boiled down to a single word: trust. No one, it seemed, was sure whom in the office they could trust. Moreover Stanley was seen as hell-bent on running everything himself, having every buck stop at his desk. That of course did little to generate self-confidence among his crew, not to mention keeping Stanley bogged down in a mire of minutiae.

By the day's end it was clear to us that there were a couple of serious problems. One of them was Stanley's ego—his exaggerated need to do everything himself and to believe he could do it better than anyone else. The other was that the group lacked any Feeling types whose position and sense of worth could be viewed by others as having leadership qualities.

Stanley had early on told us not to mince words, so when we confronted him with all this, we tried to help him understand how, as a strong Thinker, he was out of touch with his own people-oriented Feeling side and therefore how difficult, if not impossible, it was for him to find energy for "all that interpersonal stuff" in day-to-day operations. In fact, this is what led to his high control needs. It was a case of his overdoing some things to compensate for things he wasn't doing well. In this case what he wasn't doing well was affirming people, letting them work on their own and make mistakes (and learn from those mistakes), and nurturing and encouraging his employees to do their best.

All of this falls under the umbrella of trust.

Though it was painful for Stanley to hear this, we did get his attention and helped him understand that there were others in the office who by virtue of both preference and talent could do some of "that interpersonal stuff" with greater ease than he. In fact, we concluded, it was all right to delegate those tasks and to hire F consultants periodically to lead team-building skill-development sessions. This would not reflect his weakness but rather would be seen as a strength—that he was so much in charge that he could put others in charge of these important tasks.

In the end we managed to show Stanley and his crew that

both Thinkers and Feelers bring very different needs and skills to the workplace, all of which are necessary for effectively working together. For the Ts that includes such things as analysis, logic, clarity, productivity, objectivity, and, as Isabel Briggs Myers puts it, "appearing firm-minded in day-to-day situations." For their part Feelers bring an awareness of other people and their feelings, an enjoyment of pleasing others, a need for harmony, and a great deal of sympathy for individuals' daily bumps and bruises.

It's so obvious that all of these qualities are essential to a successful team. Yet it's so easy, as Stanley found, to block one half of the equation completely and to try to compensate for it by emphasizing the other half. The good news is—as Stanley also found—that, using Typewatching skills, it often doesn't take a great deal of time and effort to resolve some seemingly intractable problems. Moreover Typewatching's objective, conceptual framework appealed to Stanley's T nature. Thus it legitimated his implementing a clearly "touchy-feely" dimension without compromising his own sense of objective behavior. That's called a win/win solution.

Four Steps to Effective Teams

As you have realized by now, the benefits of Typewatching in team building are limited only by your imagination. There are as many techniques and solutions to team problems as there are teams themselves.

Still, there are four questions to ask about any team effort that can help to keep you on track and to diagnose the potential problem areas.

1. **Are the types represented on the team the best ones to get the job done?** Let's look at a team formed to raise money for an alumni association. Getting this job done—the job being fund-raising—requires a diversity of types and skills. For example, you'll need Extraverts to sell the program to the alumni. You want to make sure that you have types that will

generate alternative ways of raising the money (iNtuitive-Perceivers), but there must be a balance of types who will pound the pavement and follow through on the commitment cards (Sensing-Judgers). If these fundamental types aren't members of the team, their best efforts could go awry. The time taken to determine the types of each team member will be well worth it.

Not all teams require every preference. Some types of goals are best achieved with a team that is more type-alike than different. For example, if the goal of a group is to generate ideas in a brainstorming session, the more Extraverts and Perceivers you have, the better. If the goal is to inventory all the supplies in the storeroom, the more Sensors, and especially Sensing-Perceivers, the better.

2. **Within the team, are the right types doing the right jobs?** Often, because of either loyalty or habit, people don't announce that they have special talents that are not being tapped. Those talents may be perfect for the task at hand, if only the talents are recognized and the individual encouraged to put them to work. The fund-raising group, for example, may have an Introvert whose good writing skills would make that person ideal to craft a top-notch fund-raising letter. But if that Introvert is traditionally a number cruncher within the organization, he or she will not likely volunteer—or be called upon—for this job. Before the team gets very far down the road, it may be worthwhile for the team leader to call for an assessment of the different resources: who has special talents for this assignment; who thinks he or she would like to try something different (and would be good at it)—writing, phoning, selling, and so on. By the way, don't forget to include yourself in the assessment. If it turns out your natural abilities may be hindering more than helping, don't be afraid to get out of the way and let others with better-suited abilities take over.

3. **How, typologically, will we check our progress along the way?** Failing to keep track of progress is the downfall of

many teams. It's important not only to have a healthy sprinkling of Judgers to make sure you keep on course but also to have enough Perceivers to ensure that the team doesn't make good time going in the wrong direction. You need enough Introverts to keep your listening skills sharp and enough Feelers to make sure that people's ideas aren't dismissed out of hand. Our alumni fund-raisers would do well to have some Feelers and Perceivers—for example, individuals who can help get them through the discouraging times, such as getting everybody to take a break and going out for pizza when people are working too hard with too few results.

4. **Is there someone who can help determine when the job is done?** One of the common dilemmas of any group is that committees (teams) have a way of hanging around forever. They can take up people's time with meetings that go nowhere and reports that no one will read. Even if the job was completed months ago—or even years ago—the committee can keep meeting, if only out of habit and the camaraderie that has grown over time. This occurs regardless of the group's success or failure: If the team reached its goal, it wants to sit around and pat each other on the back; if it didn't make the goal, the team members want to stick around and lick each other's wounds. So, it's helpful to have some Judgers and probably some Extraverts to speak up and tell the group, "We're done. Let's split up and get on with the rest of our lives."

Using the Type Table

One of the most useful tools for using Typewatching in team building is the Type Table, which begins on page 277. The table can give you an instant look at an organization typologically. It can also give you a way of keeping team members aware of the

Typewatching dynamics within the organization. (The Type Table is also symbolic of our individual similarities and differences. Any type that is adjacent to another type shares three letters; the ENTP, for example, shares three letters with the INTP, the ENFP, the ESTP, and the ENTJ. As such the table helps to demonstrate our interrelatedness, at least typologically.)

In using the Type Table, write the names of those who know their type or who are at least pretty sure of it in the appropriate squares. (Make sure you have each individual's permission to do this. Each person's type is his or hers to choose to disclose.) You might consider turning the table into a wall poster. We know of one organization that has sixteen twelve-inch-square cork tiles arranged on a central wall. The group has not only placed each employee's name in the appropriate square but the table has grown over time to include the names of spouses, friends, and significant others. So, when someone is about to do business with an ISFP, he or she could approach a team member and ask, "Your husband is an ISFP. Give me three or four pointers about communicating with an ISFP that will help me in my meeting." The success—not to mention the camaraderie—has been enormous.

You may not want to go quite this far, but the message is implicit if not explicit: Given the inevitability of teams in the workplace and the necessity of making the most of your investment in human capital, anything you can do to maximize each employee's contribution will pay big dividends.

Team Building

IF YOU ARE AN . . .

	EXTRAVERT	INTROVERT
EXTRAVERT	• Avoid talking over each other. Take turns. • Allow time overnight before making any decisions or before finalizing anything. • Listen more, talk less.	• Beware that your silence may be mistaken for consent. • If others claim that you did not say something you thought you had, consider that they may be right. • Allow others to use you as a sounding board.
	EXTRAVERT	INTROVERT
INTROVERT	• Remember that others' silence is not necessarily consent. • If others say, "I told you that" or "I already said that," consider that you may not have been truly listening. • Don't invade others' space. Allow for privacy and reflective time.	• Be animated and assertive, and try to read each other's behavior. • Talk more, edit less—share spontaneously. • Teamwork is team building—don't wait until you are alone to deal with stuff.
	SENSOR	INTUITIVE
SENSOR	• Be sure you agree on details, facts, and specifics. • Remind yourself that there's more to the life of the team than the task at hand. • Find three stumbling blocks and work toward avoiding them.	• Be clear and concise. • Show where specifics fit within the grand scheme. • Remember the old adage, "Tell them what you are going to tell them, tell them, and then tell them what you have just told them."
	SENSOR	INTUITIVE
INTUITIVE	• Push for specifics—then push again. • As often as necessary, ask, "What do you mean by . . . ?" • Before saying that something can't be done, think of ways to do it.	• Concentrate on what is practical. • Try not to get lost in strategizing. • Be sure you have a way to implement your strategy.

LEADING AN . . .

IF YOU ARE A . . .

THINKER	FEELER
THINKER	
• Don't contest every point with which you disagree. • Push for each individual's personal reaction and give it credibility. • Manage your competitiveness.	• Realize that criticism of others' ideas may seem a challenge to their sense of competency and bring on a fight. • Keep in mind that conflicts can lead to newfound respect and new levels of competency and performance. • Cut some slack if others don't engage with you on all of the personal stuff.

THINKER	FEELER
FEELER	
• Keep in mind that too much criticism of an idea may be devastating. • Remember that engaging others with sincerity builds their trust. • Talk about what is important to others.	• Remember that it's not all about you. • Try hard to see simple disagreements as something other than personal attacks. • For the sake of the team, confront conflicts as soon as they happen.

JUDGER	PERCEIVER
JUDGER	
• Schedule time for brainstorming without feeling you must decide or judge the outcome. • Delay making decisions on team issues until members have had time alone to consider all sides—even if there seems to be consensus from the start. • Practice asking open-ended questions to explore options and decisions.	• Remember that some enjoy following an agenda. • Try to impress on others the need for flexibility and options. • Recognize that sometimes structures and procedures are necessary.

JUDGER	PERCEIVER
PERCEIVER	
• Remember that others will be productive only if they are allowed to be spontaneous. • Try to impress on others the necessity of structure and order for better teamwork. • Recognize that there are other ways besides your own for doing things.	• Write and distribute an agenda before each meeting—and stick to it. • Conclude each meeting by collectively setting the next meeting's agenda. • Practice making closed-ended, definitive statements and decisions.

LEADING A . . .

8

Problem Solving

"But if it works, why should I change?"

You know the adaptation of that old adage, Always put off till tomorrow what you absolutely, positively don't have to do today. And then there's "Peanuts'" Charlie Brown's corollary: "No problem is so big and insurmountable that it can't be run away from." Some of you immediately saw the humor in the above statements. For you they are part and parcel of your problem-solving model. But we can say with some certainty that the majority of you shudder at these thoughts. You know that there is nothing funny about these statements and that anyone who believes these are problem-solving models are themselves the problem. They need to be "fixed" immediately.

The fact is some people are problem solvers and others are problem makers. Ironically each party sees the other as the problem, at least when it comes to ironing out life's differences. Certain personality types are solution-oriented, while for others the orientation is only toward generating alternatives and letting the parties involved select their own solutions. For some personality types problems come from indecisiveness, while for others the problems come from deciding too early, then having to live with the consequences.

At its essence Typewatching is problem solving. By keeping differences in focus and putting them in a positive, empowering frame of reference, it not only heightens your awareness of the problems but gives you more powerful tools with which to solve them. In this chapter we're going to provide one additional tool specifically designed for problem solving in any situation that will further facilitate the process.

You may ask, "How does problem solving differ from conflict resolution?" Liberally defined, "conflict" involves mutually opposing forces in which one force seeks to win over the other—a win/lose model. Problem solving comprises a broader array of issues, some of which may indeed lead to conflict, but many of which involve no conflict at all. For example,

- How can we continue to maintain profits during a period of economic slowdown?
- How do we integrate the new division manager effectively into all aspects of the organization?
- Should I accept the promotion and relocate or stay here at a lower level?
- Should we spend the money to rearrange the office so that more people have access to windows?
- How can we make a product that's better and cheaper than our competitor's?
- How do I make sure my portion of the budget passes intact?
- How do we convince management that the proposed merger will be counterproductive?
- How do we heighten the company's awareness of ingrained racism and sexism?

As this admittedly random sampling shows, the nature of problem solving is broad-based. As a result we've found that the quality of solutions is directly related to the amount of diversity brought to the problem-solving process. Of course, that's easier said than done. Just as personality differences provide the key to more creative and dynamic solutions, so, too, do they intensify and sometimes hamper our ability to work through problems effectively. So, Typewatching, with its naturally affirming quality, provides a basis for solving problems in a constructive and effective fashion.

PROCESSIONARY CATERPILLARS

One of the realities of the workplace is the preponderance of Judgers. And one of the trademarks of Judgers is that they sometimes mistake activity for action. If a problem can be filed away, organized into meaningful components, or otherwise "disposed of," it is no longer of concern. And for the J the problem has been "solved." In fact, if you merely suggest anything to the contrary, we have known Js to become defensive, rigid, and abrasive.

That brings to mind a story we heard years ago about a French naturalist who experimented with a group of caterpillars. He enticed a group of them onto the rim of a flowerpot, one behind the other, until they formed a complete circle. The caterpillars began moving around the flowerpot.

The naturalist expected that after a while they would catch on to the "joke," get tired of their useless march, and go off looking for food. But through sheer force of habit, they kept creeping around the pot at the same relentless pace for seven days and nights. They would doubtless have gone on had it not been for sheer exhaustion. Despite the fact that an ample food supply was close at hand, they ultimately starved to death.

Of course, all of us are creatures of habit. But Judgers, whose watchwords include habit, custom, tradition, precedent, and standard operating procedure, tend to follow a course blindly, often feeding off each other's sense of purpose. The result: a chain of Judgers going around in circles.

Clearly, when it comes to solving problems, the processionary-caterpillar model simply won't do. What's needed is to slow down the process, consider some alternatives, perhaps live for a time with ambiguity—none of which is particularly oriented toward immediate, bottom-line results, but all of which is geared toward generating long-lasting solutions.

The bottom line: The more people involved in solving a problem, the longer it may take, but the higher the commitment and the better the end result.

How the Eight Preferences Solve Problems

Before we demonstrate how Typewatching can help, let's first take a brief look at the eight preferences and how they approach problem solving.

Extraverts and Introverts

As with everything else, Extraverts solve problems best when they talk them through with someone else—or even with no one in particular. They appreciate others' input and reactions, even if the listener doesn't say a word. A simple head nod or a frown may be sufficient to tell the Extravert something about the other person's reaction. We know of one extreme Extravert who entered a room, rambling to others about a problem: "Gee, I don't know whether to call the gas station about my credit card or just drive up there to see if that's where it is. I can probably do either—I have plenty of time this afternoon—I think I'll drive and check it out. Thanks for your help." At which point he turned and walked out of the room. The amazing thing is that the Extravert really did feel that the "listeners" were helpful, while the "listeners" were mostly amazed at the spectacle. That's an important Extravert-Introvert difference. Without the benefit of Typewatching you are likely to perceive such an Extravert as anything from superficial to borderline psychotic.

Introverts, on the other hand, do their best problem solving after they can take the external input of others away to some private space where they can reflect and contemplate internally. Introverts bring to problem solving listening skills as well as the ability to step back and carefully consider the problem before leaping to a solution. Although we don't claim to know any such circumstances, it wouldn't be beyond an Introvert to walk into a room of other people, look reflectively at each of them, say nothing, nod affirmingly, turn, and leave the room, feeling helped by the situation. And indeed he or she may have been.

While others may perceive such behavior as being cool and aloof, the Introvert, by using the moment to sharpen his or her awareness of the problem, can come to a resolution.

Sensors and iNtuitives

Sensors deal best in problem solving by trusting the facts and evidence. They are most adept at solving problems that they can get their hands on, literally, and move toward some practical and tangible results. To spend too much time designing a solution or theorizing about alternatives seems a waste of time and will lead to little that's productive. If the problem is in front of you, solve it and move on, even if it's just to another problem. If it's not in front of you, don't waste your time worrying about it. Fortunately for the Sensor, there always seem to be enough immediate and tactile problems to solve.

The iNtuitive, on the other hand, won't touch a problem until all of the alternatives have been considered and various schemes have been drawn to cover every aspect of the situation. Problems are best solved when they are set in a context that gives perspective to a bigger picture. A dripping faucet, the iNtuitive may perceive, is part of a larger problem—water pressure, perhaps, or temperature, or even the design of the kitchen or bathroom. Thus a proper solution involves acquiring books on home

HOW TO KEEP Ss FROM GETTING STUCK ON SPECIFICS

- Think of a bottom-line reason for the change.
- Remember the sensory origins of the idea.
- Find a short, memorable way to say it.
- Make up an action plan.
- Look around for something already in existence that is similar.
- Run it by Ss informally to find the practical pitfalls.

HOW TO KEEP Ns AWAY FROM NEVER-NEVER LAND

- Before giving them details, let them talk about their personal vision and tie the details into that.
- Trace the details back to when they were a new and exciting idea.
- Give them the Christmas tree before the ornaments, the framework before the details.
- Don't judge their progress by the amount of tangibles produced. Look instead at how the concept has progressed.
- Don't listen for your agenda when iNtuitives are imagining possibilities. Just try to identify the dream.
- To get them grounded, don't shoot them down. Throw them a line instead.

repair, perusing catalogs of new fixtures, perhaps drawing a schema of the entire system. All of which is exciting as the dickens to an iNtuitive and will probably keep him or her from remedying the actual drip for days, if not weeks or months. Sensors, meanwhile, will be driven up the wall by such inaction. To them the solution is a matter a few turns of a wrench and a new washer.

Thinkers and Feelers

In problem solving, the Thinker's contribution is to keep everyone aware of the potential consequences of any given action. They tend to see problem solving much as they see everything else: as a chessboard. It is a model in which figures can be moved and strategized in such a manner as to weigh carefully the cause and effect of each action. This allows them to stay removed from the problem-solving process so as not to become overly involved with the personal aspects of the issues. Someone once defined the difference between "major" and "minor" surgery by suggesting that minor surgery is an operation made on someone else; if made on oneself, it's always major. In a positive way, problem solving is something like that to Thinkers. They are able to separate themselves from the problem, offering an objective perspective. "Here are the solutions, here are the consequences, here is a good route to take—bite the bullet and move on; let the chips fall where they may." Because they're human, when confronted with the same problem themselves, Thinkers have a more difficult time staying objective.

Feelers bring to problem solving the reality of how the process affects people. So even if it isn't a Feeler's own problem, he or she can still give pretty accurate readings of how those involved will react. In problem solving, the Feeler is the barometer of what the interpersonal reaction to the solution will look like. While we must emphasize again that both the Thinking and Feeling dimensions are essential ingredients for effective problem solving, it is important to underline that if the best solution in the world does not take into account how it will be received by the parties involved, it works only on paper and is doomed to fail. Of course the opposite is also true: If people are relatively happy with the solution but certain objectives aren't being met, things will also run aground.

Judgers and Perceivers

In any problem-solving situation, if a person's last preference is J, his or her nature is to be solution oriented. Consequently the Judger's strength is in his or her ability to come to a conclusion and implement it relatively easily. However, this preference can get in the way more than any other because of the Judger's premature need for closure—to choose a solution even though all the alternatives and implications have not yet been fully explored. In other words, the Judger's strength is in seeing the end and moving toward it; the danger is that, to the Judger, reaching "the end" may be more important than the quality of the solution.

The Perceiver's strength can also be a weakness in that he or she can massage a problem and generate new problems even after deciding on a course of action. It is not unlike Perceivers to interrupt themselves in the middle of a solution to try an alternative to the alternative, thereby avoiding any real implementation and action. In the ideal world there would be enough Ps to keep the Js from coming to premature solutions and enough Js to keep the Ps from overworking solutions.

Coping with Crises

None of this would even be worth discussing if workplace problems were announced and planned in a timely fashion. Of course that's not the way things happen. In some organizations a crisis mentality is the norm, with everyone in a reactive rather than a proactive stance. When this happens, it is human nature to fall back on what we know works. In Typewatching terms that means that we trust our preferences. And while that may be comfortable, it fails to draw upon all of the resources available to us in any crisis situation.

Consider the simple act of throwing and catching a ball. If you know the ball is coming, you have the time to consider the options: Do you want to catch it with your preferred hand or your nonpreferred hand or some combination? Do you even want to catch it? Forewarned is forearmed: With the luxury of time you can increase your chances for success.

But what if you have no warning that the ball is coming? All of the above is suspended in favor of going with what works. You must react rather than plan. In most cases that means opting for your preferred hand either to catch the ball or at least to protect you from harm. You do that because it's what has worked all your life.

The process is much the same at work. When the ball comes flying unannounced—in the form of an accelerated deadline, an absent key player, a missed shipment, a dissatisfied customer—we always go with what works. Typologically that means that if you are an ISTJ, to pick one example, you'll close the door, think it through privately, get your facts in order, stay objective, and above all make a decision about what to do. Even a poor decision is better than none, and you can always revise it tomorrow. In contrast, if you're an ENFP, you'll trust sharing the problem with everyone within range, bouncing it around the office, brainstorming alternatives, keeping everyone involved, and above all, hanging loose in case some new information comes along.

You may be saying, "But if it works, why should I change?" The fact is, you have gotten by, perhaps even succeeded, based on trusting what works for you. And that's fine. But we believe that you can increase your success rate—and reduce your stress rate—by understanding how personality type plays a role. (Recognize that if you're happy and successful at work, you're already in a class by yourself. All of the studies indicate that work and the workplace are the number-one source of stress in most people's lives. Far too many of us are just getting by, barely coping, walking invitations to anything from headaches to heart attacks.)

Coping with Sameness

We've already pointed out that an ongoing, recurring organizational problem is not differences but sameness. In corporate America it is quite common to have a management or work team that is 100 percent Judging and as high as 90 percent Thinking. We already know their problem-solving model: Analyze the situation objectively, consider the consequences, and above all, do something. That's what we call a "Ready, Fire, Aim" problem-solving model. In the best J tradition, the result may be that if you hit a target, it may not even be the one you were shooting for.

When you put all of this together, you can readily see the problem: a world of primarily Thinking-Judgers confronted with a constant barrage of announced and unannounced problems and who, being human, tend to fall back on what works for them. All of which results in a corporate culture that at best may have difficulty maximizing alternatives and at worst fails to meet the challenges of today by insisting on applying yesterday's solutions. The best-managed companies are those that observe George Santayana's adage, Those who do not learn from history are destined to repeat it.

The Z Factor

The ideal, win/win problem-solving model would minimize failure, increase success, and allow everyone involved to maximize his or her own potential and satisfaction.

Typewatching can help turn this ideal into a reality.

The method we've found most effective we call the Z Problem-Solving Model. We did not develop it. It is the brainchild of Isabel Briggs Myers. In her development of type theory, she found that good problem solving involves four things:

1. **Gather the facts**—use Sensing to look at the details of the problem at hand.

2. **Brainstorm possibilities**—use iNtuition to develop possible causes of and solutions to the problem.

3. **Analyze objectively**—use Thinking to consider the cause and effect of each potential solution to the problem.

4. **Weigh the impact**—use Feeling to consider how the people involved in the problem will be affected by the suggested solutions.

As you can see from the following diagram, taking this route involving the two middle letters of your type—from Sensing to iNtuition to Thinking to Feeling—forms the letter Z, hence the name.

It doesn't matter what type you are. Anyone can use this model. Keep in mind that each of us has all eight personality traits—Extraversion, Introversion, Sensing, iNtuition, Thinking,

The Z Problem-Solving Model

| Look at the **Facts and Details** | **S**ENSING → **IN**TUITION | What **Alternatives** do the facts suggest? |

· What are the facts?
· Be specific and actual.
· List all relevant details.
· Be clear.

· Let your imagination run wild.
· Brainstorm.
· Consider various solutions.

| Can it be **Analyzed Objectively?** | **T**HINKING → **F**EELING | What **Impact** will it have on those involved? |

· Consider the consequences of each alternative.
· If you weren't involved, what would you suggest?
· What is the cause and effect of each action?

· Is it something you can live with?
· How do you feel about the action?
· What hunches do you have about others' reactions?

The Z Problem-Solving Model is used with the written permission of the Publisher, Consulting Psychologists Press, Inc., Palo Alto, CA 94303.

Feeling, Judging, and Perceiving—but each of us prefers only four of them. The Z model asks you to tap into four of these traits, including two of your nonpreferences, to solve problems more effectively.

This is easier said than done during the heat of a crisis. As we said before, when you know the ball is being thrown at you, you can prepare accordingly. And when the ball comes as a surprise, you go with what works. Similarly our natural tendency in problem solving is to use our preferences. So, in the stress of a crisis,

- STs will likely rely upon facts (Sensing) and will translate them analytically and objectively (Thinking).
- SFs will likely rely upon the facts of the situation (Sensing) and translate those facts as they affect people (Feeling).
- NFs will likely rely upon the possible alternative solutions of the situation (iNtuition) and translate those possibilities as they affect people (Feeling).
- NTs will likely rely upon the possible alternative solutions (iNtuition) and translate them analytically and objectively (Thinking).

It's also important to point out that while we are dealing with only two of your four preferences here, the other two preferences (E/I and J/P) do come into play. An Extraverted SF will react to a problem differently than an Introverted SF. And an SFJ will react differently than an SFP. But all of these Sensing-Feelers will be motivated by the same two factors.

Let's consider a hypothetical crisis. It's Friday at three o'clock. A customer calls to inform you that a major shipment you sent a week ago has not arrived, and they must have it by noon Monday. While it is not said, it is clear that your failure to deliver will result in the loss of business to this important client. There's no way around it: You must either find the shipment or reship it and make sure that it arrives on time.

As with all crises, this is far from a convenient moment for this to happen. Since it's a Friday afternoon, things are gearing down, and a few folks have even left early. Still, there are enough people left to get the job done. But how to get it done?

Let's look at how each of the four preference combinations would likely cope:

- **STs** would be inclined to accept the reality that the original shipment is lost and that there's no time to waste tracking it down. There's no alternative: A new shipment must be assembled and shipped immediately. And everyone will have to stay late and pitch in to get the job done.

- **SFs** would also write off the original shipment and support the reality that there's no time to waste looking for it. Given this, they would poll the rest of the company as to who did not have other obligations and could work late, fully aware that if no one else could do it, they'd have to do it themselves.

- **NFs** would consider the possibility that the original shipment might still be recoverable, saving everyone the trouble of having to do it over again. They would attempt to organize and motivate a team of co-workers to fan out and track down the shipment. At the same time they would organize a second team to develop a backup plan. The NFs' energy would be spent moving back and forth, motivating both teams, and perhaps doing the bulk of the work so that as few people as possible are inconvenienced.

- **NTs** would also try to track down the original shipment (because it will have to be located in any case), and would simultaneously begin assembling the second shipment (because that's the only reliable solution). At the same time the NTs would also develop a strategy for evaluating the shipping operations to ensure that this problem wouldn't happen again.

Each of these is a perfectly valid approach to resolving the crisis. Which of these is most likely to succeed is anyone's guess; all of them could potentially prevail. We would probably put our money on the STs as having the cleanest, most direct, and simplest solution. The bad news, however, is that the STs' approach will bruise the most egos, disrupt the most personal lives, and probably cause the greatest number of absences on Monday morning. The bottom line is that by relying only on your two strongest preferences, you are likely either to reduce your chances of solving the problem or to increase your chances of alienating others in the process.

The Z model, by incorporating both preferences and non-preferences, increases the chances of success without upsetting either the process or the people.

Putting the Z Model to Work

Let's look at how the Z model might have worked in the above scenario:

1. **Gather the facts.** Start with the facts of the situation, trying to be as specific as possible. In this case the facts are that the original shipment never arrived, according to the customer. What are the facts about that process? What do shipping dates, times, logs, and personnel tell us about the shipment? Is the customer correct? Perhaps the shipment is sitting in his warehouse but the shipping label was written in such a way that it was misdirected. What specific information can the shipper provide? Again, push for details.

2. **Brainstorm possibilities.** Given the information you've collected, it's now time to figure out what it all means. In this case the facts lead you to conclude that the shipment has definitely been shipped properly by you but has not yet arrived at the customer's warehouse. So, what are the possibilities concerning what happened? The shipper would certainly seem a likely suspect. But that's not the only possibility. Another scenario is that the shipment was properly delivered but misdirected by the recipient so that it did not end up in the proper place on the warehouse floor. A third,

albeit less likely, possibility is that the shipment "fell off" the truck and into the hands of a band of thieves. Finally, it's entirely possible that there's no answer to this question and the shipment will have to be reassembled and reshipped.

3. **Analyze objectively.** A careful consideration of these possibilities is now in order. You start with the reality that you ought to begin assembling the backup shipment. With every tick of the clock, the reality that you will need to send it becomes greater. You will need to assemble the personnel to get it done by the end of the day, even if it takes until seven or eight o'clock at night. You know that some people will resent having to work late on a Friday, but that's life; there's a job to be done. Another conclusion is that if organized (or unorganized) crime indeed hijacked your shipment, there is nothing you can do about it that will help the customer's immediate problem. Still another conclusion is that the misdirected-shipment theory is worth pursuing because this has happened in the past, and it will be much more cost-effective if you can find and deliver the original shipment on time. Your final objective conclusion is that you must do whatever it takes, because this is such an important customer you don't want to risk losing them.

4. **Weigh the impact.** Before you can make a final decision on a course of action, it's important to consider how the various scenarios will affect the work force. You know from previous experience that some employees will be available but others won't. So, a poll of the work force will find out whether there are enough bodies available to pursue the various courses of action without upsetting anyone's weekend. During your poll you may also want to determine the extent of the commitment to the project, the client, the company, and anything else that may motivate an employee to put in the extra effort or make him or her angry about the whole thing. For example, someone may really want to help but simply isn't available because of previous family commitments; you may determine that this person may be of use

during the first few hours of the crisis and can then be relieved by others. This way you'll get their best work without guilt or anger on anyone's part. The important part of the process is that as many people as possible feel that they have a say in the decisions you ultimately make.

Whatever the final solution—whether you determine that the shipper's truck broke down but will be fixed in time to make the Monday delivery or whether you indeed have to reship—the wear and tear on your company will be far less for having gone through this process. We'll be the first to point out that the Z model may add a few minutes, or even an hour or so, to the problem-solving process. But inevitably you will get a better end result, and there's a greater likelihood that the next time you have a crisis, your employees will be there when you need them. Moreover, the more you use the Z model, the easier it becomes and the less time it takes to implement.

Here's a bonus: As you begin to use the Z model, you'll understand that you can rely on others to provide your nonpreferences in problem-solving situations. If you're a Sensing-Thinker, for example, you may want to rely on a trusted iNtuitive-Feeler during a crisis situation. His or her advice will help to ensure that you are covering all aspects of the Z model. For that matter you may want to have a sort of typological crisis team on hand—with a smattering of each of the preferences—to leap into action when the situation demands.

In problem solving, as with so many other things, Typewatching will broaden your approach to a situation in such a way that your strength is maximized and your weaknesses are covered.

Maintaining Perspective

All of the insight we've provided is of little use if you aren't tuned in to your group's typological blind spots. When each of the eight preferences is respected, solicited, encouraged, affirmed, and used, solving a problem may take a bit more time, but it will always yield better results.

Problem Solving

IF YOU ARE AN . . .

	EXTRAVERT	INTROVERT
EXTRAVERT	• Repeat what you have heard for verification and ask that others do the same. • Try not to speak at the same time as another. • Pause after a comment or question before resuming—if need be, count to five before speaking.	• Ask for quiet time and space. • Work at being direct and expressive. • Raise your voice if you need to make your point heard—don't wait to be asked.
	EXTRAVERT	**INTROVERT**
INTROVERT	• Make private time and reflection—sitting in silence—part of the problem-solving session. • Now and then, put it in writing instead of saying it. • Raise issues and problems prior to a meeting to allow time for reflection and consideration.	• Speak out, even if it seems awkward. • Edit yourself out loud, not internally. • Share more than you think is necessary and request the same from your colleague.
	SENSOR	**INTUITIVE**
SENSOR	• Work on stating the obvious in general terms. • Share your hopes and visions with each other. • Try to keep each other from interpreting what is being said too literally.	• Remember that much of what you say might be taken literally. • Correlate your interpretations with others' so that you are satisfied. • Keep in mind that precision and facts are key to formulating a response.
	SENSOR	**INTUITIVE**
INTUITIVE	• Correlate interpretations and meanings so that you are satisfied with what is being said. • Be prepared for your colleague to give general responses to your specific questions and statements. • Expect others to be irritated with overly specific or detailed questions, plans, or data.	• Be sure to double-check the meaning of what each of you is proposing. • Be mindful that the solutions you seek need to be attainable in the here-and-now world. • Push for specifics about what each person is saying, answering the who, what, where, when, how, and how much.

LEADING AN . . .

IF YOU ARE A . . .

LEADING A . . .

	THINKER	FEELER
THINKER	• Be sure to consider each person's emotions in your exchanges. • Be careful not to become too competitive in your drive to solve the problem your way. • Ask yourself about possible solutions: "How will this affect the people involved?"	• Don't be afraid to argue now and then. • Once in a while, express something negative without feeling guilty. • Avoid saying "I'm sorry," taking blame, or giving in for the sake of harmony.
	THINKER	**FEELER**
FEELER	• Make an effort to connect personally with others—acknowledge their circumstances outside of the problem you are solving. • Keep in mind that others may want support, not analysis, when issues are raised. • Be prepared to confront the fact that any criticism may be taken personally.	• Try not to rescue your colleague or to take what he or she says personally. • Remember that establishing and maintaining an open dialogue and relationship is not necessarily solving the problem. • Be mindful of your tendency to avoid confrontation and to accommodate others in problem-solving situations.
	JUDGER	**PERCEIVER**
JUDGER	• Try to raise a question instead of giving an answer or offering advice. • Give in now and then, even when you *know* you are right. • Actively seek new data by asking, "What could we be overlooking?"	• Know that your openness and tendency to generate options may create more irritation than admiration. • Help others to see that there is more to any conversation than just answers and directions. • Remember that what others are saying may not be their final position on an issue, even if they say it is.
	JUDGER	**PERCEIVER**
PERCEIVER	• Avoid putting others in a corner conversationally. Allow room for them to move. • Know that your tendency to organize, decide, and control may create more resentment than relief. • Take some downtime—by yourself—to consider others' options and ideas before coming to closure.	• Be sure that one of you makes a decision and follows through with it. • Work to finish solving one problem before moving on to another one. • Try whenever possible to finish your sentences.

Perspective is key. If you know at the start what preferences are missing from your problem-solving team, you'll be better equipped to find appropriate solutions, whether the problem is large or small, expected or unexpected. By compensating for the group's nonpreferences or underrepresented preferences, you'll ensure that the solutions you reach are the best ones available.

To paraphrase "Peanuts," with Typewatching no problem is so big or insurmountable that it can't be effectively handled with a little help from your friends.

9

Conflict Resolution

"Now, now, let's not get emotional."

Conflict can take many forms, not all of which are obvious. There's the traditional knockdown drag-out, of course, but there are also much subtler forms of dispute: the passive-aggressive nod intended to indicate agreement when in fact that is far from the case; the saccharine smile that belies intense bitterness and resentment; the silent treatment, in which one party simply refuses to acknowledge the other's presence; the long-standing rivalry that when ignited—often over the most trivial of issues—makes the Hatfields and the McCoys look like a family reunion.

Conflict can also have many different outcomes. For some it is a creative and dynamic force that can move the parties involved—perhaps even the whole organization—to a new level of productivity. Others see it as a necessary evil that you can only grin and bear and hope that everything turns out okay. Still others see conflict as devastating, something to be avoided at all costs because of the long-lasting ill will that can ensue; for them there are no benefits at all to be derived from the process.

Conflict, like it or not, is inevitable as long as humans try to coexist in the workplace. While very few healthy individuals actively go out looking for a fight, fights seem to find us anyway. Our differing values, opinions, definitions, and perceptions set

us up for seemingly endless possibilities to have misunderstandings or differences with others. Try as we may, we can't avoid
such conflicts—at least, not for long.

The problem starts with the fact that different types define
"conflict" in different ways. One person's "making a case" can
be another's "starting an argument." One person's relatively
mindless statement can be viewed as a thrown gauntlet by
someone else. Your "simple misunderstanding" can be our "major affront."

One might think that certain types would have distinct abilities to deal with conflict. Thinking-Judgers, for example, would
probably be good at remaining objective and unemotional during a stressful encounter. Extraverts, because of their verbal
prowess, would be able to smooth-talk their way through almost
any situation. The relative silence of Introverts, on the other
hand, would be likely to lower the intensity of a heated situation.

In our experience, though, no type excels at dealing with conflict. In fact, for whatever reason, conflict tends to bring out the
worst in all of us. Thinking-Judgers, for example, tend to become even more rigid, not only convinced that they are right but
closed to alternative points of view. Extraverts, instead of being
smooth talkers, can become loud and needlessly aggressive. Introverts can often simply close the door on the outer world, all
but shutting out any communication that could lead to resolution.

So we've become resigned to muddling through conflict, using whatever techniques have carried us through in the past, for
better or for worse.

It's our inability to cope with conflict effectively that causes
companies to spend great sums of money to bestow upon their
employees "conflict resolution skills." Please understand: Not
all of these programs are worthless, or even bad. Many offer
valuable insights into the process of dealing with conflicts and of
avoiding them in the first place. But there is often a rather large
gap between the theory preached by many of the purveyors of
these programs and reality. Their ten or twenty conflict-
resolution principles, while perfectly valid and insightful, may

WHEN SIMILARITIES DIFFER

So far we've concentrated on what happens when people of opposite preferences disagree—Introverts vs. Extraverts, Sensors vs. iNtuitives, and so forth. But a great deal of conflict arises when people share the same preferences and thus magnify each other's strengths. (Remember the Second Commandment: Your strength maximized becomes a liability.) And while you'd think that people who are alike could get along, that's often far from the case.

Consider two Extraverts—each talking over the other, with neither hearing the other. As the volume goes up, listening goes down. Or consider two Judgers—each with a set of unbendable rules. One's definition of "neatness" may differ substantially from the other's. While one party has straightened up and knows exactly where things are, the other finds the situation lacking—or simply different than expected. Both parties know they're right, setting themselves up for a no-win argument. If both Js are Introverts, the dispute can lead to a long period of mutal avoidance. If they're both Es, it can lead to an escalating exchange of bad feelings.

We were once called in to do time-management training for a company that was almost 100 percent Judgers. Our first reaction was, as organized as Judgers are, why would they possibly need time management? What we learned was that each had his or her own time organized and they were totally rigid about anyone else's imposition on that schedule. So, forty managers worked on forty different time schedules, pulling rank on each other, arguing that their time or schedule was the most important. You can imagine the chaos!

There's no reason why the five steps we've outlined can't work in such situations. But a quicker resolution may come simply from bringing in a mediator of a different type. Ask the mediator to hear both sides and to offer his or her own analysis. Because they are different types, the analysis can't help but bring a different dimension and probably some helpful insights.

not always be applicable to the almost endless array of conflicts that arise.

We believe that any conflict-resolution model that does not consider personality differences is doomed to fail. In case after case we have seen Typewatching lead to a heightened awareness that affords those in conflict better coping skills and more accessible alternatives—during and immediately following the altercation.

How Thinkers and Feelers Deal with Conflict

We'd like to discuss the T-F dimension first because we believe that this comprises far and away the most crucial differences in dealing with conflict.

In the simplest of verbal exchanges a Thinker's need for objective clarity can push an issue to a level almost immediately interpreted by a Feeler as hostile. Remember, it is the F who prefers to make decisions based upon whatever will create the greatest harmony.

For example, a T might ask an F, "What do you mean by that?" simply seeking to clarify a point.

The F, though, responds defensively to what he or she feels is a curt demand, saying back, "I don't know" or "You seem angry" or "It doesn't really matter."

None of these replies produces the clarity the T is seeking, and each causes the T to push harder for a more desirable response: "How can you not know what you mean?" or "I'm not angry at all, but I must understand what you're trying to say," or "It matters a lot because it's imperative that we have a common starting point."

To which the F takes further offense and is liable to blurt out something like, "You can define it any way you want."

Then follows the ultimate T put-down: "Now, now, let's not get emotional. I can't define your words."

What started out as a simple exercise in seeking clarity can turn, in barely a few moments, into a full-fledged fight, with both parties scratching their respective heads as to how it all happened so quickly.

To illustrate how important the T-F differences are in resolving conflict, we've taken total strangers, couples, managers, work groups, and even boards of directors and separated them into groups of Thinkers and Feelers. We give each group a series of experiential exercises to heighten their differences in addressing conflict by listing on a large piece of newsprint their responses to the following:

- How do you define conflict?
- How do you deal with conflict at work?
- What would you like others to keep in mind when conflict arises?

In the first question the Thinkers almost always define conflict as an inevitable process that leads ultimately to creativity. Their definitions include such things as "creative tension,"

BOX SEATS

In the course of working with a group of managers who had just concluded an intense, head-to-head confrontation, we were trying to help the group understand what had happened and to see what they could learn from the experience. There had been some hurt feelings and bruised egos. An ENTJ who had been very vocal shared with genuine enthusiasm how exciting the event was. He said, "It was like driving a family camper to the edge of a battlefield and watching one person get harpooned, another catch a sharp blow to the midsection, and another limping to the sidelines." The Feelers in the group were stunned that he could be so involved and yet removed and consider such an intense personal experience as a spectator sport. But as a Thinker, there was a certain consistency to his behavior: He participated as much as was needed for clarity and candor, but not so much as to get personally involved.

"when two minds do not meet," and "opposition between energies." The Feelers, for their part, have a recurring theme based
on disharmony and the desire to avoid it at all costs. They are
likely to define conflict using such words as "stressful," "emotional," and "upsetting."

In response to the second question Thinkers tell us that they
deal with conflict at work by learning, discussing the issues, and
strategizing solutions, whereas Feelers say that they reflect on
their feelings, blame themselves for the conflict, and often react
physically—sweating, yelling, and crying, among other things.

As for what each of the preferences would like others to keep
in mind when conflict arises, Thinkers would like Feelers not to
personalize things, deal with just the facts, and keep hysteria to
a minimum. Feelers would like Thinkers to consider their feelings and to remember that there is anxiety on both sides and
that there must be respect for other people's positions.

You can easily see the enormous differences here. For example, while Fs deal with conflict by getting emotional, Ts would
prefer that they not personalize things and minimize emotional
reactions. It's easy to see how some conflicts never get resolved
simply because the individuals' approaches to resolving them
are equally at odds with each other.

We've been doing this exercise for the better part of a decade
with every imaginable configuration of groups—husbands and
wives, executives and underlings, parents and teenagers, even
church groups—and the results are always the same. And the
amazing result is that both Ts' and Fs' biggest concern is over the
same thing: losing control, albeit for different reasons. Ts don't
want people to personalize things; they're afraid that they might
"lose control" if they admit that they have been personally
wounded by what's just been said. And Fs are afraid that in a
conflict they'll "lose control" and say things that will do ir-
reparable harm to interpersonal relationships.

Whatever the exact words used by Ts and Fs, the responses to
these exercises are always true to type. As the sheets of
newsprint are unveiled, the participants inevitably respond with
one of the following reactions: nervous laughter (because of the
inner secrets that have been revealed) or stunned silence (from

the near disbelief that people could produce such dramatically different responses to the same questions). It is exactly these insights and differences that we intend to bring to the forefront and use as the basis for subsequent lessons on this subject. The ultimate insight, of course, is the one at the very basis of Typewatching itself: There are no good or bad approaches to resolving conflicts, there are only differences. That understanding alone can be liberating and can unlock previously closed doors to resolving problems.

How Extraverts and Introverts Deal with Conflict

You won't be surprised to learn that Extraverts, usually unwittingly, prefer to move a conflict to the external arena, where it can become a point of discussion, if not argument. This happens whether the Extravert is arguing with an Introvert or with another E. In the process Extraverts will likely spray everyone with their verbalizations of the moment, usually refining their points of view while speaking them. Most Extraverts *know* that with one more word "we can clear this matter up." ("One more word," of course, often becomes a paragraph, if not a rambling dissertation.) Introverts, on the other hand, *know* that if they hear just one more word, they're going to go stark-raving mad.

One problem with Extraverts is that they can say so many things in so little time that they scarcely remember what they've said. Indeed they may be surprised—perhaps shocked—to learn that others have not only paid attention but taken offense. This creates at least two problems. The fact that the remark caused offense is one, ironic in that the statement might have been merely a trial balloon designed to sort out, if not solve, the conflict at hand. In addition, the Extravert's forgetting exactly what was said may lead to an additional conflict—a debate over whether the remark was spoken in the first place, was said in the exact words heard by the other party, or was intended to convey the message that was ultimately heard.

This whole phenomenon is exacerbated if an Extravert is also

HERE'S TO A GOOD FIGHT

Some types simply deny the reality of conflict, preferring that it will just go away. Take the case of Murray, an ESFJ rabbi working in a military organization. He could not stand the different staffers engaging in even friendly disagreement. Murray assumed any raising of voices in argument would escalate to all-out war. For such occasions Murray would keep a bottle of schnapps in his desk drawer. As conflict surfaced, Murray would run around the office, bottle and glasses in hand, forcing each party involved in the dispute to join in a toast. As he would pour the good cheer, he inevitably said, "Now, now, we're all professionals and we all love one another." The group always indulged him and toasted one another. They knew that, following the toast, Murray would leave, believing he had resolved everything. Without Murray around they would be free to resume their argument.

a J. Judgers, we know well, are prone to utter decisive statements: "I like this." "My answer is no." "Do it now." Such statements may be spoken by an EJ with little or no commitment or regard for their impact. But if heard by a P, particularly an EP, that statement might generate a question: "What do you mean?" "Why did you say that?" "Do you really feel that strongly about it?" In the meantime the EJ, who may not even remember making the statement, may respond to the question by giving yet another answer. (We've long believed that if you are an EJ, you will spend an inordinate amount of time in your life defending things you don't necessarily believe.) In the course of about three question-and-answer exchanges, the two parties find themselves defending or arguing positions that are just slightly to the left of absurd.

When arguing with an EJ, remember this cardinal rule: EJs already know the answer; the question is irrelevant.

We can't think of a better example of this than the EJ army colonel we know who was about to leave the office for a three-day trip. Standing in the doorway about to depart, he looked back at his staff and in his commanding EJ way said, "Just in case something comes up while I'm away, here are five nos that will take care of them: No, no, no, no, and no." He saluted and departed.

Imagine how difficult all this can be to Introverts. As you'd expect, they deal with conflict by saying (to themselves), "Go inside and work carefully on your next move. Don't expose yourself, don't make a fool of yourself, and don't say or do something you will regret. Above all, stay aloof, cool, and quiet."

Nothing is more physically stressful to an Introvert than conflict. During an argument, while an Extravert dumps his or her problems into the outer world, an Introvert internalizes them. As a result during conflict an Introvert's insides resemble those old TV ads for Bayer and Bufferin: hammers pounding on the head, ropes knotting in the stomach, screws tightening all over. Boom, boom, boom. Tension. Anxiety. Stress. Studies have shown that Introverts are more prone than Extraverts to such stress-related maladies as ulcers and lower-colon problems.

As we've said many times, Introverts get ulcers; Extraverts give ulcers.

Clearly, when in conflict with an Extravert, an Introvert is yielding home-field advantage. This is because, with Extraverts representing 70 percent of the population, most of our conflicts are played out verbally. It rarely occurs to one party, in the heat of a disagreement, to say to the other, "Hey, put it into writing and I'll get back to you tomorrow." Not that this is necessarily

MIXED MESSAGES

We have one Feeler and one Thinker supervising our production shop. When asked how things were going, the T said he often had to reprimand one man who did not follow instructions. The F said, "Yeah, and every time you yell at him, I have to go over and make up for it."

the best tactic, but the point is valid: There is more than one way to deal with conflict.

Introverts would do well to level the playing field a bit. We'll offer some specific suggestions later in this chapter, but the idea here is to realize that in tense or conflictual situations, there are alternatives to merely shouting about them. In fact, talking problems through—without allowing sufficient time for introverted reflection—is probably the least effective way to resolve a conflict.

How Sensors and iNtuitives Deal with Conflict

When two people perceive the same thing differently, it can become extremely difficult to untangle how those different perceptions fuel subsequent communication. If you believe the problem is centered around specific wording on a memo, and we see the problem as the substance of the memo itself, then we have a conflict about what the real conflict is. Remember that the S-N difference revolves around how we take in information, which becomes the basis for the decisions we subsequently make.

The information that Sensors take in deals more with the specifics of what has been said or has taken place. Precise words and events are key here and are subject to subsequent recall and scrutiny. For iNtuitives, implications and meanings about what's transpired are far more important. This difference leads to a variety of "yes, buts," which sound something like this:

> Sensor: "Yes, but, this is what you said. . . ."
> iNtuitive: "Yes, but, this is what I meant. . . ."
> Sensor: "Yes, but, if that's what you meant, you should have said it."
> iNtuitive: "Yes, but, I shouldn't have to speak the obvious to intelligent people."

How Judgers and Perceivers Deal with Conflict

Once again, the J-P difference can play a major role here. When a Sensing-Judger or an iNtuitive-Judger *knows* what he or she has perceived, there will be little room for negotiation on their perceptions. Indeed, an ongoing organizational dilemma is that there are far more Js than Ps in management positions, setting up this obviously conflict-laden situation.

We've already covered some of the J-P differences during conflicts, but they are worth reviewing.

We know that Judgers like structure. So any unplanned or unannounced change can lead to some abrasive responses, which are often interpreted as anger or disagreement, even when that's not the case. The J's initial negative response to your idea or statement may have more to do with the fact that you've just interrupted the J's schedule—even if the J appeared to be just sitting around doing nothing—than with the J's actual response to what you said. (That "just sitting around" may well be part of the J's schedule for that point in the day.)

We also know that closure is important to Judgers. Their statements often lead us to believe that their positions are very fixed, with little room for negotiation—"The boss said it, I believe it, and that settles it." It is in the nature of Js to sound right (or closed), even if they don't know whether they're right or wrong. But the fact is Js aren't always right, and they may even recognize this, but they may have difficulty dealing with unresolved issues in an open-ended way.

We've talked with several Judgers, especially Extraverted-Judgers, who are shocked, flabbergasted, and amazed when, in the peak of a "discussion," they are told that they sound angry. In fact, this couldn't have been further from the truth. At such times they were enthusiastic, loud, their position sounded fixed, and they were counting on the other person to push back so that some sort of a satisfactory resolution would result. But that aggressive, intimidating behavior gets the opposite response: The other person shies away, wanting to avoid going to battle with such an "angry" person.

When Js seem closed and not open to negotiation, Ps are clearly at a disadvantage. They may have opinions on the issue, too, but their P nature is continually to redefine things, to stay open-ended about alternative solutions, and to maintain real flexibility. The more tense the situation becomes, the more the P can swing between blurted-out opinions (which may in fact be only additional options to explore) and questions (perhaps designed to generate still more options). During the conflict a Judger can read such scattered behavior as undependable at best, outright spaciness at worst.

All of which creates a vicious circle of behavior: As the P con-

THE SERIOUS BUSINESS OF SEXUAL HARASSMENT

When you consider the fact that most managers are male and that at least 60 percent of managers are Thinking-Judgers, you can see how sexism and sexual harassment can become institutionalized in some organizations.

We're not going to be audacious enough to suggest that Typewatching can solve or eliminate sexual harassment—that would require a major transformation of human nature—but there may be some ways that Typewatching can help. The first thing, of course, is to have a heightened awareness of yourself in relation to the people with whom you work. What kind of messages are you receiving? What kind of messages are you giving? What kind of attitudes do you bring to work each day about people? Are they potential friends as well as co-workers? Are they potential conquests? Are they resources that can help you get your job done? Can and should your relationships with them combine work and play? Whatever your answers, once you've considered these things, you can be more direct in your day-to-day dealings with others.

tinues to generate options, the J becomes more fixed in a definite position. So, to the J's assertion that "The boss said it, I believe it, and that settles it," the P might respond, "Are you sure? What if the boss meant . . . ?" The J will inevitably insist that his or her initial interpretation was the right one. And the P likely won't be able to resist the bait to find additional alternatives around such a fixed position. The two find themselves locked in a hopeless conflict that may reflect positions that are far removed from the initial issues that began the disagreement.

Learning to Dance with the New Boss

We could cite from literally hundreds of real-life cases in which Typewatching skills have resolved conflicts. One of the more dramatic situations involved a very successful group of high-tech engineers at a Fortune 500 company whose reputation was well established in the aerospace industry.

Here's the background: With the retirement of the CEO, the board of directors began a search for a replacement. True to human dynamics, each of the eight talented division directors was sure that the board would hire from within and that he would be the choice. However, the board felt the group to be too ingrown and sought some new talent with no previous history or political ties within the company. Such a pick, the board felt, would give new life to the corporation. So they hired a top-notch retired general with impressive credentials from a thirty-year career in the military.

When the shock and dismay among the favored eight settled, there was a pool of anger and frustration at the board's decision that soon became directed at the new CEO. Because the eight were party-line team players, there was no way to express their anger and frustration at the board. Further, because it is not generally accepted behavior to express such anger within a company, the assumption of everyone—the board, the new CEO, and the eight engineers—was that things would return to business as usual.

Without a meeting, without a spoken word, without any overt behavior among the eight engineers, there soon evolved a wide range of aggressive behaviors: backstabbing, sabotaging, and outright revenge. Sure, they gave lip service to teamwork, but nothing was further from the truth. Behind everyone's friendly smiles was fast-growing resentment to every new decision that came along.

What made it more insidious was that the engineers denied being angry. "I certainly have no problem with the new guy," one of them told us later. "It's just that military types just don't understand the business world." But it didn't take a genius to read between the lines.

The CEO, in fact, *was* reading between the lines. And what he saw was resistance to almost everything that was happening. He was having trouble not personalizing it all; the anger seemed directed at him.

The CEO had heard about Typewatching and believed it might help to clear the air. He called us in, and we gave the MBTI to the nine individuals involved and arranged a one-day retreat at a nearby resort.

One of the first things we were shocked to find was that none of these nine individuals—all of whom held advanced degrees from very prestigious institutions of higher learning—had ever taken a single psychology course, let alone a psychological instrument like the MBTI. As a result all nine came to the retreat with incredible levels of anxiety. They assumed they were about to be psychoanalyzed, stripped of their innermost secrets, and ultimately "found out."

We quickly calmed them down with a classic exercise. We asked them to write their names on a sheet of paper. Then we asked them to put their pencil in their other hand and repeat the exercise. As typically happens, they began laughing nervously and expressed how difficult it was for them to do this. We told them that this was analogous to the day ahead: Just as the exercise had dealt with physical preferences, we would be dealing strictly with psychological preferences, not with pathologies or intelligence. This always seems to warm a group up.

Though many insights occurred that day, certainly the most

dramatic of all was that the new CEO was a four-letter opposite of the other eight's predominant group type. The group consisted of five Introverts and three Extraverts, making it an Introverted group. There were five iNtuitives and three Sensors, six Thinkers and two Feelers, and five Judgers and three Perceivers. Taking the largest number of each preference, you can see that the predominant group type was INTJ. The new CEO was an ESFP.

When this revelation came to light, a lot of things started to make sense. When both sides became aware of how naturally different they were, a lot of the anger began to dissipate. It became clear, for example, that the CEO's constant thinking out loud grated against the engineers' need to retreat to their drawing tables and calculators. The CEO's call for detailed plans for everything was heard as nitpicking and riding herd, when engineers would rather be left to themselves. (After all, the engineers knew the system; they didn't need him to show them the ropes.) The CEO's willingness to hold decisions in favor of more information was seen as indecisiveness and lacking direction. And so it went.

Now, this is not what you might call a typical case. It is rare that individuals in conflict differ on all four preferences. But it is instructive nonetheless. *It is the preference differences that create communication problems and give rise to conflict.*

In this case, with four typological differences, the conflict was deep and wide. Perhaps the engineers would not have accepted anyone the board had picked as CEO were it not one of them. Perhaps whoever came on board as CEO would soon be made to feel like an outsider. But since every idea, statement, directive, or program was at opposite ends of the typological scale, it was little wonder that tension, stress, and distrust abounded and continued to enflame a variety of counterproductive behaviors.

When each side could see and experience the opposite types, tension was significantly reduced, and they began to trust one another.

At our retreat we initiated a series of exercises designed to heighten awareness of their differences. For example, we split the group into Sensors and iNtuitives. We asked them to view the same slide for twenty seconds and to compile a group report of what they saw. (These "reports" consisted of using markers to write on large newsprint sheets that the group could later view and discuss.)

The differences were so dramatic that there was a stunned silence. The four Sensors tried to reproduce the slide—it was a slide on leadership with some stick figures, some colors, and a couple of vague messages about vision—even to the point of attempting to reconstruct the arrows, figures, and colors. In the meantime the five iNtuitives were caught up in the meaning of the slide and tried to analyze its message. The group quickly came to see not only how different their interpretations were but how the two reports combined were more accurate portrayals of the slide than either individual report.

From that point on, the group was committed to learning how to communicate.

Among the other exercises we tried that day were the following:

- The Extraverts and Introverts, asked to describe an ideal weekend, couldn't believe how different their ideals were. This led to some insight on how Es shoot from the lip and don't always mean the first things they say; they speak so that they can think and ought not always to be held accountable for it. It further underscored how much the Introverts appreciate their own space and resent others invading it—audibly, physically, or visually.

- Because a central area of concern was the inability to deal with conflict effectively, we divided the group into Thinkers and Feelers and asked them to define the word *conflict*. Again they put their results on newsprint for everyone to see. The T engineer types' definition was not unlike something you'd read in a dictionary and was almost completely devoid of specific references to the situation at hand. In essence their definition was "Conflict is something that happens when opposing forces meet." The Fs, meanwhile, personalized the assignment. They suspected this assignment was directed at them, designed to push them to deal more effectively with conflict situations. Their definition included only personal references; conflict was something that happened to them and something they preferred to avoid.

- The J-P exercise was almost laughable. We divided the group into Js and Ps and asked each to discuss "the economy," without giving more specific directions. True to type, the Ps rambled on: "Which economy? Do we know anything about it? Do we even want to talk about it?" In less than five minutes they raised nothing but questions that ranged from the ridiculous to the sublime. The Js, in contrast, didn't need further explanation. The first J to speak set the tone; the subject would be the U.S. economy. The rest chimed in, either agreeing or disagreeing with the previous speaker, but all being very clear on where he or she stood on the subject. The Ps were astounded that the Js never sought a more specific definition, while the Js couldn't believe that the Ps could wander so far away from what the Js thought was a specific assignment.

Each of these exercises produced some small but significant insight that at once created a heightened awareness of differences while they opened up avenues of communication. One of the most important benefits of all this was that the blame being heaped on the CEO could be better defined and understood, as could the CEO's frustration with his underlings. For example, the engineers began to understand that as an Extravert the CEO did hear what they said, but he tended to talk over them, making it appear that he wasn't listening. The J engineers wanted specific directions, but the P CEO tended quite naturally to offer more questions than answers. The more they talked, the more insights they got and the more they were willing to lay aside those things that were blocking their effectiveness. That allowed them to stop bickering and start doing.

Overcoming the Obvious

Now, all of the above may seem like just so much common sense. Indeed it is. But in the heat of a conflict, common sense is one of the first things to go out the window. Granted, even common sense isn't always easy to follow. If you are surrounded by people like you, your common sense will tell you, "That's the way the world is." So, if you are among a group of Introverts, "common sense" would dictate that while people don't always speak their minds, when they do, others will listen. So, an Extravert's behavior seems to defy common sense; obviously there's something wrong with this "bad apple." You'd be surprised to learn how difficult it is for some people to truly understand that a different point of view can be worthwhile. They may understand this intellectually and even in their hearts, but their experience tells them otherwise.

If you can consider the type of the person with whom you are in conflict, you will find while the resolution may take longer and be somewhat more arduous than you'd prefer, the end result is always better. For one thing, if we solicit feedback from you, we will hear your criticisms much differently than if you were to offer the same comments unsolicited. For another, the more we know each other's natural styles, the more we can help each other with our natural shortcomings. We can tell you if you're talking and not listening; you can tell us that we're being too rigid or that we've personalized things too quickly.

Still another roadblock to constructive conflict resolution is answering the question, Whose problem is this? Thinkers would naturally like to believe that it's the other guy's problem, although that's right only about half the time. Feelers, meanwhile, would naturally like to believe that it's their problem; again, there's about a 50 percent accuracy rate to this assumption.

For some reason all of us—whatever our type—have a hard time sorting out who's right and who's wrong in a given conflict and how it can best be resolved. Fs quickly try to personalize a dispute, thereby rescuing everyone else, and Ts just as quickly depersonalize a problem and analyze it to death without ever getting involved in it. Extraverts want to talk their way through a situation without realizing that it's not even their problem, while Introverts tend to mind their own business, often keeping to themselves ideas and information that could lead to resolution. And so it goes.

Conflict Resolution

IF YOU ARE AN . . .

	EXTRAVERT	INTROVERT
EXTRAVERT	• Have one party listen while the other talks and then switch roles. • Remember that the last word is rarely the final word. • Try to argue the other's viewpoint; repeat what you heard the other say.	• Demand that your colleague be silent for a while and listen. • Try to blurt out the first thoughts that come to mind without editing them in advance. • Commit yourself to sharing your thoughts, even if you need to write them down first.
	EXTRAVERT	**INTROVERT**
INTROVERT	• Avoid overkill and redundancy. • Say your peace, then back off and allow the other time to respond. • Jot some thoughts down on paper and share them with your colleague.	• Force yourself to speak on issues. Above all, do not avoid conflict by being silent. • Commit yourself to working out the issue together, rather than internally. • Assume that your colleague is experiencing at least as much stress as you are over the conflict.
	SENSOR	**INTUITIVE**
SENSOR	• Beware of overloading each other with facts and specifics. • When you disagree on details, stop the action and check each other's accuracy before continuing. • Try to explore the implications of what you say before you say it.	• Respect the fact that it may be necessary to consider specifics in order to resolve the conflict. • Help your colleague to see the meaning and implications of the details he or she is presenting. • Avoid trying to win an argument by focusing only on the big picture.
	SENSOR	**INTUITIVE**
INTUITIVE	• Keep your colleague grounded and specific. • Try to grasp the implications and meaning of what is being said. • Avoid introducing so many details that you lose sight of the bigger picture.	• Recognize that you both tend to avoid facts or to bend them in order to prove your case. • If you disagree over perception, stop and check for accuracy before the conflict escalates. • Work hard to stay grounded, precise, and in the present.

LEADING AN . . .

IF YOU ARE A . . .

LEADING A . . .

	THINKER	FEELER
THINKER	• Know when to stop analyzing and competing. • Recognize that you both have emotions and that hurt feelings may result from your disagreement. • Remember that it is okay to lose the argument. Life will go on.	• Try to remember that not all criticism is directed at you. • Stand your ground. State your position and try to stay objective. • Avoid saying "I'm sorry" or "You're right" too often. It's okay to argue. Life will go on.

	THINKER	FEELER
FEELER	• Keep in mind that whatever you say may be taken personally, even if you don't mean it that way. • Remember that it is good to say "I'm sorry" when you mean it. • Try to show your human side during the conflict.	• Face the conflict. Stand tough and don't avoid it. • Don't give in early for the sake of harmony. • Remember that conflict can be a positive, learning experience.

	JUDGER	PERCEIVER
JUDGER	• Keep in mind that conflicts can't be scheduled, but the resolution of them can be. • Bring up the issues, then schedule a time to deal with them later. • If an issue isn't yet resolved, don't say that it is just to bring closure to the situation.	• Recognize that your colleague may sound more angry than he or she really is. • Seek alternatives to win-lose situations. • Hit and run: Drop the topic of the conflict and leave, then come back and deal with it later.

	JUDGER	PERCEIVER
PERCEIVER	• Allow some latitude to explore different aspects of a subject. • Make a positive resolution the goal, rather than winning. • Help your colleague to stay focused and to deal with one issue at a time.	• Help each other stay focused on one topic at a time. • State your opinions and needs as clearly as possible—no waffling. • Try to negotiate win-win solutions. Or decide which one of you can "win" and "lose" each issue.

10

Goal Setting

"If I did speak up, would anyone even hear me?"

Goals confront us at every turn of the screw. For some people goal setting takes the form of establishing formal objectives, mission statements, PERT charts, and the like. But goal setting takes place in other ways on a day-to-day level. To-do lists, meeting schedules and agendas, even a stack of phone messages, comprise a set of goals and put us into a goal-oriented frame of mind. A goal might be something as simple as "I'd like to leave today by four o'clock." It is phenomenal how much that goal determines the rest of the day's activities. Managers and others take courses and read books to learn how to set and reach goals of all kinds. From our earliest days we have been taught the psychological values of not biting off more than we could chew.

Yet with all of this emphasis goals are still severely misunderstood, very elusive, and often send individuals and groups going in opposite directions. This isn't just a matter of not being able to reach consensus. Frequently, dynamic leaders starting with the same goals and visions end up taking very different routes, ultimately reaching very different destinations. The result, rather than being a product or a service, can be frustration, conflict, and high levels of stress.

Why does this happen?

We'd like to suggest that the problem has less to do with what we have in common and more to do with our differences—specifically the differences among our personality preferences. Some people are comfortable working within a chain of command, even finding solace in the knowledge that "the boss is the boss" and of where the buck finally stops. It never occurs to these soldiers not to work within that frame of reference, and when someone of a different type pushes against the system, bringing in new ideas and methods, the soldiers become rigid and resistant, even questioning the "rebel's" loyalty. In the process good ideas can die on the vine.

Their counterparts are those for whom the chain of command only means one thing: confinement. These types are not as bound by time, preferring to respond according to when and how the spirit moves them. They tend to think of goals more in general terms than in specifics and as a result are less concerned about specific deadlines so long as the overall project is in the ballpark. Such individuals can find having to march in step a setup for tripping and stumbling.

The same dilemmas happen with leaders. There are those drill sergeants who live and die by the rules. Don't look for creative or alternative interpretations—there's the right way and the wrong way to achieve a goal. Such individuals not only accept the goals they set, they embrace the challenge of their position and often believe that it's their duty to impose the goals on others. Management for them is a one-way street: from the top down. Goals must follow the same route. Clearly not everyone lives and dies by these same rules—or by any rules, for that matter.

And then there are those leaders who are so open-ended that their followers never know what's going to happen next. Today's goal might be increasing widget production; tomorrow it could be a whole new product line. Such wide swings can leave a workforce on edge and confused, with efficiency and loyalty taking a backseat to covering one's backside.

The challenge, then, in goal setting is to get everyone throughout the organization moving in the same direction (ideally at the same time; more on that in Chapter Eleven, on time management). To do that, however, requires that you first understand how different preferences approach the very meaning of "goals."

How Extraverts and Introverts Approach Goal Setting

As we said before, Extraversion and Introversion have to do with where you focus your energy—outwardly (E) or inwardly (I). For Extraverts the process of setting goals is done the same way they do everything else: They talk them through. Goal setting, therefore, is a group experience for Extraverts. Everyone shares, often talking over one another, and things get massaged and modified out loud. By the time everyone walks out the door, the assumption is that everyone is on board. Their assumption is that if everyone is involved in the goal-setting conversation—and for Extraverts that means simply speaking up—they will be committed to the end product.

But will they? One of the pitfalls of this Extraverted process is a second assumption: that silence equals consent. In other words for an Extravert, the simple act of your being present at the goal-setting session assumes that you will be in accord. That immediately puts Introverts in the middle of a dilemma: Should they give in to their desire to reflect awhile, perhaps even overnight, thereby keeping their thoughts to themselves and risking that they will be consenting tacitly, or should they speak up despite the fact that they're unsure of how they feel, risking that they'll later change their mind and be labeled wishy-washy?

This Introverted dilemma sets Extraverts up to widen the gap with Introverts farther. In an effort to involve everyone, as Extraverts are wont to do, they become more assertive, verbal, and louder. Some Extraverts may even go so far as to take an opposing or controversial point of view just for the sake of "involving everyone." Introverts, for their part, do get more involved—in their own Introversion. The added noise level and verbosity makes them even more reflective and causes them to wonder, "If I did speak up, would anyone even hear me?"

Another ongoing problem for Extraverts is that because they need to hear what they're going to say before they can be sure of what they think, they are constantly crowding airspace with words to which they have little or no commitment. They may become totally surprised to find that people not only were listening to them but actually were ready to implement what for them was "just an idea."

Consider, for example, the case of an army general we worked with, who one morning, staring out the window, mused, "I wonder what would happen if we moved that ditch about six feet back." To his amazement, a few hours later he looked out his window to find a cadre of troops busily filling in and digging out. He said, "What the hell are they doing?" totally forgetting his earlier thinking out loud. (Like many Extraverts, he wasn't even listening to himself.) To which the chief of staff replied, "General, you said you wanted the ditch moved."

GOOD AS GOALS

Having clear-cut goals is one thing. Managing them, and keeping them in perspective, is another. Consider Parris N. Glendening, Governor of Maryland. According to the *Washington Post*, in his early twenties Glendening was hemorrhaging from a stomach ulcer. His doctor told him that he would likely face a lifetime of internalized stress, of stretching himself against rigorous self-imposed goals. Simply put, he was quietly killing himself. So at age twenty-three he decided to change his ways. Each day, he decided, would have a manageable schedule. That rule is so strictly enforced that even now his secretary pencils in "family time" in his official calendar. His life has been structured around a series of goals, each carefully weighed and analyzed, with an appropriate fallback position.

"Someone once said, 'You've got to know where you're going, or how will you know when you get there?'" he told the *Post*. "You've got to know what it is you want to do, or how will you know if you ever achieved anything?"

Introverts, like Extraverts, want a sense of having personally influenced the goal-setting process so that they can then "own" it. But they do it in a different way. They want to reflect on what's transpired, massage it a bit internally, recognizing that for them the richest part of any such encounter is ultimately an internal experience. At goal-setting time Introverted managers find it far more appropriate to disseminate a written draft "for your advance thinking and preparation," which will later become the basis for the goals at hand. For an Introvert it's important that everyone arrive prepared, and that means thinking about what you're going to say, not shooting from the lip. The goal-setting process doesn't end when the meeting's over. That presents a chance to reflect on what's been discussed and to formulate some final thoughts. (The process doesn't necessarily end for Extraverts either: They'll simply talk about it *ad nauseam* to whoever's within reach.)

The difficulty for both sides centers around one essential difference: the Introvert's desire to "get it in writing" versus the Extravert's need to "talk it through." When the result is a stalemate—the Extravert wants to talk more and the Introvert wants to reflect on it—it places them 180 degrees from each other, a clear adversarial model in which the goals become increasingly elusive, and seemingly insignificant matters ("Okay, but we'll have to do it in my office.") take center stage. What started out as a well-meaning process ends up as an exercise in interpersonal nitpicking.

The most effective goal-setting process, then, would be one that gives Extraverts the opportunity to verbalize—and reverbalize—their ideas and Introverts the time to reflect on what has been discussed. (We'll offer more specific tips and exercises for each preference later on in this chapter.)

How Sensors and iNtuitives Approach Goal Setting

Sensing and iNtuiting, as you'll recall, have to do with how we prefer to gather information—in hands-on, here-and-now fashion (Sensing) or in a theoretical, futuristic way (iNtuition). This preference differential is the starting point for all goal setting. After all, without an initial perception there's no basis for further communication. However, if in examining a goal one person perceives it one way and someone else sees it differently, it becomes the basis of missed goals and opportunities.

Let's look at a typical Sensing-iNtuitive goal-setting problem, this one between Sally, a Sensor, and her colleague Ned, an iNtuitive. The two are planning a marketing seminar to launch a new product from their division, and among the many things to anticipate is the relatively simple matter of how many people will attend the seminar. The question has an impact on a number of things, including how many marketing kits to have on hand, how many chairs, the amount of coffee and donuts—and how much all this is going to cost. But the key question is the attendance figure. Ned is trying to get a rough estimate. He wants a general plan that will cover a wide range of options. Sally, in all good faith, is having trouble speaking in generalities.

> Ned: "Sally, how many people do you think will show up?"
>
> Sally: "Well, let's see. The Chicago group will be sending twelve. Milwaukee is sending six. And St. Louis will send fourteen. But I haven't heard from Los Angeles, Phoenix, and—would you believe—our own office. That could be anywhere from twenty to about fifty-two."
>
> Ned: "So, if everyone were to show up, what would that total be?"
>
> Sally: "I don't know. As I said, I still haven't heard from some of the groups. And there may be some executive guests. So it's hard to say."
>
> Ned: "Well, can you give me a ballpark figure?"
>
> Sally: "Gee, that's difficult. I don't know if I can."
>
> Ned: "Look, are we going to have three hundred, two hundred, or one hundred?"
>
> Sally: "I just can't answer that yet. It's too early to tell."

By now Ned is nearly apoplectic. All he wanted was an estimate, and all he got were nonanswers, at least by his perception. He still doesn't have the basic information he requested, so he feels paralyzed as to what his next move should be. And he's more than a little irritated at Sally.

Sally, for her part, is none too pleased with Ned. She has tried to provide him with specifics and has done her best to prevent him from being misled by bad information. She, too, feels that her detailed analysis has gone unappreciated.

We've encountered many Sallys and Neds in organizations, and such dialogues, while perhaps funny to read about after the fact, are quite painful, costly, and counterproductive to the parties involved. But when you examine the goal-setting differences between Sensors and iNtuitives, it's no wonder that Sallys and Neds disagree.

Sensors prefer goals that are simple and attainable. "Simple" means straightforward, no-frills, and understandable by everyone by any level of intelligence. They are the inventors and implementers of the "KISS"—Keep It Simple, Stupid—model of life. And for a Sensor, there is nothing like a good KISS when it comes to goal setting. "Attainable" means that there is enough challenge in the goal to inspire and motivate but not so much challenge as to appear absurd. Goals that are out of sight—however inspirational they may sound—border on the ridiculous and for them become exercises in futility. An attainable goal is one in which the Sensor can get his or her hands on it and get to work, and receive some gratification en route to the finish line. So, unless a goal fits all these criteria, a major portion of the workforce—Sensors comprise 70 percent of the population—will reject a goal from the start.

For the iNtuitive, goals need to be inspirational, challenging, and set within a clear conceptual framework. There is no motivation or movement without inspiration, so the goal needs to be a broad-based idea that will lift the organization to the next higher level—of productivity, achievement, profits, or whatever. No matter what has transpired to date, there is only opportunity ahead, and goals are one of the keys that unlock that potential. For iNtuitives goals that are too simple or too clear are pointless because they are considered to be obvious—and the obvious is the bane of the iNtuitive's existence. In goal setting, the obvious needn't be planned; it will take care of itself. The purpose of a goal is to go beyond that which is already being done. Hence, even if the sound of a goal seems a bit out of reach, it's better to try for it, because even if you fail, the system will be better off for trying. It is an iNtuitive's ongoing quest to "dream the impossible dream."

So, let's take another look at Sally and Ned. In the above dialogue Ned kept pushing Sally for the conceptual framework of the attendance. No doubt, Ned thought, once he had a handle on that, he would be ready for anything, able to adjust the facilities and services upward or downward as needed. The obvious—that there would eventually be a specific number of people—was a given and a waste of time even to consider. The more he pushed for generalities, the less helpful and more confining her specifics seemed to be. For him the exact numbers were simply a case of data overload.

Sally meanwhile perceived the question as unanswerable because it called for exact data she didn't have. Moreover she knew, based on previous experience, that there would be costs involved for everything from coffee to chairs, so it was important not to spend more than was needed yet still have enough of everything. And that required exactness.

So what Sally and Ned experienced was another situation of two bright and committed people starting at the same place with good intentions ("How many people do you think will show up?") and moving in opposite directions. Even simple awareness of the difference might have allowed them to laugh at the situation rather than permit it to accelerate into a full-fledged snit. It's very important in goal setting that Sensors keep in mind that some of the ballpark quests of the iNtuitive can be responded to without exactness, and for iNtuitives to remember that the specifics that Sensors offer are an effort to provide necessary information, even when such exactness isn't called for.

How Thinkers and Feelers Approach Goal Setting

The decision-making function—Thinking versus Feeling—plays a major role in how committed everyone will be to the goal, even if everyone agrees on what that goal is. It's the decision-making function that says, "I like that goal and I'm going to work like crazy to achieve it," or "I don't like that goal, and I'm not going to play on the team, or maybe I'll play half-heartedly." So it is crucial to understand the difference between an objective (Thinking) commitment to an objective goal and a subjective (Feeling) commitment to a subjective value.

Let's look briefly at just one moment in business history in which one preference's style of decision making—in this case Thinking—predominated to the neglect of the other. The year was 1958. Ford Motor Company's goal was to introduce an exciting new car. In preparation the Thinking-oriented engineering department had designed a car that was technically sound, architecturally innovative, and chock full of state-of-the-art amenities. The engineers knew they had a car that would rise to the top of the marketplace because of its structural excellence.

But no one adequately considered the subjective (Feeling) impact of the car. How would people feel about a car whose front-end design was substantially different from anything known in recent years? Would Americans appreciate the dramatic changes from other Ford models, such as the push-button shift and overstated design? The feelings of the consumer were not taken into account. The company felt the car would stand on its own by virtue of its objective capabilities.

The Edsel, as everyone knows, didn't sell. It did not appeal to car buyers. It wasn't attractive. People simply didn't like it. So all the objective engineering in the world couldn't carry the car to that part of the population that would rather have something they liked than something that worked well.

How do you ensure commitment? It begins with bringing consensus about goals to both Thinkers and Feelers.

For Thinkers, a goal must be the result of an exhaustive thought process. Goals must reflect "the best there is" and "the state of the art" and should lead ultimately to a good product. Thinkers are driven by the *what* and the *how* behind a goal: what is to be achieved, what good is to come from it, how will it fit into the rest of the world, and how will the world be affected by it? The answers to these questions should be able to produce a logic that makes the goal one to which a Thinker can commit.

For Feelers, goals must reflect a concern for everyone involved—those who must meet the goal as well as those who will be affected by it. Feelers want the most—and sometimes even the best—for everyone. In contrast to Thinkers' goals that reflect the state of the art, Feelers want goals to reflect the state of the people or organization—to be effective, a goal that leads to esprit de corps. The question for the Feeler is not *what* or *how* so much as *who*: Who will be affected by this goal, and what will be the quality of life as a result? Will people be better off or live differently because of it, and will humanity—whether the office staff or the world at large—come to some new level of growth as a result?

Aside from their different sets of needs, Thinkers and Feelers approach goal setting in very different ways. A Thinker can be committed to a goal but not necessarily in agreement with it or with everyone on the work team. "I don't have to like you to work with you" is a familiar Thinker refrain. For the Feeler that notion is abhorrent. The whole purpose of a goal is to achieve harmony in the workplace and to move the organization as a team. Clearly both parties will have to compromise: Thinkers will have to realize that it is important for Feelers to have some modicum of harmony in the workplace, and Feelers must recognize that not every goal needs to be fully embraced by all in order to be achieved. Good things can still be accomplished despite these differences.

How Judgers and Perceivers Approach Goal Setting

All that we've said so far notwithstanding, everything having to do with goal setting comes to rest with the Judging-Perceiving difference. It's on this dimension that push comes to shove. For one thing, this is the most obvious of our four preferences, the one that reflects our outward lifestyle. So if you're a Judger, your lifestyle is structured, scheduled, and ordered, and your speech is even directive and opinionated. And if you're a Perceiver, your lifestyle is flexible, spontaneous, and adaptive, and your speech is open-ended and inquisitive. Therefore, because setting goals is a decision-making process, it gives an obvious edge to the more decisive Judgers, for whom a good day is one in which a series of both large and small goals are set and accomplished.

Another area in which push comes to shove is when Perceivers modify a goal based on new information. For Ps this is exciting and reflects good common sense—after all, why stick with the old goal when things have changed? Unfortunately Js see this as a failure, because you didn't accomplish what you set out to do. So it is a quintessentially Judging philosophy to believe that "It is better to accomplish the wrong thing with dispatch than not to accomplish anything at all." As we've said, Js aren't beyond making good time going in the wrong direction.

The goal can be just about anything. Today's goal might be to plan for the company picnic on Saturday. If by Friday half of the company couldn't make it because of deadlines and on Saturday it rained cats and dogs, the Judgers would still want to proceed with the original plan because it was part of the team-building goal of the company. And besides, "We committed ourselves to do it." For the Perceivers the change in circumstances, however disappointing, is ample reason to cancel the event. The "new information"—the absent employees and the weather—was sufficient to reassess the goal of having a picnic. For the Ps it had nothing to do with commitment—it's just plain common sense.

HOW TO KEEP Ps FROM PROCRASTINATING

- **Give them your plans in advance so that they can think about them when they are alone.** "I wrote out my plan so far. Would you look at it tonight and give me your reaction tomorrow?"

- **Move to closure by acknowledging the worthwhile new information beneath their aggravating style.** "Thank you for that feedback. Those are all things I should consider and probably wouldn't have on my own."

- **Make it clear when you have made a decision, set a deadline, or intend to act, and when you want them to do the same.** "I'll be informing the client that we'll have a report by May 10, so our reputation as a reliable firm depends upon our finishing by then."

- **Ask questions that lead them to think about the order and direction of their thoughts.** "There are many ways this could be wrong. It could be the wrong idea, the wrong people, the wrong market, the wrong time. Do any of these stand out in your mind?"

- **Set up frequent feedback sessions so that they can talk about what they are thinking.** "Let's meet every week just to talk about the project." Or "When are we going to get back together to discuss your progress?"

For the Js such behavior is simply another demonstration of the Ps' lack of commitment to the program.

Judgers don't need a formal process to set goals. Indeed it is a natural part of life. Each day's awakening brings a new list of goals to be met by the end of the day—including the goal of crossing everything off the list by day's end. In group goal setting,

Judgers want goals explicitly defined so that all involved can agree to them. And when consensus is reached, the goal-setting process is finished until at some future time it may need reassessment. Until that time the goals are carved in stone; accountability and commitment will be measured against them.

For Perceivers, goal setting is an unfolding process with different levels of agreement. Goals for them are always emerging. While most Ps would readily agree that you need goals to be successful, the goals they reach are only guidelines, open to reevaluation and additional information. Interestingly, Ps' success rate is not significantly different from Js'; they are equally

HOW TO KEEP Js FROM JUMPING TO CONCLUSIONS

- **Give them new information in advance so that they have time to think about it when they are alone.** "I put my comments on the sidebars. Let's meet tomorrow morning to discuss them."

- **Keep the dialogue moving by acknowledging the worthwhile judgments beneath their aggravating style.** "You've envisioned a whole new organization. That's exciting."

- **Make it clear when you are only speculating and when you want them to speculate.** "I'm only thinking out loud now. I just need a good listener."

- **Ask them questions about their decision process.** "Tell me from the beginning what led you to this conclusion."

- **Let them organize the data-collection and review process.** "How should we organize our research? When should we meet again? What should we prepare for the next meeting?"

capable of reaching the same heights. But their methodology couldn't be less alike.

A Final Word About Goal Setting

As one of our commandments reminds us, your strengths maximized can become liabilities. This is certainly true in goal setting. One way we see this problem is in the tendency of many organizations and professions to become typologically similar. For example, 60 percent of the managers of the world share preferences for Thinking and Judging—they are objective, oriented to the bottom line, decisive, and accountable. A minimum of 80 percent of the entire corporate world is comprised of iNtuitive-Thinkers and Sensing-Judgers. Those who are administrative will be more SJ than NT. Those that are more entrepreneurial and research-oriented will be more NT than SJ.

The point is that we can get so tunneled in the goal-setting process that we can forget our nonpreferences. The result can be goals that are too single-minded, specifically focused, or simply uninteresting to the other types in the workforce. That leads to apathy, sabotage, or simply poor productivity. So even the best goals in the world can go nowhere if they don't appeal to personality differences.

In our experience the most successful organizations are those that recognize their typological blind spots and involve all types in the goal-setting process. So, if your group is heavily weighted toward Sensors, it's crucial to seek the insight and inspiration of iNtuitives lest the goals become too short-term and mundane. And a heavily Judging group needs Perceiver input so that goals reflect potential changes in the marketplace and the business world. And so on.

In the end, goals that involve each of the preferences are much more likely to succeed.

Goal Setting

IF YOU ARE AN . . .

	EXTRAVERT	INTROVERT
EXTRAVERT	• Try to listen without interrupting, verbally or nonverbally. • Repeat the essence of what the previous speaker said before stating your point. • Let a pause or silence occur now and then.	• Allow for some fluff and redundancy. • Don't hold others to their first impressions or to the first words they say. • Help sort out the conversational wheat from the chaff.
	EXTRAVERT	**INTROVERT**
INTROVERT	• Establish methods to achieve clarity and mutual agreement. • Now and then, allow things to remain unsaid. • Speak only for yourself, and allow everyone else a chance to speak.	• Push yourself to speak without editing yourself first. • Though silence may be comfortable, do not assume that it means there is agreement or that nothing remains to be said. • Practice redundancy.
	SENSOR	**INTUITIVE**
SENSOR	• Generate some "way-out" material and wait twenty-four hours to revisit it. • Consider the facts—but not as a first step. • Reflect and improve upon previous goal-setting experiences.	• Stress the facts and specifics as much as possible. • Allow time to consider a mock-up vision that is firmly rooted in reality. • Temper your tendency to be impatient and even arrogant with regard to tedious and time-consuming reality checks.
	SENSOR	**INTUITIVE**
INTUITIVE	• Establish each person's contribution to the goal-setting process and use identified strengths. • Feel free to contribute specifics and facts that enhance the strategy or vision. • Before determining that a goal is unrealistic, live with the idea and play with its specifics for twenty-four hours.	• Try to flesh out general goals with costs, time lines, and other details. • Avoid discussing and defining the concept of "goal setting"—just do it. • Wait twenty-four hours before "improving" goals and ideas that have been established.

LEADING AN . . .

IF YOU ARE A . . .

LEADING A . . .

	THINKER	FEELER
THINKER	• Keep reminding yourself that the personal and interpersonal dimensions of goals are important. • Now and then, ask the people working toward a goal whether they feel committed to it. • Spend a little time discussing the broader issues surrounding your goals.	• Push others to see how important the human element is in setting goals. • Remind the group that it takes people who have direction to reach goals. • Remember that happy people who do not set goals go nowhere.
	THINKER	**FEELER**
FEELER	• Try to establish and make known how each of you experiences and defines goal setting. • Recognize how important people are in working toward realizing goals. • Remind yourself that setting goals, though important, is not everything.	• Keep reminding yourself that effective goal setting involves impersonal as well as interpersonal approaches. • Measure the value of each goal with objective, impersonal criteria. • Spend a little time discussing "What are the central issues in goal setting?"
	JUDGER	**PERCEIVER**
JUDGER	• Be careful not to set the goal too rapidly. • Check the goal for reachability and flexibility. • Remind yourself that swift completion is not the goal in goal setting.	• Be directive even when your proposals may not go as far as your colleague wants them to. • Push to avoid hasty completion. • Help others see that the process of setting goals is as important as the goals themselves.
	JUDGER	**PERCEIVER**
PERCEIVER	• Be aware that others may be more interested in the process of goal setting than in the goal itself. • Keep things on target when they start to wander. • Lend enthusiasm to a task that may be seen as boring to others.	• Remind yourself that you must come up with a goal, as meaningless as that may sound. • You can alter any goal, but allow at least twenty-four hours to pass before doing so. • Now and then, push for closure.

11

Time Management

"We don't have time to do it right.
We only have time to do it over."

When it comes to managing time, it's a Judger's world, hands down. Beginning in grade school, the spoils go to those who have their homework in on time and who complete tests and other assignments "under the clock." Punishments are meted out to those who are late, no matter what the quality of the work may be. The reward is not to do it right but to do it on time.

The rewards continue throughout academic and professional life. In high school an overachiever is invariably a Judger and an underachiever is invariably a Perceiver. Of the latter it is frequently said that he or she "is such a bright student but is not working up to potential." Classes that involve structure, homework, and deadlines give the edge to J students, while P students excel in self-directed and more loosely structured situations. Independent study is a P's dream come true.

In adult life, airlines reward those who manage their time, with special discounts for early ticket purchases. Banks offer incentives for those who can plan sufficiently to lock up their funds for extended periods of time. Whatever the incentive, the more you plan and manage your time, the more rewards will be available to you in our time-conscious world. Learn to meet deadlines and be punctual, and you can probably go far—even if you're only mediocre.

Simply put, it's a conspiracy of Judgers. And most key time-management issues are rooted in J-P differences.

The conspiracy is part and parcel of the work world. Whether you must punch a clock or simply get through the day, we all eventually become slaves to the clock. So significant is the conspiracy that in some psychological theories time is seen as an authority figure. Those who are chronically late are judged as having deep-seated problems with authority. Your tardiness is your way of thumbing your nose at the system.

Our J-oriented preoccupation with time and schedules can be very costly. It's a hardcore J's slogan that "We don't have time to do it right. We only have time to do it over." Repeatedly we work with organizations that are bent on delivering a half-done, ineffective program on schedule rather than running late but taking the time necessary to do things right the first time. How many times have you said to yourself, "I wish I had taken a bit more time to do it right"? Or "If only I knew how much work was involved, I would have allowed more time for this." It doesn't take a degree in accounting to recognize the dollar costs involved in doing things over or repairing the waste that is born of haste.

The Judging-Perceiving preference is only part of the story when it comes to understanding how people deal with time at work. The three other preference pairs are also important. Keep in mind that the differences don't necessarily translate into greater or lesser productivity. When time is a concern, it's more method than results. Still, the differences can cause a great deal of friction, which can be disruptive and costly.

Let's take a look at how each of the preferences deals with and ultimately manages its time.

How Extraverts and Introverts Relate to Time

Given that there is a finite number of hours in a day—and even fewer in a workday—there are rewards available to those who use that time efficiently. The advantage here goes to the

WHAT IS TIME?

Extraverts: Time is to be overpowered and used.
Introverts: Time is spatial, a concept.
Sensors: Time is now; there is no time but the present.
iNtuitives: Time is possibilities; there's always time for one more thing.
Thinkers: Time is an object, a resource.
Feelers: Time is relational and interpersonal.
Judgers: Time is to be scheduled and controlled.
Perceivers: Time can be adapted and added to.

Introverts. The reason, simply put, is that thinking about something usually takes less time than talking about it. When it comes to processing information in order to formulate thoughts and opinions, Introversion is an efficient process: You can do it anywhere, at any time, as long as you aren't interrupted by the external world. Extraverts, as they formulate their thoughts and opinions, need external stimuli and constant engagement and can be given to redundancy, repeating the obvious in the name of clarity. All of which can consume precious moments. Extraverts not only use up their own time, they use up that of others—Introverts and other Extraverts—by invading their space and demanding responses, whether those responses are verbal or simply the occasional nodding and smiling. One way or another, Extraverts demand that you listen to them.

Things even out somewhat when it comes time to communicate one's thoughts and opinions to others. Extraverts don't need to take additional time to communicate these things—they've been doing so all along, beginning with their initial perceptions and continuing through their final conclusions. Introverts, while more efficient, communicate a great deal less. You may only get the tip of the iceberg—the conclusion without an understanding of how it came to be. A great deal of good material may be lost in the process.

So, for purposes of using time efficiently, both Introverts and Extraverts would benefit by monitoring their own preference as well as understanding that of others. Introverts, for example, should recognize that sooner or later—preferably sooner—they must stop thinking and start talking. Moreover, when scheduling time with Extraverts, they should allow time for Extraverts to extravert.

The process works in reverse for Extraverts. They should recognize that sooner or later—preferably sooner—they must stop talking and start listening. Moreover, when scheduling time with Introverts, they should allow time for reflection and contemplation. A solution can be as simple as scheduling a five-minute break during an hour-long discussion, to give Introverts a moment to recharge. That will make better use of the Introverts' second half hour.

How Sensors and iNtuitives Perceive Time

Many problems begin with differing perceptions of time. To a Sensor, a minute is sixty seconds—no more, no less. To an iNtuitive, a minute is what you make it—it's more than a few seconds, but far less than an hour; for iNtuitives time is relative. Both parties have trouble understanding the other's perspective. Sensors can't believe that you can ignore the obvious, and iNtuitives can't believe that you mean only the obvious. It's an age-old conversation: The Sensor says, "I thought you said you'd be there in a minute." The iNtuitive responds, "I didn't think you'd take me literally."

It's a relatively simple problem, with a relatively simple solution. When it comes to scheduling, both preferences must make accommodations for the opposite. Whenever possible, Sensors should give iNtuitives a little leeway when it comes to allotting time to get something done. "An hour-long meeting" might take anywhere from forty-five to ninety minutes; the "hour" is simply a rough guideline. And iNtuitives need to remember that when Sensors speak of a time frame, they usually have an exact one in mind.

The fact is we need both perceptions of time to be efficient. The two preferences together comprise a complete picture of time and keep us from falling into a time-based trap. Although they are the bane of iNtuitives' existence, there are those moments when time should be exact. And there are other moments when time should be a rough concept that can be added to or subtracted from as the situation demands.

How Thinkers and Feelers Use Their Time

Consistent with other aspects of their lives, Feelers and Thinkers base their time around either people or things. Feelers set up and prioritize their time around the people with whom they must interact in the course of the day. So, if a Feeler is confronting an unpleasant task—an encounter with an individual with whom he or she is in conflict, for example, or a reprimand of an employee—it will inevitably fall to the bottom of the day's list and may get continually postponed to the next day's activities.

A Thinker's use of time, in contrast, is driven by the events or things that are deemed necessary for the day's success. While a Thinker may not relish the unpleasant confrontation or the reprimand any more than a Feeler, he or she may schedule it high on the list to get such a task out of the way. Then the day is free and clear to pursue the rest of the agenda.

This is not to say that Feelers are chronic procrastinators and Thinkers always deliver the goods. Feelers will tend to make the time to listen to an employee's concern, resolve an issue that's gnawing at the staff, or deal with other interpersonal issues. And Thinkers are perfectly capable of procrastinating, especially when it comes to doing such things as giving praise for a job well done or tending to other things that might inspire motivation. If an entire department goes bowling every Thursday night, believes the T, that will likely fulfill the quota for camaraderie. Some of this of course has to do with whether the Thinker is an

Introvert or an Extravert. But the basic model holds true: The Thinker will invariably pursue those activities and events during company time that require the least amount of personal involvement or vulnerability.

It's important to keep in mind that Thinkers and Feelers need each other. Ts need Fs to remind them that process is as important as product. In other words, if you get through the day but alienate people in the process, your bottom-line productivity is questionable. And Fs need Ts to keep them from getting too embroiled in daily interpersonal dynamics. Getting through the day means more than simply everyone getting along and liking you—you have to get something done.

How Judgers and Perceivers Cope with Time

As we said earlier, this is where the rubber meets the road when it comes to time management. Because Judgers want to control their environment, they are naturally prone to control their—and everyone else's—time. Because Perceivers want to understand their environment, time is only a vehicle that helps in that understanding; it is merely something to be aware of, not something to be imposed on others. For Perceivers the whole notion of managing time flies in the face of their need to be flexible and adaptive.

For a J, having established a schedule, it's clear how much free time is left.

For a P, all time is free, except what is scheduled.

Once again, both preferences need each other to be productive and effective in their use of time. Js need Ps to keep them from becoming rigid and compulsive in their use of time. Clearly Js run the risk of making great time going in the wrong direction. In a time-sensitive situation, Ps can help Js to stay open to creative alternatives and to understand that the clock isn't the only criterion by which the job will be judged.

Ps, for their part, need Js to get a job done within some realistic

TEMPERAMENTS AND TIME*

ASSETS	LIABILITIES

Sensing-Judgers

Good at time management	Rigid about schedules
Most grounded in sensate realities	Hooked on responsibility
Most realistic	Can't relax
Able to throw things out	Hate to wait for others

Sensing-Perceivers

Can meet immediate needs of a situation	Efforts get scattered
Flexible and pliable	Changes direction often
Handle emergencies well	There's always tomorrow
Adaptable about scheduled changes	Bowled over by the moment

iNtuitive-Feelers

Sensitive to people and their time	Difficulty saying no
Give people all the time they need	Feel guilty if they don't give others time
Time oriented toward others' needs	Neglect own time needs
Time is useful for finding life's purpose	Waste time searching for self

iNtuitive-Thinkers

Time is conceptual, impersonal	It is enough just to think it through without taking action
Time is part of a bigger system	Time is in the mind only
Time is a tool to accomplish things	People's needs may suffer

*For a discussion of Temperaments, see Chapter Five.

SEE, I TOLD YOU SO

It has always been one of our theories that life unfolds for each of us to support our preferences. So, Judgers schedule their lives, and they're glad they do because life happens to them on schedule. Perceivers, on the other hand, respond to life as each day happens, and they're glad they do because that leaves them open to each day's surprises.

A few Thanksgivings ago, the two of us were arguing over how we were going to spend the holiday. We had received a couple of invitations, and the Judger (Otto) wanted to bring closure to the event by accepting one and turning down the other. The Perceiver (Janet) wasn't quite sure what she wanted to do and implored Otto to delay making a decision. The closer the holiday came, the more contentious things got.

Just before Thanksgiving the phone rang, and we learned that Janet's father was seriously ill. We needed to drop everything and get to Michigan. Because nothing had been scheduled yet, it was very easy for us to move swiftly and respond to the family need. Within a few hours we were on the road.

En route Janet said, "See, it's a good thing we didn't have any commitments, because we would have had to call and redo them. That sure would have complicated things."

To which Otto responded, "That sounds simple enough. Pass the Maalox."

time frame—and to resist the temptation to revisit what's already been deemed complete. Left to their own devices, Ps tend to overwork the obvious, massaging a solution long after it is productive to do so. Js can help Ps see that making a list—and sticking to it—needn't be a stifling experience.

A New Lesson Learned

Although procrastination is a common affliction, it isn't always the key time-management issue. Some people's problem is that they take on too much, sometimes not finishing anything and neglecting other important matters in the process. Consider Irene, an INFP schoolteacher who was so involved with taking care of everyone else's needs that she was totally neglectful of her own needs throughout the school day. Everyone else came first. Everything else—from eating lunch to making lesson plans—took a backseat. (Indeed "lesson plan" was an oxymoron: Irene believed that learning was spontaneous and shouldn't be planned.) As a result Irene's own health was less than perfect, and it seemed as though she was constantly being reprimanded by the administration for failing to submit paperwork—lesson plans, evaluations, test scores, grades—in an orderly fashion.

Interestingly, Irene's students loved her, and that tended to make her even more devoted to their needs. Because she was so iNtuitive and Perceiving, her quest of endless possibilities kept her chasing one impulsive vision after another. Irene would stop a discussion to help a student in need, skip lunch to tutor, or stay late to listen to a student's family problem. This was always done to the near-total neglect of her private time.

By the time she came to us, Irene was sharply self-critical and felt like a failure. Her employer, the administration, reinforced her negative self-image, and her family felt neglected. As we worked with her, it became apparent that Irene needed some forced Introverted time alone. This would allow her the opportunity to complete some reading or assignments, or just attend to her personal life. Very slowly we tried to help her accomplish—bring closure to—just a few of these things. (Knowing she needed help, all of these things appealed to her. Her tendency was to jump in and do them all at once. That of course would have led to her accomplishing none of them and would only have exacerbated her stress.) We started with one, and only one, of the items and stayed with it until she had a sense of completion within a given time frame. We decided that she would finish the book she had started within a week and would then turn to creating a lesson plan for the following two weeks.

As Irene began to accomplish a few things, she began to see the need to limit her inspirations and pace herself by doing one thing completely before starting something else.

Success bred success, as she began to discover the appeal of completion. She still found a strong call to deal with whatever "emergencies" happened along, but she also started to realize that the emergencies would always be there. In fact, Irene learned that she was better able to help others if her own needs were attended to. We had no intention of turning this Perceiver into a Judger. We simply wanted to instill in her the need for closure in some parts of her life.

The Art of Planned Spontaneity

Another case involved Arthur, a compulsive ESTJ whose obnoxious, controlling behavior was irritating everyone around him and whose rigidity was driving him crazy. Anything unscheduled or spontaneous opened a floodgate of self-criticism and anger. Arthur's motto was I don't like surprises, and he backed this up with outrage toward anyone who dared mess up his neatly packaged day. Every plan had a backup plan, and even some of those had backups. As others would laugh in disbelief at his behavior, it made him only more determined to prove the folly of their whimsical responses. This was all the more complicated because by all management standards Arthur was Mr. Success. He was looked upon as a leader and had moved up to high levels of responsibility within his company.

When we first met Art, we tried to reason with him through humor: "Will any of this really matter in ten years?" He was clearly not amused, and we concluded that Arthur would best be served by a more scheduled, structured route to relaxation. With such an extremely rigid person as this, it often takes a heart attack, a major accident, a threatened divorce, or some

MISSION: DIFFICULT

"The difficult we do immediately; the impossible takes a little longer."   —a P management model

other physical or psychological sledgehammer to help him or her see that the compulsive behavior is ultimately destructive.

Fortunately Arthur was spared through Typewatching and its ability to help him see how extreme his behaviors had become. We asked him to schedule some quiet time and to add to his list such open-ended activities as smelling the daisies, enjoying some music, or appreciating some other restful experience in which no accountability was demanded. This allowed him to back off a bit, but to do so in a scheduled fashion. As we did with Irene, we started simply, one step at a time, so that Arthur soon began to enjoy the relaxation and even allowed his schedule to take a backseat to the experience of the moment occasionally. As everything from planned deep breathing, to open-ended relaxation, to sensory indulgence became more therapeutic, Arthur became less compulsive.

Again, we did not try to transform Arthur into a Perceiver— nor could we; he would never be as impulsive as Irene—we only wanted to make him a little less rigid, and this was best accomplished through scheduling.

Wait Problems

No one of any type is exempt from procrastinating. It is a natural human trait. The issues that cause strife on the job have to do with priorities, the different issues around which each type naturally procrastinates.

The fact is that every type procrastinates around its nonpreferences. So, for example, Extraverts delay things that involve reflection and contemplation. It's not that they're against it, it's that they'd rather be doing something else (such as talking about the fact that they need to sit quietly and think things through). Introverts, for their part, may postpone returning phone calls, attending social gatherings, and may be late getting to meetings that they view as superficial or redundant. (They might spend the time thinking about what they'll tell so-and-so when they finally get around to calling him.)

And so it goes for the other six preferences:

- Sensors procrastinate around futuring and visioning; they would rather pay the bills, enter some immediate data, or engage in some other constructive activity.

- iNtuitives procrastinate around dealing with the here and now; they would rather imagine how the finished project will look, speculate on what's going to happen tomorrow, or create a new system to improve productivity.

- Thinkers procrastinate around the "touchy-feely" side of the workplace, such as dealing with interpersonal tension or someone's personal problems; they would rather work on the computer, have a hearty discussion about the new marketing program, or do some other analytical activity.

- Feelers procrastinate around facing negative office issues directly, such as criticizing someone's work or delivering bad news; they would rather spend time building esprit de corps, making sure everyone's got what they need to do the job, or something else that will be socially enhancing to the workplace.

- Judgers procrastinate around relaxing or any other activity that distracts from getting the job done; they would rather stay on schedule, tidy up, or do any other activity that will help them cross things off their list.

- Perceivers procrastinate around getting organized; they would rather be looking at options, exploring alternative ways to get something done, or anything else that brings some freshness to a routine.

It is important to realize that there's more to procrastination than just being lazy. Putting things off has to do with avoiding what doesn't come easily. Understanding this alone can make us less critical of those who get excited about some things and endlessly put off others.

Adapt or Control?

When time-related issues surface, it helps to know whether you have a need to control time or adapt to it. That awareness alone determines whether you will be stressed by a situation or empowered by it. For example, let's say you are on the verge of missing an important meeting, or at least you are going to be quite late for it. You're stuck in traffic, delayed at the airport, or dealing with a family emergency. If you are a Judger, being late to this important meeting can nearly paralyze your ability to deal with the situation constructively. Judgers can't easily generate alternatives, they often deal with the people around them with anger, and they tend to lose perspective, compounding an already difficult situation. In short, Js don't deal well with "circumstances beyond our control."

If you know that about yourself, as you see the time crunch emerging, you will be better equipped to make accommodations, both in your own behavior and in the present circumstances. You can seek alternative transportation, take a different exit, or reschedule the meeting. Perhaps the most constructive thing you could do is to simply recognize that you're not going to make the meeting and that a month from now it probably won't make any difference.

Let's replay the late-for-the-meeting scenario through the eyes of a Perceiver. Realizing that you're not going to make it to the meeting, you could react in any number of ways. At the extreme you could say, "Thank God, I wasn't ready for the

WIGGLE ROOM

Here's a handy way we've found for Judgers more easily to be flexible. Js often schedule things so tightly—including free time—that there is little room to "wiggle" within the schedule. They plan free-time reading, for example, to be followed by a nap and then on to the next activity. We know Js who can be thoroughly engrossed in what they are reading but will put their book down because their schedule says it's time to stop.

By scheduling things with some space in between, it allows Js to expand a given activity as needed or desired. Such wiggle room is not only refreshing and rewarding but, in the bigger picture, helps to create a much more flexible notion of scheduling. In the long run it can also be a stress reducer because the individual can control the schedule, instead of the other way around.

meeting anyway. I'll just stay here and use this reprieve to watch HBO." In fact, you might not even bother to let anyone know about your new plan, assuming that if you're late, the meeting isn't even going to happen. That certainly demonstrates the P's adaptive nature, albeit not in a particularly constructive way. But by being aware of your adaptive nature, you could deal with the bad situation much more productively. For example, a simple phone call might determine whether the meeting will actually take place or should be rescheduled or whether you can participate by phone. Getting closure on this matter itself can bring direction and satisfaction to everyone involved, because everyone won't be just hanging loose.

We tell another story, this one about a farmer who is a clear Perceiver. Today he has scheduled himself to paint the fence. He heads to the barn to get the paint and en route notices that the blades on the tractor mower need sharpening. He takes the blades off and sets them against the bench and realizes that his drawer of sharpening equipment needs straightening and cleaning.

The first thing he picks from the drawer reminds him to call the hardware store about a coupling he had ordered. When he calls the hardware store, he learns that the part has arrived, so he leaves for town to pick it up. In town he runs into an old friend, and they decide to have a cup of coffee. And so it goes. Before long it's time for dinner and bed, and the fence—not to mention the mower blades and the equipment drawer—remain unattended to. All starts and no finishes. That's the classic P scheduling dilemma.

So, if Perceivers could better control time and be somewhat less adaptive to every new circumstance, and if Judgers could better adapt to changing circumstances and be less controlling of the world around them, both would handle themselves and their time more effectively.

The Three Key Points About Time

So, you can see that dealing with time issues through Typewatching is relatively simple because, as we said earlier, the issues usually deal with the J-P preferences. While the other preferences can still play a role—for example, a Sensor's literalism about time can differ considerably from an iNtuitive's relativism on the subject—in the end most of our issues about schedule, timeliness, deadlines, and productivity center around one's J or P preference.

Here are the three key things to remember:

- People procrastinate around their nonpreferences. When someone is continually putting off a job that needs to be done, consider that he or she might need some extra help or support.

- Recognize that everyone has a natural need either to control time or to adapt to it. A lot of time-management problems can be solved by getting the adaptive types to be a little more controlling and getting the controllers to be a little more adaptive.

■ Don't try to change people. Adapters will never become controllers, nor will controllers become adapters. However, they do have the ability to make accommodations. When they do this, be supportive; when it doesn't happen, respect the differences.

Type Preferences and Time Management

EXTRAVERTS
- Can get distracted and pulled by the outside world
- Need to get others involved
- Are invasive of others' time
- Procrastinate about being alone to think and reflect

INTROVERTS
- Can get into their own projects and forget deadlines in the outside world
- Desire to work alone
- Tend to let their time be invaded by others
- Procrastinate about engaging with social groups

SENSORS
- Are here and now—in the present
- Regard "time" as *this* moment
- Tend to have either too much or too little to do
- Procrastinate about envisioning or dreaming of the future

INTUITIVES
- Are then and there—in the future
- Regard time as endless
- Believe that they can always do more
- Procrastinate about really enjoying today

THINKERS
- Objectify time
- Organize presentations that progress from subject to necessary points to conclusion
- Seem more terse (especially Introverted-Thinkers)
- Procrastinate about working on their relationships

FEELERS
- Believe that time is relative
- Organize presentations to meet others' needs
- Are more chatty (especially Extraverted-Feelers)
- Procrastinate about working to resolve conflicts

JUDGERS
- Make lists of items to be done, and overlook things not on those lists
- Don't want to be caught at the last minute without a schedule or plan, fearing that then things won't work out
- Want themselves (or at least someone) in control
- Manage time
- Read books about time and follow their advice
- Work first and play later
- Procrastinate about making time for leisure and play

PERCEIVERS
- Make a list of options, then reject those options in lieu of a more compelling one, should it appear
- Are prone to last-minute starts and the belief that things will work out
- Question whether there is such a thing as control
- Adapt to time
- Buy books about time and think about applying their advice
- Mix play and work
- Procrastinate about completing laborious tasks

12

Hiring and Firing

"How can we trust each other not
to screw up each other's jobs?"

When it comes to selecting the right person for a job, we usually talk out of both sides of our mouth. While we espouse that in putting together a staff "variety is the spice of life," what we actually do tends to look a whole lot more like cloning. The reason? It's a perfectly normal thing: At work, at play, even at church, it's smoother and easier to be with people like ourselves.

The fact is, whether hiring is done in individual departments or by a centralized personnel department, most staffs invariably resemble typologically those at the top. And more often than not, those at the top share the preferences for objective decision making (Thinking) and structure, schedule, and order (Judging). It's not that the other types are incompetent. It's just that in a system driven by profits and productivity, Thinking-Judging types have the edge. Other types, however qualified, are destined to leave the organization prematurely.

Consider the following:

- Sixty percent of managers throughout the world are Thinking-Judgers, according to data compiled by Otto Kroeger Associates as well as by the Nippon Recruit Center in Japan and the Center for Creative Leadership in North Carolina.

■ Eighty percent of the corporate world is made up of iNtuitive-Thinkers and Sensing-Judgers, according to our own data. But NTs and SJs comprise only about 50 percent of the general population. The higher up you go in an organization, the greater the concentration becomes. We've seen organizations where NTs and SJs made up over 90 percent of the upper echelons.

None of this is to say that other types—iNtuitive-Feelers, for example—can't cut it in the management world. They do. In fact, you can find all sixteen types in management positions of major corporations and government agencies. Still, the overwhelming majority fall into the statistics cited above. We strongly believe that to be successful, companies increasingly will need to bring more Feeling and Perceiving types into the upper echelons.

There's both good news and bad news about the current homogeneity. The good news is that when people resemble each other typologically, they can be fairly productive. The bad news is that when like types disagree, the source of the disagreement can be vague and difficult to define and often leads to a lot of misplaced blaming. That's because when you're angry, it's either a projection of your own personal issue or an issue over which you have little control. In either case you lack a clear focus on the source of the anger. And a group of people just like you, all angry about the same thing, can reinforce your confusion.

Example: An office full of TJs will view the world in largely black-and-white terms; things are either right or wrong. When two TJs disagree—when one sees black and the other sees white—there are few alternative solutions short of pulling rank and status, shouting more loudly, or becoming increasingly more stubborn. Sometimes the source of the disagreement can become obscured—are the parties disagreeing with the matter at hand, or are they reacting to the fact that they can see themselves in each other? Often it's hard to tell. In the end, productivity becomes curtailed.

Contrast this to a working environment in which there is a

broader mix of types. Studies show that diversity engenders creativity. The more diversity of personnel on any given task, the better the final product will be, if (a) differences are respected, authenticated, and integrated; and (b) communication remains open. Clearly, with so many opposing points of view, projects may take longer to accomplish, but the end result will have more people committed to it (because more people had a chance to influence the process) and there will be a greater sense of pride.

At one time or another most managers have been through the following management training exercise: You are lost at sea (or in a desert or on the moon) as the result of a crash. All that's left is a handful of specific items, ranging from a case of vodka to a small mirror to a piece of cheese. Your task is to rank-order the items for importance to your survival.

In this exercise each manager must independently come up with his or her own rank order. Then groups of managers are assigned to arrive at some consensus of the ranking. This process parallels real-life group decision making—you arrive at the meeting with some opinions, a little knowledge, and your reactions to the people with whom you must work to reach a group decision.

The final scores in this training exercise are usually set against some "expert" criteria. Repeatedly those groups that have the widest diversity of knowledge—for example, a group ranging from a former Marine who's an expert in desert survival to an accountant who's never spent a night under the stars—yet respect that diversity and communicate openly about their differences come up with the closest to "correct" answers.

We've conducted this same exercise typologically many times over the years, and we've always gotten similar results. For example, a J-dominated group is likely to come to a quick decision, but does so by a simple majority, thereby ruling out alternatives in the process. Decisions come down to a process of "Five people are in favor, four people are opposed, so the item passes." Never mind that four individuals may have had good points that they articulated effectively. The closure-driven

BUSINESS AS USUAL

While it's part of Typewatching philosophy to "think opposite" and respect differences when hiring, this is easier said than done, even among Typewatching pros. A case in point is a human resources consulting group outside Washington, D.C. The name-brand group, which has decades of experience with Typewatching, not long ago had to replace a thirty-year senior staffer, who was given total freedom and the final decision in hiring her replacement.

She elected not to use the Myers-Briggs Type Indicator or any other instrument, but decided to hire based strictly on her instincts. After she was hired, we gave the new person the MBTI. Lo and behold, the new hiree was the exact type as the person she was replacing.

Both parties were surprised at the finding, because they felt they were so different from each other. But we weren't surprised. Deep down all of us are more comfortable with people who are more like us than different.

Judging process didn't allow for many alternatives; "That's tough," they were told. "Majority rules." As a result nearly half the group ends up frustrated and a lot less willing to contribute their ideas in the future.

The problem is reversed for P-dominated groups. They spend so much time generating alternatives that they never reach consensus in the time allowed. The Js in the group become frustrated, and the overall group fails to complete the assignment.

Extraverts, Introverts, and the other preferences all have their own style of behavior in the decision-making process. The point is, when any organization or process is driven by only one or two typological preferences, tunnel vision is inevitable. The creative process will be limited, and alternatives may be stifled.

Which is not to say that an organization that is heavily type-alike is doomed to fail. There are a great many examples of highly successful companies whose leaders are virtual typological clones. The point here, however, has to do with awareness. By being aware of the concentration of types in various parts of your organization, you will become aware of its strengths. That in turn will provide insight into its potential weaknesses—its blind spots, where creativity and productivity may be lacking. So Typewatching becomes a valuable tool for balancing strengths and weaknesses.

Such a tool will be even more important in the years ahead. The workplace is increasingly filled with people who reflect a vast range of backgrounds, lifestyles, and values: singles, married, divorced, widowed, gay; young and old; native English speakers and those for whom English is a second (or third) language; high school dropouts and multidegreed individuals; and on and on. While we've always had some of this diversity, it is fast becoming more the rule than the exception.

Along with such diversity comes a variety of perspectives to just about every situation. Not everyone will have the same view of punctuality. There will be increasing differences in work styles. A single parent will have a different perspective on what constitutes "full-time work" than will a married person with grown kids. A sixty-year-old employee will deal with a fast-paced travel schedule differently than a thirty-year-old.

All of this will particularly affect the work lives of those in the personnel department, who typologically tend to be Introverted-Sensing-Thinking-Judgers. The ISTJ is, as we've said, the predominant corporate model. ISTJs have several strengths and weaknesses. Those strengths include their ability to be objective and impersonal when handling sticky personnel problems. (They have to be: If the people in personnel let these problems get to them, they'd be basket cases.) Their Introversion permits high confidentiality, which is a clear asset in this area.

Maximized, these strengths become liabilities. Those in personnel are often seen as uncaring, harsh, and rigid in the imposition of their duties. Their J characteristic can make them appear impatient and unbending in meeting employees' needs. Their impersonal approach to life can result in ways of communicating

ILL AT Es

Sometimes people get promoted up through the system into places they probably shouldn't be. Take the case of the Introvert we know who outlasted his colleagues to become head of a public relations division of a multibillion-dollar organization. By the time he got to the top, he was in charge of twelve Extraverted professionals responsible for communicating the company mission to the public.

Problem was, working for the Introvert, the twelve Extraverts worked as hard as ever but received virtually no recognition for their efforts. (Remember, you can't give an E too many strokes.) It wasn't that the Introvert wasn't pleased with the work. It's just that he never communicated it.

layoffs and other personnel changes that demoralize the whole workforce.

The Case of the Positive Bank Balance

There's no question that wonderful things can happen when organizations are typologically balanced. And there's no better illustration of this than the consumer services division of a major worldwide bank headquartered in New York City.

We were called in on something of a lark. The chief lieutenant to the division president had read about us in *Fortune*. At about the same time, the division was planning its annual three-day retreat, traditionally a reward for exemplary achievement for the entire ninety-person staff. She decided that we would be the keynote for the event.

Everyone took the Myers-Briggs Type Indicator in preparation for our one-day workshop, which focused on self-awareness and interpersonal similarities and differences. By the end of the day the group decided to print each individual's name and type on an organizational chart, to be distributed throughout the division. We've reprinted the chart below, minus the individuals' names.

What struck us about the group is that while it was typologically representative of a bank—mostly Thinking-Judgers—there were some notable exceptions. For one thing the head honcho was an ENFJ, hardly the commanding-officer type usually associated with the pin-striped world of bean counters. His deputy

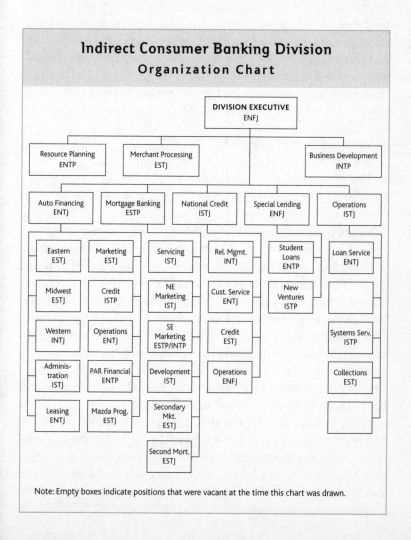

Indirect Consumer Banking Division
Organization Chart

		DIVISION EXECUTIVE ENFJ			
Resource Planning ENTP	Merchant Processing ESTJ				Business Development INTP
Auto Financing ENTJ	Mortgage Banking ESTP	National Credit ISTJ	Special Lending ENFJ	Operations ISTJ	
Eastern ESTJ	Marketing ESTJ	Servicing ISTJ	Rel. Mgmt. INTJ	Student Loans ENTP	Loan Service ENTJ
Midwest ESTJ	Credit ISTP	NE Marketing ISTJ	Cust. Service ENTJ	New Ventures ISTP	
Western INTJ	Operations ENTJ	SE Marketing ESTP/INTP	Credit ESTJ		Systems Serv. ISTP
Administration ISTJ	PAR Financial ENTP	Development ISTJ	Operations ENFJ		Collections ESTJ
Leasing ENTJ	Mazda Prog. ESTJ	Secondary Mkt. ESTJ			
		Second Mort. ESTJ			

Note: Empty boxes indicate positions that were vacant at the time this chart was drawn.

was a female ENTP—again, not one readily given to the high level of detail demanded in an executive assistant's role. Moreover, each of the branch chiefs represented still more diversity than is often the case at that level—another ENFJ and an ESTP, for example, in a part of the company that is traditionally TJ.

Note in particular the mortgage banking branch, headed by an ESTP, with an overwhelmingly Judging staff. During the retreat this group's criticism of their boss was that he was rarely where he should be when they needed his direction. His seat-of-the-pants management style frustrated everyone in the operation (except the two Perceivers, who found his style familiar and refreshing). As the day unfolded and the group began to understand and appreciate differences, the group discovered that the boss expected them to act on their own; he didn't want constantly to oversee their every move. And in good J style, once the staffers understood the rules, they felt liberated.

So, what started as hostility and frustration had, by the end of the day, become both freedom and empowerment.

The organizational chart created by the division offered benefits long after the retreat was over. Because the members of this division were not all in the same building—indeed they were scattered all over the country—many of the group reported using the chart to facilitate communication with others in the group—even by phone and fax. So when the ENTJ heard the INTJ at the other end of the phone say, "I've heard you. Just tell me when you want it done," the Extravert understood that the conversation was over and it was time to hang up. Prior to his understanding of type, he might well have fallen into the Extraverted trap of conversational overkill—if saying it once was good, then saying it twice would be better, and once more for the road would guarantee results. In fact, the Introvert would have stopped listening several sentences earlier.

Now, we should point out that this dynamic and typologically balanced group wasn't put together by any forward-thinking whiz-kid in the personnel department. It was more serendipitous than that. The ENFJ division chief was hired because he was a personal friend of the bank's CEO. He, in turn, brought

STOP, LOOK, LISTEN

Extraverts, as we've said, tend to talk their way through silences. And while that may be good at a dinner party or on a date, that doesn't necessarily cut it during a job interview. An ESTJ client told us about a job interview he went on in which he was meeting with an Introverted senior executive. While the executive sat and listened, the ESTJ rambled on. During occasional pauses, when the Introvert didn't quickly respond, the Extravert would go back to what he did best: extraverting. Midway through the experience, recalling his Typewatching training, he finally realized, "I'm doing all the talking without giving this guy a chance to reflect or respond. I think I'm blowing it."

So he stopped talking. In fact, he at one point told the interviewer, "You may want to think about this for a while." Things immediately turned around. He got the job.

his own branch managers from a previous job. So a variety of types were already in place at a high level of the organization.

We should also point out that this typologically ragtag group was no bunch of shirkers. In fact, their division was responsible for the bulk of the bank's annual income. They were management's pets, respected and rewarded; witness the three-day annual retreat in a posh setting.

The point is that this successful group defied the stereotypical personnel configuration found in the banking world—a world that is overwhelmingly type-alike. And that makes our case for diversity. Had matters been left to regular personnel practices—outside recruitment and internal promotions—the group would likely have been largely Sensing-Thinking-Judging. And, as we said before, such type-alike groups can get swept away by their apparent success, lacking the tools necessary for changing and emerging situations. Remember the Second Commandment: Your strength maximized becomes a liability.

THE ABCs OF LIFE

Personnel professionals tell us that increasingly job seekers' resumes feature a few extra letters besides their academic and professional credentials. So, for example, an insurance salesman's resume might read, "John Smith, MBA, CLU, INTJ." For that matter we've seen individuals' four-letter preferences become the foundation of job applications, college applications, and personal ads seeking dates and mates.

Diversity is only part of the answer, of course. After all, the banking division was diverse long before we met them. What turned this from a potential liability to an asset was the understanding that came with Typewatching.

You might conclude from all this that the ideal organization would consist of a group of sixteen people representing all the types. But that's not necessarily effective either; indeed, such a group would likely be counterproductive. The problem would be that there would be so little agreement on most issues that progress would be next to impossible. What we're talking about here may well be the flip side of the Second Commandment of Typewatching: Diversity maximized may be a liability too.

What's key here is a combination of putting the right types together and making sure that they communicate. Whether we are alike or different, if we have a common language that serves as the basis for understanding, we can survive almost anything.

A Few Words of Warning

As much as we believe in and practice Typewatching in our personal and professional lives, we can't stress strongly enough the danger of hiring strictly on the basis of a person's four-letter type. For one thing, the Myers-Briggs Type Indicator does not measure skills and abilities; it only measures personality preferences. So, a personnel officer who knows Typewatching may interpret the model very correctly—that a specific job opening is a natural for an ENFP, for example—but may not necessarily hire the best person for the job. While the assessment may be correct in theory, there also may be an ISTJ who applies or volunteers for the assignment and who, because of many factors beyond typological theory, may do the job perfectly.

A psychological instrument such as the Myers-Briggs Type Indicator was never intended to be used as the only criterion of employment. Ethically and even legally, using type as the basis of a hiring or firing decision would be inappropriate. Legally, companies and labor unions must determine what, if any, instruments or tests can be used by personnel. There may also be legal implications relative to administering a psychological test without proper credentials. Such credentials are often determined at the state level, with each state setting its own criteria. Finally, using type to fire—or not hire or promote—someone could be seen as a form of discrimination. There is a growing body of laws that speaks loudly and clearly to that issue.

None of this is to say that Typewatching can't be used as an effective tool in the personnel department. If the department elects to use one or more instruments as part of the hiring process, certainly the MBTI should be included among them. But it is at most a basis for validating other results and conclusions. Type literature continues to affirm that any of the sixteen types has the potential to be successful at any job. Some types in certain positions may have to work harder, but they can be just as effective. (Indeed, Isabel Briggs Myers herself cautioned that you should never tell a person, "You are an ISTJ, so you'll never make it as a priest," or any other such limiting kinds of statements.)

The bottom line in personnel is this: You are never hiring a type for a job. You're hiring a person.

Playing the Cards You're Dealt

Now, all of this assumes that you've got the luxury of choice: that you can handpick your staff from a diverse pool of applicants. Real life, of course, isn't quite that convenient. Managers are brought in from outside; companies are bought, sold, and traded like baseball cards. Most bosses inherit staffs, and most staffs inherit bosses.

Given this reality, how can you make the best of the people you've got? The goal here is what the military calls allocation of resources. In business, that translates into making the best use of everyone, what we call a total-participation model. To accomplish this demands that everyone have a clear sense of what the organization has to do. That requires answering the following four questions:

- Of the things that need to be done, who does them well?
- Who would like to try something different?
- What things are still left to be done?
- How can we divide them up in a way that produces the most satisfaction?

This represents a declining model of satisfaction: We start by people choosing their ideal tasks—matching square pegs with square holes—then give everyone a chance to stretch themselves a bit. Finally we attempt a reasonably equal distribution of the grunt details faced by any organization.

This model is also consistent with the philosophy of type. It doesn't try to change anyone. Rather it takes everyone's existing talents and attempts to align them more with personal interests than personnel's interest.

We saw this realignment work beautifully at a government agency we worked with in Oklahoma. The senior-ranking executive was an Introvert, who very much disliked the Extraverted demands of his position—attending Rotary Club and other community functions, for example, and keeping the agency's mission in front of the public. Interestingly his deputy was an Extravert, who loved those assignments but whose job description did not call for her to do these things; instead she was more deskbound, usually buried under a pile of administrative details. Two other key staffers, in the finance and human resources development branches, also found themselves at odds with their job descriptions. One, an ENF, had a degree in finance. (ENFs typically aren't suited to finance and engineering, but they may seek degrees in these fields because they wish to follow in the footsteps of their heroes and heroines, such as parents, teachers, and other influential people in their lives.) The human resources guy was an ISTJ, who would much rather have been in (and would have been much better at) the finance department.

As consultants we asked why these people couldn't change around to do what they wanted to do—in other words, changing jobs outside the personnel process. Their responses were immediate and typical. "It's against personnel practices," they said. "Besides, it's never been done before. And how can we trust each other not to screw up each other's jobs?" For example, the Introverted boss was concerned that his Extraverted deputy would grab the limelight and run away with the glory. In fact, it was a valid concern.

We spent some time weighing the pros and cons. We also determined that the people involved were highly responsible and concluded that it was a very workable model. In the end we successfully managed to realign each individual's missions with his or her personality type and interests, rather than following seemingly arbitrary personnel practices.

Are people and jobs really that malleable? We think so. The advancement process and our continued academic pursuits move us way beyond our original vocational choices. So a competent Extraverted accountant, pursuing an interest and an MBA degree along with twenty years of growth and community activity, can become skilled at a variety of jobs. In other words, no one should be considered "locked into" a specific task, no matter how perfectly he or she may be suited for that task. For managers charged with the responsibility of finding the right people for the job, the possibilities are limited only by the degree to which one is flexible enough to recognize each employee's potential.

On the Firing Line

Let's start with a basic assumption: No one is comfortable when it comes to firing another person. It's unpleasant and stressful, which is probably why in recent years we've come to do it more in writing than face-to-face. The notorious "pink slip" has absolved us from the pain of being the messenger of such bad tidings.

Some Typewatching professionals believe that Thinkers are adept at and can more easily cope with the firing process. But our own experience tells us that this simply isn't so. Thinkers— logical and analytical though they may be—may indeed be less personally embroiled in the process, but they still agonize over the painful reality that they must deliver the news.

However difficult it may be, personality preferences still play a dramatic role in how an actual firing takes place.

Let's start with Es and Is. Extraverts often need to rehearse the firing speech on anyone within listening range. During the actual delivery he or she may take twenty minutes to say what should be said in five, filling the extra time with a seemingly random rambling—about the weather, last night's ball game, whatever. After it's all over, Extraverts may have a high need to talk it through—yet again—with colleagues, friends, veritable strangers, reliving it, second-guessing it, perhaps still "rehearsing" it after the fact.

Introverts, on the other hand, also agonize over the firing before the fact, but they do so internally, perhaps jotting down a few notes about what they want to cover in the "exit interview." In the actual event they may in fact say much less than they intended, with long, screaming silences that can intensify both parties' embarrassment and discomfort. They, too, will relive the experience, albeit internally, for hours, days, or weeks—typical of the inner turmoil that can give Introverts ulcers at a much higher rate than Extraverts.

Or take Thinkers and Feelers. Thinkers, in their objectivity, can be read as very uncaring in the firing process, although this may be far from the case. In their awkwardness with emotion, they tend to emphasize their coolness; it's axiomatic that during difficult times Ts must stay rational, no matter what. Feelings, no matter how genuine or deep, simply play no part of the process. As a result the Thinker is perceived as not giving a damn. An Introverted Thinker will direct that frustration internally; an Extravert will dump it onto anyone who's around.

But it is the Feeler most of all who is least capable of keeping the firing process in proper perspective. Feelers, you'll recall, almost always put themselves in the other person's shoes—"How would I feel if this news were being given to me?" The attempt to answer that question can blow everything out of proportion for the Feeler, even if the firee is guilty of the most egregious behavior. It's a very F thing to blame oneself, even institutionally— "What has the company done that's allowed this person to fail?"

The discomfort of Feelers is so great that they are prone to say just about anything short of "You're fired." We know of no better illustration than that of Charlie, the ENFJ executive who faced the task of firing Sam, the janitor. Three times Charlie told Sam that he was being terminated, and each time Sam returned for work the next day. The problem? It turned out that Charlie was so circumspect in his termination speech that Sam thought that it was *Charlie* who was on his way out the door.

You can just imagine the scene:

Charlie says, "Well, Sam, I'm going to miss seeing you every day. Things aren't going to be the same. There's a lot of changes everywhere these days, you know. And if you're going to improve yourself, you've got to keep moving. That's life." And on and on. Furthermore this was all done over a cup of coffee, preceded by small talk about Sam's family and last night's news. It was all so warm and friendly. It's no wonder that Sam had no idea that it was time to pack his bags.

We've seen similar things happen in our own company, an organization that is heavily staffed with Fs. At one point we hired an ESTJ because typologically we felt the organization was too NFP. (Indeed we didn't practice what we now preach: We tried to hire principally on the basis of type. We've since learned from our mistake.) Though the person's credentials were impressive, her skills, abilities, and commitment just didn't work out. And we, the F owners, had to face the reality of letting her go.

For the first month we coped with the situation by more or less terminating ourselves—or at least our presence in the office. We came to work later, found reasons to be elsewhere, even managed to extend a work trip into a two-week vacation. Talk about avoidance! But finally the time came to bite the bullet. Otto worked up the courage to confront the individual, rehearsed the speech, and planned a specific moment to deliver it—Tuesday at 3:00. At 2:55 on the appointed day, Janet came into Otto's office and said, "Perhaps we're being too harsh. Maybe we haven't considered all the alternatives. Shouldn't we give her two more weeks to prove herself?" Otto came close to agreeing, until sanity prevailed. The deed was done. But it took the better part of two months to do what should have been done quickly and efficiently.

In an effort to heighten Thinking-Feeling differences in the workplace—with the aim of making them so obvious that they can begin to be addressed—we use an exercise that has produced dramatic results. We split a group into Ts and Fs and ask each group to develop guidelines for terminating employees pursuant to a mandated downsizing or reduction in force. (We sometimes encounter trouble right from the start. Some organizations have such a paucity of Feelers that it's impossible even to create two distinct groups. But if there are three or more Fs present, this exercise can be insightful.) Each group writes its answer on a sheet of newsprint, which we hang up and display for discussion.

The Ts' criteria inevitably include an impersonal imposing of a company policy—for example, "Last hired, first fired." They'll also develop a list of various measures of productivity—sales per week, forms processed per hour, timeliness, and so on. Those who measure highest on the list have the most job security. Those who rank low are the first to go.

The Fs, on the other hand, include in the dismissal criteria such things as family needs, an employee's total household income and family size, child-care needs, employability, years of service, age, health, and the like. It is common for the Fs to include company policy and productivity, but these are rarely guiding forces. (Similarly, Ts often consider such things as seniority and an employee's personal needs, but these are just additional factors to consider.) The Fs often want the guidelines to be based upon each individual case and extenuating circumstances, while the Ts are far more likely to create blanket policies and principles.

The discussion that follows each group's presentation is always enlightening. In the process both sides learn the necessity for the other's point of view. They'll rarely agree completely on a single set of criteria, but these simple sharing exercises can move both parties toward a policy that works better for everyone, including the company.

Three Tips for the Personnel Department

1. **Think opposite.** Because we know statistically that type begets type in the hiring process—that people are more inclined to hire individuals who are more like themselves than different—then it is incumbent upon the personnel department to think in terms of opposites and differences in every respect: gender, race, age, academic achievement, personality types, and so on. So, in other words, if you're hiring someone into an all-white-male organization, you need to explore black female candidates. Such diversity, combined with Typewatching understanding, will always produce a better product.

2. **Know thy company.** It's up to personnel to know what the organization wants and expects of its new hires. It is also up to personnel to challenge the organization from time to time to ensure that the results continue to be in line with expectations. We knew an organization that had a formal policy of hiring minorities and women, for example, but the policy was never made known to the personnel department, which

Hiring and Firing

IF YOU ARE AN . . .

	EXTRAVERT	INTROVERT
EXTRAVERT	• During the process, allow time for both of you to speak and listen. • Enjoy the few silences during the interview. • Separate yourself from the person—don't try to clone yourself.	• Allow space and time to be used as a sounding board. • Though you may have little need to speak or listen, others may need to do so. • First words are first words—they're only the beginning. There may be much more to follow.
	EXTRAVERT	**INTROVERT**
INTROVERT	• Allow extended reflective time—don't rush the silences. • Listen now and then to who is doing most of the talking. • Consider a second meeting in a day or two.	• The nervousness of the situation is normal. Keep in mind that dialogue may be accentuated by longer silences. • Push both yourself and the other person to share more than is considered "enough." • Stay in touch with the other person by staying in touch with yourself.
	SENSOR	**INTUITIVE**
SENSOR	• Consider whether there is too much or too little attention being paid to details. • Push both yourself and the other person to speak about the implications and meanings of specific job duties and areas of experience. • Separate your personal preferences from the other person's, though they may be similar.	• Stay grounded—facts, specifics, and the like are helpful and confidence-building. • Remember that skills and past experience are strengths that can help you cope with the present. • Recognize that forecasting impact beyond one month is worthless to the other person.
	SENSOR	**INTUITIVE**
INTUITIVE	• Be clear about the facts and specifics, but emphasize the big picture. • Be sure to relate the issue at hand to the future. • Remember that the unknown can be exciting and filled with possibilities.	• Remember to state and restate the bottom line. • Overemphasize the facts, specifics, and tangible issues. • While strategizing may be exciting, it must still relate to the present.

LEADING AN . . .

IF YOU ARE A . . .

LEADING A . . .

	THINKER	FEELER
THINKER	• Remember that the emotional element is important. • Try to imagine yourself as the candidate: What parts of the process would you respect? • Get to the point early and often.	• Stay direct and objective. • Recognize that a strong reaction may be more your issue than the other's. • Don't be too touchy-feely—too many frills can bring out the ills.

	THINKER	FEELER
FEELER	• Speak positively as much as possible. • Be aware that directness, though often appreciated, may invoke a strong reaction. • Remember that "a spoonful of sugar helps the medicine go down."	• Remember that avoiding the negative—or overworking the positive—is not helpful. • If delivering bad news, rehearse with someone else first. • Recognize that even when you feel you are being direct and confrontational, you probably could be more so.

	JUDGER	PERCEIVER
JUDGER	• Work against your urge to argue or defend. • Be aware that closure does not always mean agreement. • Consider options and alternative points of view.	• Keep in mind that no matter how direct you think you are, you probably aren't direct enough. • Remember that bottom lines are more important than options. • Recognize that decisions are good—they allow things to move on.

	JUDGER	PERCEIVER
PERCEIVER	• Accept options and arguments; avoid being defensive. • Beware of sounding angry, even when you are just stating the obvious. • Keep in mind that a little "go with the flow" may help the situation.	• Avoid beating dead horses. • Bear in mind that too many options, though interesting to consider, may obscure the point. • Recognize that some decisions really are final.

in turn couldn't communicate this to the headhunters, which provided a steady stream of white male candidates. The same goes for expectations of type preferences and everything else.

3. **Beware of blind spots.** Similarly, it's up to personnel to know the organization's typological blind spots. Are there too few Extraverts, so that the world may never hear about your good ideas? Are there too few Introverts, so that everyone's talking and no one's listening? Rather than merely hiring a warm body, it's crucial that those in personnel try to view how that person will fit into the fabric of the organization.

13

Ethics

"Why do we spend so much company time talking about a problem that doesn't exist?"

Many people consider ethics to be an overworked and tired, albeit sensitive, issue. The mere mention of the word can evoke groans in management circles: "Oh, no. Not another lecture on the evils of white male bosses," or "Why do we spend so much company time talking about a problem that doesn't exist?"

The very nature of such comments indicates that—as with sexism, racism, and the weather—everyone seems to talk about ethics but no one does much about it. Which is not to say that everyone is unethical (or racist or sexist). But nearly everyone is confronted with ethical issues on a regular basis at work.

We're not necessarily talking about big-time scandalous affairs—kickbacks, influence peddling, or wiretapping, for example. We're talking about a host of everyday activities, many of which seem innocuous and acceptable in today's society. It is an ethical issue, for example, to have your secretary tell a caller that you're not in the office, when in fact you are. It is an ethical issue to embellish a resume, to add a few dollars to a restaurant receipt before submitting it for reimbursement, or to come in late for work when you know the boss won't be around. And a million and one other things.

We don't intend to argue the morality of these situations. That's not within the scope of this book. But we strongly believe that one's personality preferences play an integral role in the development of one's ethics. Each personality type has its own unique value system. None is more or less ethical than the others, but they differ widely in their approach to ethical issues. Typewatching, then, can provide a lens through which to view each type's ethical stance. The ability to understand these differences can be a powerful tool in helping you sort through your own ethical motivations and rationalizations and those of your subordinates, colleagues, and superiors.

Ethics, Morals, Values, Integrity

What exactly are ethics? There's no simple answer, to be sure. Ethics are a complex set of ideas that include morals, values, and integrity. Each plays a part in a discussion of ethics and certainly impact upon one another.

- *Ethics*, from the Greek word *ethos*, meaning "character" or "moral state," refers to the moral judgment you exercise in the day-to-day arena in which you live your life.

- *Morals* reflect customs that have been handed down to us in our society. You take your morals and set them against your daily living—ethics—and from that develop a value system.

- *Values*, then, are your personal interpretation of society's customs.

- *Integrity* represents the congruity between your values and ethics and the responsibility that accompanies that congruency.

It's one thing to have a value system based on society's morals that is for or against something. It's another thing to believe in that system—to establish an ethical code of behavior for one's daily living. How you actually behave when confronted with these issues defines your level of integrity. Ethics means nothing unless backed up by integrity.

As you can see, there is very little that is concrete in the above paragraph. Some of these notions are relative and highly subjective. And that's exactly the point: Each personality type interprets ethics, morals, values, and integrity in different ways. And of course each type strongly believes that theirs is the right interpretation.

Why is all this even important? Don't we seem to get through the day just fine without confronting these sticky issues? Perhaps, but not for long. Eventually one or more ethical issues is bound to trip you up. With life getting increasingly complex, sticking one's head in the sand won't work for long.

Take a look at what's going on around you. The newspapers are filled with tales of ethical misconduct involving billions of dollars, each story more sensational than the one before—the stock market, the savings and loan industry, the Pentagon, and all the rest. The individuals involved aren't just highly placed officials and executives. The webs extend to neighborhood real estate brokers, mom-and-pop subcontractors, and countless mid-level bureaucrats. The mere existence of the Defense Department's toll-free "800" whistle-blower number for reporting infractions involving waste, fraud, and even reckless driving is a barometer of the broad cross-section of society involved in such behavior. There's even a toll-free number near where we live to report commuters who drive in the carpool lane without the requisite number of passengers!

Another problem is that we're having trouble keeping up with our own technology. Computers and telecommunications facilitate lightning-fast movements of seemingly innocuous bits of data that can have multibillion-dollar impacts. Even the office photocopier and a bottle of Wite-Out™ can enable clever souls to doctor receipts, letters, and resumes. Each new technological innovation seems to bring with it a new set of opportunities for circumventing ethical behavior.

Added to all this is the fact that as the workplace has gotten more complex and the workforce more diverse, it has created new ethical dilemmas for each of us. Take the issue of pregnant women working behind computer terminals. Some evidence has suggested that radiation emitted by computers may cause miscarriages or birth defects. So, given the lack of conclusive evidence, should a pregnant data-entry specialist be laid off, moved to a different job, or forced to stay at the terminal or lose her job? Similarly, should safety directions be printed in Spanish, Korean, or other languages to make them more comprehensible to all workers? Or should everyone be forced to speak the native

FIDDLING WITH THE TRUTH

Popular culture is filled with treatments of ethical issues and the creative ways in which they are resolved. Consider, for example, a scene from the musical *Fiddler on the Roof.*

Tevye, whom we believe to be an NF in an SJ world of Jewish tradition, found himself with a crisis of conscience. Having promised his daughter to the butcher, Lazar Wolf, for a wife, he learns that she is really in love with someone else. His duty to honor his pledge to Lazar is in direct conflict with his sense of responsibility to his daughter's happiness.

Striving to undo his commitment and not burden his conscience, Tevye concocted a "dream," in which Lazar Wolf's deceased wife returns to implore him not to let his daughter marry her widowed husband. Tevye "wakes up" and reveals the "dream" to his wife, who responds with the predicted answer: "Obviously the wedding is off."

Now, with his wife's blessing, he feels righteous in telling Lazar that the marriage contract is null and void.

As a good NF, Tevye has given in to his love for his daughter and will allow her to marry the man she really loves. And he has done so without breaking any rules or going back on his word because his wife has relieved him of his contractual responsibility. To Tevye, it was an entirely ethical bending of the rules.

tongue at their peril? The largely white male English-speaking workforce of a quarter century ago didn't have to deal with these issues.

As things have gotten more complex, one concept has become increasingly simple: There is no single agreed-upon ethical frame of reference.

This lack of ethical unanimity extends to companies themselves. Just as individuals differ in their ethical stances, the companies they run reflect this diversity. A company that is predominantly ISTJ, for example, will take a very different ethical position from a company that is largely ENFP. And each company gets branded with an identity of having strong ethics, questionable ones, or perhaps none at all. We label them as conservative, liberal, progressive, reactionary, Republican, Democratic, young, or old. All of these are only quick labels that miss the mark. Each is symbolic of some ethical culture.

In recent years company ethics—and individual ethics, for that matter—has moved out of the realm of religion and family life and into the legal system. Where we used to rely on clergy and loved ones to help us sort through these daily quandaries, we now turn to lawyers, juries, and judges as the arbiters of the many interpretations surrounding a single ethical issue. Thus an inflated resume is no longer merely a matter of questionable ethics; it is now a legal issue involving liability, conspiracy, and fraud. (So, too, is the resulting dismissal of the employee who embellished a few job descriptions.) Some would say that the introduction of lawyers itself has caused a raft of new ethical concerns.

How the Preferences View Ethics

Before we examine some of the specific ways Typewatching can respond constructively to ethical situations at work, let's take a quick look at how each of the eight preferences views ethics.

- **Extraverts** focus outward, so ethical situations are seen as external events that touch many people. Es, especially EJs, have a high need to control the ethics of everyone within reach, and even some not within reach.

■ **Introverts,** in contrast, have a high need to control only themselves, perhaps including their immediate families. For them ethical accountability is an inner-directed activity. Their motto: To thine own self be true.

■ **Sensors** see ethics as specific and immediate. Whether right or wrong, the ethics center around a specific event, not some larger problem, and are best dealt with as soon as possible.

■ **iNtuitives** view ethics as part of a grand system that is connected to universal truths and principles. Ethics are relative, and each situation must be set in its context.

■ **Thinkers** see ethics as objective principles that, when violated, must be punished. It's nothing personal, it's just that if someone fails to live up to the code of behavior, they must be dealt with.

■ **Feelers,** in contrast, see ethics as an outgrowth of human interaction, and each determination of right or wrong must be weighed against one's personal value system.

■ **Judgers** see ethics as black or white. Once ethics are determined, they are not negotiable.

■ **Perceivers** are always questioning ethics, even issues they thought they were sure about. In the light of new data even the toughest ethical stance can be reconsidered.

Obviously when you combine preferences, you compound the interpretation of any ethical situation. So, an ESTJ may have the ethical stance that "the end justifies the means"; this combines the attitudes of four preferences: externalization (Extravert), immediacy (Sensing), objectivity (Thinking), and decisiveness (Judging). Harry S Truman, for example, whom we believe to be an ESTJ, had no other choice than to drop the bomb on the Japanese. The end justified the means, he believed, so it was the only thing he could do.

Truth, Beauty, and Contact Lenses

As we get older, not only does our hair get gray, but so, too, do the ethical issues that once seemed so black or white. Ethics—like truth, beauty, and contact lenses—are not only in the eye of the beholder but in the beholder's personality type. So, what may appear ethically reprehensible to an ISTJ may, to an ENFP, be the only humane, ethical thing to do.

The typological possibilities are endless. For example, here are the ways the four Temperaments approach an ethical situation:

- NFs may look at you and lie boldly if they think you cannot take the harsh truth or rejection. ("You really were the best person for the job, but company politics made us pick someone else.")

- NTs never lie, they simply tell Jesuitian truths, framing words or statements so that you the listener hear whatever they want or need you to hear. ("There were so many excellent candidates competing for the job.")

- SJs frame their ethics from company policies and procedures. ("The job required two years' previous experience. You only had eighteen months'.")

- SPs' ethical responses are governed largely by the events of the moment, so are very unpredictable. (Any of the above, as well as "If we add a few things to your resume and resubmit tomorrow, there's still a chance.")

Each of these responses represents the individual's best effort to deal with the situation in a way that reflects his or her type's ethical frame of reference.

The Two Fundamental Points

No matter what your type or who you are, there are two fundamental points that govern our ethical behavior:

1. The only ethical behavior for which you can be responsible is your own.

2. Your perception of someone else's ethical conduct may be more a reflection of your own value system than a reflection of that person's behavior.

This may sound obvious, but in the turmoil of daily life the obvious can easily become obscured. Indeed, if there was only one person living on the face of the earth—you—there would be no ethical problems. The problem comes when a second person shows up with a different interpretation of life's values. You fall into the trap of unconsciously policing the other person rather than recognizing that his or her conduct is triggering some reaction in you. It is much easier to see ethical "problems" in others than in yourself.

Now, you may be concluding from this that there are no rights or wrongs, that your employees' blatant lying, cheating, or stealing merely represents an ethical interpretation different from your own. That's not what we're saying. There certainly are absolute rights and wrongs in our society, but even they are tempered not only by the sixteen personality types (and even variations within each type) but also by ethnic, cultural, religious, and class differences, not to mention personal circumstances.

For example, a military officer and a Quaker, both ISTJs, can differ 180 degrees on the issue of violence. The officer may believe that the only responsible thing to do is to follow orders, which direct him to find and kill the enemy. The Quaker may believe that the only responsible thing to do is to follow conscience, which directs him to avoid the taking of any human life. Keep in mind that as ISTJs, both individuals are being true to their personality type, which directs them to be responsible and duty bound. But their religious differences give them a very different sense of "duty."

Another example, closer to home, illustrates how two people of the same type can arrive at two different ethical conclusions: Two women, both ENTJs, work side by side in the same office. Mary is a single mother with a child in day care. Sue is a career-bound married woman with no plans to have children. Their boss is of the school of management that believes that all employees should do a day's work for a day's pay and, short of being bedridden or deceased, should be at work from nine to five every day. However, Mary from time to time faces some real parenting crises—a sick child, last-minute day-care cancelations, even car troubles—that require her to be absent from work, or at least tardy. To avoid being fired, she believes that she must lie about these absences; so, whether right or wrong, Mary believes her lying is for the greater good. Sue believes that the lying is simply wrong.

So the obvious dilemma arises. Should Sue confront Mary or her boss, or should she do nothing despite her belief that it is wrong?

To resolve this dilemma ethically, let's review our two fundamental points through Typewatching:

■ We earlier pointed out that the only person for whom you can be responsible is yourself. So it is Sue herself that she must first answer for. Her job is not to be a policewoman or to control her co-worker's behavior. Recognizing this, she still feels she must take some action on her belief. Because she is an Extraverted-Judger, her conviction is that the dilemma should be directed externally—to someone with some intended resolution. The dilemma, of course, is precisely what that action should be.

BUCKLE UP

Here's the scene: You've just crossed the state line, and the sign on the highway says SEAT BELT USE REQUIRED BY LAW. FINE $300. The person sitting next to you hasn't buckled up. Here's how four different types might respond:

NF: "Put on your seat belt, or I'll do it for you. I don't want to lose you."
NT: "That sign bothers me. I think it's an invasion of privacy. Don't you think what you do in your car is your own business?"
SJ: "I won't drive another inch until you buckle up. It's the law."
SP: "I bet it would be an amazing sensation to fly through the windshield."

■ In determining the appropriate action, Sue must face the second fundamental point: Is her ethical dilemma truly based on Mary's behavior, or does it have more to do with Sue's own personal issues? As an ENTJ she has a need to control the world around her as a way of reflecting her own personal competency as a manager. In other words, Sue has a high need to mind both her own and other people's business.

Regarding the second point, Sue could look in any of several directions. For example, she might ask herself, "Is this simply my need to control someone else, or am I jealous because Mary gets time off and I'm here working?" Or, "Do I resent that she's beating the system when I always seem to get caught?" Or even, "Do I envy that Mary has a child, while I've decided that I'll probably forgo having kids in favor of my career?" If Sue determines that some such question may be at the heart of her ethical dilemma, then she would probably do best simply to let the situation go and not do anything more about it.

Let's assume that Sue has thought these questions through

and has determined that these probably aren't the issues and that Mary's untruthfulness is really the issue. Then it is imperative that Sue confront Mary and/or her boss about this issue. If she fails to do this, she is not only being unethical herself, she is aiding and abetting Mary's questionable behavior. Simply put, she is compromising her integrity.

And that, we believe, is unethical.

Putting Your Own "House" in Order

Another way of looking at the above story is through an analogy we call the House. To the best of our knowledge, it originated years ago with a Jungian analyst at Andover-Newton Theological Seminary. In essence it describes one's personality as a house. Like almost all houses it has several series of rooms that encompass various parts of one's existence.

For example, the main floor of the House incorporates the basic living area—the kitchen, living room, family room, bedrooms, dining room, and bathrooms. These are the rooms where everyday life happens, parts of which are open to display to others and parts of which are fairly private. This part of the House represents your four-letter type. It is the part that other people see about you and to which they relate. So, just as someone might describe a residence as "a red-brick three-bedroom house on the corner with a white fence, a picture window, and a family room that was added on," your personality type begins with a similar type of description: "a warm, outgoing, laid-back person who will speak freely about what she's thinking"—in this case an ENFP.

But the main living space is not the whole house. There's also a cellar-attic. (True, it may be a cellar or an attic, perhaps even both, but for matters of simplicity, we'll use this term to describe the space that includes a house's storage and utility areas.) The cellar-attic houses some basic services: the fuse box, the hot-water heater, treasured mementos from college, family heirlooms, and the like. It's the place we go to for special needs, whether it's to change a fuse, pull out winter clothes, or reminisce. The cellar-attic can also contain some of the less pleasant aspects of life: roaches, mice, cobwebs, unwanted clutter, items long forgotten or deliberately stashed away so as to avoid having to deal with them.

In our personalities the cellar-attic is represented by our four nonpreferences. So, for the warm, outgoing ENFP described above, the cellar-attic would be the letters ISTJ—a contemplative, realistic, objective, structural individual.

Of course, for an ISTJ, the ENFP's cellar-attic seems harmless enough. After all, that personality description is the ISTJ's main floor. But to an ENFP those same ISTJ traits can be scary indeed. They are scary because they are traits that are difficult for the ENFP to control, and they are ones with which he or she is not particularly comfortable. In short, they are not part of the ENFP's main floor. (Can you imagine trying to live your everyday life with just those items contained in your home's cellar-attic? It would likely be a frustrating, perhaps futile, experience, filled with a few tools, some love letters from college, perhaps a rocker that needs to be caned, and a freezer full of leftovers.)

What does all this have to do with ethics? In confronting an ethical issue, it is first crucial to determine whether the substance of the matter is based in your main floor or in your cellar-attic. If it is main-floor material, it is probably an issue that needs to be confronted because it relates to your everyday existence—and probably that of your organization, perhaps even your community. On the other hand, if the ethical issue reflects something you've stuffed in your cellar-attic, then your concern and actions may have other motives and may be far more destructive to you and the people involved.

Consider the case of two co-workers we'll call Jennifer, an ESFP, and Noreen, an ISTJ. Colleagues in a small office, the two found themselves at odds almost from the day Jennifer arrived on the scene. Noreen seemed constantly frustrated with Jennifer's work habits and would not hesitate to let their mutual boss know about Jennifer's latest antics—her tardiness, her long-distance phone calls to friends at company expense, her poor work habits, her bitching about her job—in short, her bad attitude and poor regard for the organization. Over time Noreen's policing of—some would say preoccupation with—Jennifer cut into Noreen's own time and productivity. Clearly the ISTJ had a higher need to control others than to be productive herself, a pitfall of any good TJ.

The nature of the business was that a certain number of projects had to be completed by various deadlines. Their boss, the company owner, cared less about work style between nine and five than about getting the projects done well and on time. If the work could be done most effectively between 11:00 A.M. and 7:00 P.M., or even on weekends, that was acceptable. Although it was not his ideal situation, the boss was satisfied with the fact that Jennifer's work was at least getting done. And Jennifer found this work style very compatible with her live-for-the-moment SP lifestyle.

But such unorthodox work habits were not acceptable to Noreen, who became increasingly preoccupied with Jennifer's every move. Jennifer then began to distrust Noreen and even did some questionable things simply to get Noreen's goat. Both women's productivity waned, and accusations of ethical misconduct and abuse of company rules flew back and forth.

In looking at the problem, we first attempted to sort out what were the real ethical issues and what were the personal issues of each party. In other words, we tried to separate the main floor from the cellar-attic. We concluded, for example, that much of Noreen's frustration with Jennifer was based on her own personal belief that people should work at fixed times and follow company rules to the letter. It had less to do with Jennifer's actual behavior. Clearly their personality differences were getting translated into rights and wrongs, thus becoming an ethical issue.

Noreen, it turned out, had come up through a series of companies in which work rules were both rigid and enforced. Punishments were meted out for even minor infractions. She felt that these experiences had been character building for her and that she was therefore justified in imposing them on others. But while noble, this had nothing to do with this particular situation.

Noreen's issues, we felt, were rooted in her cellar-attic, not in the main floor of day-to-day work.

Not that Jennifer was blameless. Some of her actions—such as charging long-distance calls to the company or lying about being at work when the boss was away—were clearly abuses of trust and grounds for discipline. In other words, they were main-floor issues that affected the company and needed to be dealt with.

By isolating the real issues from the personal ones, we were able to confront Jennifer and resolve the issues. Had we tried to deal with all of Noreen's issues, we would likely have been frustrated. Jennifer might have countered that because she was meeting deadlines, her hours at the office were justifiable. And she would have had a point. That would have diluted the real issue of her dishonesty and misrepresentation.

As we said earlier, ethics are in the type of the beholder. As the House analogy points out, much of what we view as a matter of others' ethics is far more a reflection of ourselves. Sorting out the difference between what is a genuine organizational concern and what is an irrelevant personal value system is the most important step in dealing with any ethical situation.

Sorting Through the Issues

Here's another story, right from the type community. A few years ago a woman we'll call Gladys, an ENFJ, brought charges of ethical misconduct against a man we'll call Walt, an ENFJ colleague, to the Association of Psychological Type (APT). Gladys claimed that Walt had ridiculed various typological differences, which she perceived as a put-down of certain types. This had taken place during a presentation that Walt had jointly led with a partner. Following the ethical procedures of the organization, Gladys talked with Walt about it the next day, saying that in his enthusiasm Walt had gone too far.

Walt explained that his statements had been made humorously and lightheartedly and that the participants' evaluations indicated that his words were taken as such. But his response was apparently unsatisfactory, and Gladys took the matter in writing to the APT ethics committee. In her letter Gladys referred to the verbatim notes she had diligently taken of Walt's workshop. Indeed her notes were copious, although not necessarily accurate: The alleged ethical misstatements she attributed to Walt had actually been made by his partner.

This is not to suggest that Gladys did not have legitimate concerns. But it points to a larger picture of how our own values and concerns can influence how we see something and how we respond to that which we've seen, perhaps even crediting to verbatim accounts things that didn't really happen or that happened quite differently.

You can easily see how this very human quality can cause a multitude of problems at work. Person A reports Person B for a wrongdoing, backing it up with a variety of evidence, including the fact that "I wrote down what she said two minutes later, so I wouldn't forget it." But Person A's account is colored by his own values, including his career track, his sense of ownership in the company, and his dislike of Person B's aggressive behavior in the office. As it turns out, such things help to color Person A's account of the incident, and by the time it gets reported, it has escalated into an international incident, which has unfairly tainted Person B's reputation. And so it goes.

Person A may have had a valid point. But the process of mixing personal values with legitimate ethical concerns can add an intensity to the dynamic that makes it difficult to resolve in everyone's best interest. It becomes a lose/lose proposition.

In a perfect world each individual would be able to step back and assess whether his or her motivation was clouded by personal biases. But that, of course, is much easier said than done. It's almost impossible, when we're embroiled in an ethical issue, to sort out what's personal, what's professional, what's organizational, and what's truly ethical. It all becomes one heap of grist for the ethical mill.

Sixteen Ways to Look at Ethical Issues

If someone has sought you out for help in "getting" another individual for an ethical misdeed, it becomes terribly important to help that person sort through the various typological dynamics that are behind the charges. In our experience we have found that when confronting and resolving any ethical issues— whether it be a personal issue or an organizational, systemic one—it helps to view it through the four pairs of type preferences. This will help you and others sort through a dilemma in a constructive way. Whether the ethical issue at hand is a festering scandal of epic proportions or a simple revelation at the watercooler, these points can help the people involved think things through more objectively and resolutely.

Danger: Dumping

Sometimes sorting through an ethical issue is as simple as discerning between dumping and a discussion that can lead to positive action. That can keep you from wasting your time with an exercise in futility.

So when Bob approaches you in the coffee room and discloses that the sales department has discovered a nifty new way to pad their travel vouchers to the tune of several thousand dollars a week, your first concern has to do with why he is telling you this. Is Bob jealous—does he want part of the action? Is he concerned that the cash drain may affect his department or even his job? Does he have it in for the sales department because they haven't been moving his product line? Is Bob participating in this scheme and revealing it to you out of a sense of guilt? Or does he believe this is a moral indignation that must be stopped? It is possible that more than one of these issues has spurred Bob's revelation. The important thing is to figure out which of these things is the driving force, and especially, is he interested in seeing something done about this situation, or is he just Extraverting? If you determine that Bob's interest is

Self-Management, Type, and Ethics

EXTRAVERTS

- Push yourself to listen closely to the person disclosing the ethical issue
- Don't get hooked into arguing with or outdoing the other person
- Beware of giving glib, offhand remarks that are not necessarily meant as serious or literal but could be interpreted as such

INTROVERTS

- Say *something*
- Through words and/or actions, acknowledge the other person's concerns
- Do not internalize the other person's problem and carry it away with you

SENSORS

- Keep the conversation focused on specifics
- Make sure the concern is reachable, doable, and genuine
- Determine whether the issue at hand is within your grasp to solve

INTUITIVES

- Push for the big picture
- Raise questions like "What will this look like in the future?" or "What will the likely outcome be?"
- Remember that iNtuitives are the world's great reasoners and can often give perspective to things that may otherwise seem hopeless

THINKERS

- Help the other person sort out whose problem this really is
- Help the other person stay objective
- Keep an eye on the difference between logical actions and righteous but subjective responses

FEELERS

- Be careful not to rescue the other person from his or her dilemma or to make it your problem
- Work hard at staying impersonal and removed so that you can be a good listener
- Point out how an unethical situation might have resulted from the other person's own behavior and values

JUDGERS

- Bring some sense of definition and closure to the issue . . .
- . . . but beware of the urge to dispose of the situation with a quick solution
- Fight the tendency to create a plan of attack that involves time lines and fixed lines of action

PERCEIVERS

- Keep the other person from taking quick actions for which he or she may later be sorry
- Help others see alternative solutions
- Know when to back off and let the other person take over

limited to passing along a juicy bit of gossip, you've just saved yourself several hours, perhaps even days, of energy spent problem solving.

The simplest way to ferret out this crucial piece of information is to ask the person point-blank. For example, "Are you really concerned about taking some action on this, or are you just extraverting for the sake of extraverting?" A less direct way might be to ask Bob, "What do you think we should do about it?" If he answers, "I don't care. It's none of my business," or "I'm worried that it's going to affect our year-end bonuses and I want to see it stopped," then you have some indication of whether you should even bother to pursue this.

If Bob is an Introvert, his initial disclosure may be cloaked in a somewhat innocuous question—"Hey, you got a minute?"—which may be followed by some cautious description of the ethical matter, including his position on the issue. The Introvert is more likely to have thought through both the concern and the course of action. Bob may be using you as a sounding board.

It's also possible that, being an Introvert, Bob will say nothing at all, but will instead become depressed or disgusted with the whole affair. Obviously until he brings it up you have no ability to respond, even if you were to ask what's bothering him. The point is, Introverts are capable of carrying deeply felt ethical issues inside without ever letting them out if they don't believe the climate will be responsive. It is possible for an Introvert to think through entire conversations or actions without either actually taking place, then assume the matter is settled, so the fact that Bob bothered to say something demands your response.

Your role is to help him to be sure his course of action is reasonable and that the words he has chosen to express it will enhance his position and not embarrass him or anyone else. Clarifying questions—"Are you sure this is what you want to do?" or "Do you think the boss will even care?" or "Do you think Jones and Smith will back you on this?"—will give Introverts much-needed focus. Often Introverts can massage a situation from a rather singular perspective—not intentionally, just naturally.

Three Steps to Confronting Ethical Issues

Before you leap into any ethical dispute, there are three essential steps:

1. **Listen and learn.** Hear what's being said, but try to stay uninvolved. Promise yourself you won't even consider a course of action for at least twenty-four hours.

2. **Consider the source.** Refer to the sixteen descriptions of how the different preference combinations approach ethical issues and ask yourself how type might be influencing both what's being said and your reaction to it.

3. **Do something about it.** Determine as quickly as possible whether you believe it is an issue worth doing something about. (Perhaps it's not as severe as originally perceived, but it still may be worthy of further action.) Then either lend your support to resolving it or see to it that the matter gets quickly laid to rest. To do otherwise would be to waste your—and everyone else's—precious time.

In the end, viewing ethics through a typological lens involves three rather simple truths. First and foremost, it is imperative to keep in mind that the only person for whom you can be ethically responsible is yourself. No matter how much you care, no matter how wrong you perceive something to be, you simply cannot change another person's basic behavior if they're not ready to respond to you. The second truth is that when it comes to ethics, your opinions about right and wrong often say more about you than about others' behavior. Your accusations toward someone else about wrongs and immoralities are often more reflective of your unresolved issues than they are of the other person's problem.

Finally, your ethical system is a reflection of a lifelong development of your personality type. So, as your personality evolves, your ethics follow it. What you might have found perfectly acceptable at one stage in life might seem reprehensible to you now, or you may be willing to bend the rules in ways you wouldn't have considered doing a few years ago.

As you can see, there are at least two kinds of ethics: yours and everyone else's. Typewatching won't make the differences disappear, but it will give you a more objective framework to find constructive alternatives to dealing with them.

14

Stress Management

"Now, now, we mustn't lose our heads."

If you've learned nothing else about Typewatching by now, it should be clear that one type's excitement is another type's stress. For example, your boss's enthusiastic rambling about the prospects of her latest project might lead to your severe worry about whether or not she'll really meet the deadline. Your spontaneous figure-it-out-as-you-go-along work style might be responsible for her sleepless nights wondering whether you really know what you're doing. In short, all the things that inspire and motivate one of you could trigger anything from headaches to heart attacks for the other.

Some basic Typewatching awareness about stress is important not only to profits and productivity but also to the physical and emotional well-being of the workforce. There is no doubt that the more stress a person experiences, the more susceptible he or she becomes to ulcers, coronary heart disease, absenteeism, and accidents. (Specific stress doesn't directly cause specific illness, but it can heighten an individual's preexisting susceptibilities.) Conversely the more one is aware of his or her personality preferences, the more one is at least forewarned of the mental minefields that contribute to harmful levels of stress.

Type and Stress Exercise

Here's a simple way to use Typewatching to gauge what stresses you on a daily basis. To begin, you'll need to do a brief analysis of how you spend your time. Depending on your style, either brainstorm with others or work up your own list of all the different things you do in the course of a typical day. What are the events, issues, and people that are the focus of your attention?

Next, try to "type" each of the items on your list around the eight preferences. For example:

■ How much of your time is spent in Extraverted activities: attending meetings, responding to phone calls, meeting the public, taking care of the demands of the outside world?

■ How much of your time is spent in Introverted activities: working behind closed doors, reflecting and contemplating, reading, just listening?

■ How much of your time is spent in Sensing activities: paying attention to details, being in touch with specifics, paying the bills (literally or figuratively)?

■ How much of your time is spent in iNtuitive activities: strategizing, anticipating, looking at the big picture, interpreting the meanings of things?

■ How much of your time is spent in Thinking activities: objectively looking at conflicts, analyzing the consequences of various actions, keeping things focused on the task at hand?

■ How much of your time is spent in Feeling activities: keeping the troops motivated, helping to make the workplace a pleasant or happy one, mediating interpersonal problems, paying attention to individuals' concerns?

- How much of your time is spent in Judging activities: meeting schedules and deadlines, fighting off distractions and sticking to your plan, organizing others?

- How much of your time is spent in Perceiving activities: responding to the unexpected, coping with distractions, staying flexible for any situation?

You might consider making eight boxes, and listing or checking off in each box each of the items on your list. In the end, you'll have a rough idea of the "type" of your day. You might find, for example, that your day is largely ENFP: It is spent responding to a constant barrage of phone calls, attending meetings, participating in community activities on behalf of the company, inspiring the troops to keep them motivated and productive, and generally dealing with whatever demands arise as the day unfolds.

That's a perfectly fine day—if you're an ENFP. In fact, it's an exciting day. But for all other types, such a day could be anything from merely irritating to downright debilitating. The ENFP's opposite, the ISTJ, would be in the latter group. Little wonder: The ideal ISTJ day would be spent working alone within the bowels of the organization, focusing on specific details, analyzing what needs to be done, keeping yourself uninvolved in other people's issues, and getting things done on time. Given this, is it surprising that ISTJs are particularly prone to burnout, fatigue, and a wide range of stress-related ills, from headaches to heart attacks?

Even for those who are only slightly different—an ENFJ, for example—the ENFP-style day can still be stressful. The ENFJ comes to work with his or her day planned and scheduled. To be bombarded with a day full of surprises will not be appreciated. An INFP, on the other hand, will be drained by the constant demand to pay attention to others—meetings, calls, personal conversations, and so on.

We've found that the higher up you go within an organization, the less control you have over how you spend your time. Others take up your time, control your schedule, and make unexpected demands. In such cases, your sense of responsibility coupled with your ego needs will constantly draw you away from your personal preferences.

Stressors and Stressees

Let's start with the basics: Stress is inevitable, and not all of it is bad. In fact, certain kinds of stress keep us on our toes, motivated, and ready for action. Stress has been likened to a bell curve—we are at our best when we're moving up toward the top. At its peak, stress gives us a sense of being out of control; at its ebb, lack of stress creates an apathy that can render us defenseless and paralyzed. So, a certain amount of stress is inevitable and healthy.

Another basic fact is that what stresses one personality type may be relaxing to another. "Easy listening" (read: elevator) music may make some workers relaxed and productive, while for others it is the musical equivalent of fingernails on a blackboard. So, too, for classical, country-western, opera, or jazz. What seems harmless—indeed beneficial—to us may send others in the office over to the windowsill to contemplate jumping.

But music is only the beginning. From personal habits (foot tapping, nail biting, pacing) to personal style (dress, mannerisms, speech patterns) to the manifestations of different preferences (thinking out loud, chronic tardiness, rigidity), there's something in each of us that can potentially drive someone else up a wall.

Of course, we haven't even mentioned the big-picture stressors—relationships, personal finances, world crises, the stock market, and deadline pressures, to name just a few. To varying degrees these touch each of us over the course of the day—and on into the sleepless night.

It's important to note that severe stress rarely results from just one or two factors. In most cases it's a building-block effect: personal issues piled on top of work issues combined with concern for the state of the world all feeding each other, building pressures. It may be one additional, perhaps trivial, matter that puts you over the top—the proverbial straw that breaks the camel's back.

Just as different types create stress differently, so, too, does each type interpret and deal with stress in different ways. Some talk their way through it—to friends, neighbors, and veritable strangers—while others work it out inside. Some types tackle their stressors and hit them head-on, while others prefer to imagine them out of existence. Some interpret stress as a personal attack on them by a specific individual (or even by the entire universe), while others interpret it as one of the laws of life, as sure as death and taxes.

The More Things Change

There's little question that stressors in the workplace will get worse before they get better. All aspects of the workplace and the workforce appear to be in flux. Predictions are that minorities, women, and those with special needs will be an increasing part of the labor force, contributing to potential interpersonal conflicts. Increased global competition combined with diminishing resources mean that virtually all organizations will have to produce more with fewer people and resources. Companies are being bought and sold, merged, broken up, and phased out. New technologies have turned industries upside down, speeding the pace of work and the way we communicate. Institutions that were once thought to be invincible seem to be crumbling before our eyes.

All of which is likely to produce stress.

As we are rather adaptive creatures, it should be theoretically possible for us to roll with these punches, to modify our institutions and behaviors as demanded by the times. The bad news is that the dominant leadership type in the workplace—Thinking-Judging—is the type least capable of coping with change. Moreover, this is a type that has a high need to control everyone and everything and views not doing so as a management flaw and personality weakness. However, the interrelatedness and global dynamic of the work world makes it increasingly impossible to control everything. Putting out a little brush fire in one part of the organization can fan fierce flames in another part. So it doesn't take a great deal of imagination to see how this increases everyone's stress.

One Size Doesn't Fit All

Ironically, many of the programs we bring in to our organizations to reduce stress are stressors themselves. They are generally designed with no regard for personality differences. As a result they tend to add stress to certain types rather than reduce it. For example, a hard-charging, compulsive Type-A ISTJ may be told to engage in an exercise regime intended to channel her stress into healthful physical release. In reality such a program merely adds one more thing to an already overcrowded, compulsively kept schedule. Or this same ISTJ may be told to relax and take time to "stop and smell the roses," a state of affairs that is anathema to ISTJ behavior. (Indeed, if it was in her nature to do so, she wouldn't be stressed in the first place; she would have scheduled this activity long ago.) It's not that the ISTJ is incapable of slowing down or relaxing, it's just that such activities must be validated by the ISTJ as significant contributions to living responsibly. As we'll see later on, there are ways to "unstress" TJs, just as there are specific ways to manage stress in all the other types.

At some point in your career you may have filled out one of the many questionnaires that are designed to quantify what is stressing you and exactly how stressed you are. In filling out the form, there are usually about thirty items, which range from death, divorce, and life-threatening diseases to the morning paper not being delivered in the same spot every day. Each stress has its own numerical value, with higher values suggesting greater needs for adjustment. When you total up your score, you find out whether you are not at risk or likely to experience an illness in the near future.

But so what? This information is important, to be sure, but

without some basic understanding of personality differences—not to mention individual values, age, religion, and the like—you may be at a loss as to how to use the information you've received from such questionnaires. If you are an ISTJ you are likely to say, "Yes, personal family issues would be a stressor at work if I'd let them, but they have no business in the workplace." But if you are an ENFP, you might respond, "I can't possibly get anything done until I get this problem with my wife off my chest." If you are an Introvert, you might respond to horrendous news at work by saying nothing to anyone, priding yourself for your stiff upper lip. If you are an Extravert, you might spend the rest of the day dumping your problem on anyone you can buttonhole or reach on the phone.

Type and Stress

Before we describe how each of the eight preferences reacts to stress, let's first point out a few dynamics that often accompany stress for most personality types. The first is illustrated in the old adage, When you're knee-deep in alligators, it's hard to remember that your original mission was to drain the swamp. In other words, stress often sneaks up on us, and it's not until we are "knee-deep" that we suddenly realize how stressful a situation is. It then acts like a snowball rolling down a hill, enlarging rapidly unless we find a way to stop the momentum. It can soon be out of control.

Another phenomenon has to do with control, especially in relation to one's own life. We have a great deal of control over some parts of our lives and little or no control over other parts. The difference between being stressed and not being stressed is the wisdom to know which things we can control and which things we can't. In dealing with a stressful relationship with a co-worker, it would make sense to be in touch with and try to control your own behavior, your own work habits, and your own job responsibilities. It would be futile—and a recipe for stress—to project your anger onto your co-workers, to burn energy trying to change him or her, or to modify your own work habits trying to accommodate a situation that may be impossible to ameliorate. You can be in charge of yourself, which can help to keep your stress in bounds. You can't control others. By the way, this same rule applies to other parts of life—everything from traffic jams to shoppers having more than the requisite number of items in the express check-out lane. You can control the route you drive or the way you respond to the traffic—you can turn on the radio or simply take a deep breath—but your anger and stress won't budge gridlocked rush-hour traffic an inch.

Often what is happening is that life has moved us, or we perceive it has moved us, to operate primarily from our nonpreferences and not from our preferences. If you are a Sensor and you are forced to spend an inordinate amount of time examining the future or creating a strategic plan, for example, and not able to do something that will produce some tangible results, you may indeed be on a nonstop bus to Stressville. If you must rely largely on your nonpreferences to cope with a situation, you are already starting off on the wrong foot. You may act responsibly and successfully in the situation, but that won't necessarily ward off stress.

So, stress attacks us in at least four ways: (a) when we're not paying attention to it; (b) when we feel we're losing control; (c) when we're trying to control the wrong or inappropriate areas of our—or others'—lives; and (d) when we're forced to use our nonpreferences more than our preferences.

Given all this, a fundamental part of dealing with stress is to understand how each of the preferences interprets and deals with stressful situations.

How Each Preference Causes and Reacts to Stress

Forewarned is forearmed. That's certainly true where stress is concerned. Here are a few things worth pointing out about each preference that may help you to avoid or to cope more effectively with stressful situations.

Extraverts and Introverts. First of all, because the workplace usually rewards Extraversion over Introversion, there is a tendency for Introverts to "sell out," giving up their natural preference in favor of living and working on Extraverted terms. So, they act Extraverted during the workday, going home at night hoping to recharge (only, in many cases, to be bombarded by family and friends). Co-workers are shocked to learn that these chatty souls are Introverts in Es' clothing. For the Is it is simply a survival technique, but it can carry a high price in the form of stress and related health issues. Indeed, Introverts more than Extraverts tend to be plagued with a range of stress-related illnesses.

Sensors and iNtuitives. When Sensors spend too much time in theorizing or abstracting uncertainties—in essence, in the world of the unknown—it is an invitation to stress. Sensors need to get their hands on something, literally, and do something. They can't abide sitting around in "Dreamland." A Sensor's retort to that classic bumper sticker I'D RATHER BE FISHING would be "Quit wishin' and go fishin'." So, one of the greatest stress reducers for Sensors is to move beyond the figurative and into action.

For iNtuitives it's the opposite. Too many details, accounts, and deadlines are all things that heighten anxiety. If you doubt this, watch a strong iNtuitive's behavior as midnight, April 15, gets closer. Their sleeping, eating, and other daily activities are negatively affected as the reality of the IRS deadline closes in. Filing extensions was made for iNtuitives.

Thinkers and Feelers. First of all, let's lay to rest the myth that Thinking types find it easy to fire people and stay objective during heavy-duty interpersonal office strife. In truth, Ts suffer just as much as Fs. And the more an altercation escalates, the more a T's anxiety rises. One big difference between Thinkers and Feelers is that Ts want to confront a stressful situation head-on, get it out of the way, and get back on track. Fs want to avoid it at all costs, hoping that it will simply go away.

For the clear T, stress centers around those things that impact on one's ability to remain objective. An abundance of displayed emotions means loss of control to a Thinker. Any emotion—joy, anxiety, tenderness, and especially affection or anger—displayed publicly just heightens the stress. It usually means the person emoting is out of control. And if the emotions continue, a Thinker may lose control. You've heard the classic T lines: "Now, now, we mustn't lose our heads." "Everyone, stay calm." "This is a time for clear thinking, not emotions." Those are all efforts on the T's part to stave off the vulnerability of getting embroiled at some personal level in someone else's stuff. "While I'm concerned that you are having a problem," the T will say, "it is your problem and I can help you most by remaining cool, calm, and collected." To be sure, Thinkers have all the same emotions as Feelers. But for Ts there is a time and place for expressing them. And stress is related to the inappropriate manifestation of anything too personal.

Stress for Feelers comes from getting overly involved too quickly in too many problems of other people, then having to remove themselves. Desertion, lack of caring, overidentification, pain, misery, nonproductivity, and avoidance surface in direct proportion to the F's stress. When Feelers are caught up in other people's problems, it can manifest itself in hyperventilation, spaciness, aloofness, or an avoidance of the situation that is totally disproportionate to their original involvement.

Over a cup of coffee, for example, an F might hear of a colleague's marital strife. In no time the F has become deeply involved, personalizing the story as though it were his own. Later that afternoon, while mulling over the conversation, the F suddenly realizes that he not only overpersonalized the problem but he just doesn't have time to deal with it. He may find it necessary to avoid his colleague, perhaps even dodge him as they approach in the hallway. If they should meet face-to-face, he might reflect sternness and disinterest so as not to be enticed into further involvement. The other party may not even have been looking for help and may be confused by this sudden change of behavior. He's encountered a strong F who is reacting to the stress of an overly personalized situation.

"YOU'RE NOT YOURSELF TODAY"

Someone may have made the above comment to you from time to time. It's often intended as a way of engaging you by those who sense that you may be stressed. We have a friend who tells the following story:

"My job involved filling out a bunch of forms once a month to make sure that I and eleven other consultants got paid as part of a government contract. It was a great deal of paperwork, and it had to be done precisely or the finance department would reject it and delay everyone's paycheck. As an ENF I enjoyed doing the job because it helped everyone get something they wanted and provided a service to the group. But each month, when the form filling took place, as I worked alone in a windowless office, I turned into a different person. Everyone would tend to avoid me. I didn't realize this was happening at the time.

"Finally one day a colleague said, 'You're not yourself today.' My immediate response was to argue, pointing out what service I was doing for everyone. The more we looked at it, the more it became clear that the work I was doing flew in the face of my Extraverted-iNtuitive personality. I was working alone, dealing with specifics, with no room for creativity.

"By changing the locale, soliciting some help, and taking a few breaks, I was able to become a bit more myself during those monthly tasks. Though the task would never be fun, I could be less stressed and more appealing to others."

Judgers and Perceivers. Judgers get stressed—and give stress—when they lack either of their most precious needs: closure and control. Work assignments that demand that they "hang loose" or brainstorm options with no intent for implementation are invitations to stress for a Judger. A workday that is one of fire fighting, one surprise after another, with few pauses to reorganize or opportunities to complete any of the "to-dos" on a list, is a recipe for a Judger's headache and in the process can lead to some decidedly irritating behavior toward others. All of which can lead to the J's stress contaminating the entire workplace.

One problem is that when stressed, the Judger works even harder at trying to control the uncontrollable. In the process the J tends to project his or her stress in the form of blame, irritation, anger, and frustration—on both self and others. It would be helpful at such points if the J could "let go" of the stressful emergency—admittedly this is easier said than done—then go organize or accomplish something from another more straightforward activity. This can be anything from straightening a desk to completing some other assignment to checking off as many things as possible on the day's list. In short, he or she is admitting, "This is one of those areas over which I have no control. So, I'm going to drop it and go finish one of my favorite projects." For a J to be that free is a major move in stress reduction.

For the Perceiver, stress often mounts in direct proportion to either the routine nature of the job or the diminishing number of options available on a given task. Something as simple as seeing next week's or next month's calendar fill up with commitments and appointments can create tension for the P, because options for "whatever comes along" are being curtailed. For the P, a simple "to-do" list can be viewed as an albatross if the Perceiver believes he or she will be held accountable for each item on the list.

Make no mistake: Perceivers can be as productive as Judgers. But their methods often include finding new ways, or at least variations, for accomplishing assignments. Just as a scattered, disorganized workplace can give a J a headache, a P can get a headache if everything seems so rigid and demanding that there is no room for movement.

We can think of no better illustration of this than a "Peanuts" cartoon in which ESTJ Lucy pontificates, "You get out of life exactly what you put into it—no more, no less!" To which ENFP Snoopy walks away looking depressed and thinking, "Somehow, I'd like a little more margin for error."

Most of the things that can stress a P, a J can find satisfying, even enjoyable. Isabel Briggs Myers was a strong P married to a strong J. Isabel would frequently seek her husband's input for items on the Indicator. She once asked him about a potential question: "When you have completed a task, does cleaning up strike you as (a) something to do right away, or (b) something that can wait until later?" To which he responded, "That needs a third choice: '(c) something that's fun to do.'" That would never have crossed the mind of a strong Perceiver. Ps have trouble seeing such routine maintenance tasks as something that could in any way be enjoyable. And if it's demanded of them, it can become quite stressful. Conversely Js can get seriously stressed if, after the work is completed, they find that no one has tidied up. If they have to do it themselves, they will, but they'll make everyone within earshot miserable in the process.

Ps work best when they can set their own pace and try alternatives. If routines or schedules are too demanding, they may need a break to work on something else or at least an option to develop a routine. Anything that can transform the experience into something that's new or a little bit different will stimulate

DEALING WITH LOSS

At the top of every scale of stress-producing events is the loss of a loved one. Clearly the initial sense of loss itself is a significant stressor. But we've found in our counseling that preferences can play a role in defining the specific source of stress. For example, Extraverts have told us that the stress is centered around being alone, not having a companion with whom to talk and interact. They feared having to spend too much time alone, looking inside themselves. Introverts, meanwhile, were more stressed over the reality of having to confront the external world of being newly single. The mere thought of having to meet new people, go on dates, and be involved in all that "social superficiality" was a source of extreme anxiety. They feared having to spend too much time "out there" relating to others.

the P into increased productivity. Ps function best when confronted with any of those many clichés that describe living on
the edge: being under the gun, burning the midnight oil, flying
by the seat of one's pants.

On Becoming Someone Else

Sometimes life becomes just too much for us, so much so in
fact that our behavior becomes altered significantly. Often these
behavioral changes, while readily apparent to anyone else, are
invisible to ourselves. It's as if we're becoming "someone else."
To make matters worse, that "someone else" is not becoming to
us; it just doesn't fit. If an Extravert is loud and raucous, no one
thinks twice. But if a stressed-out Introvert acts that way, heads
turn.

Simply put, when we become seriously stressed, we can become the worst version of our four-letter opposite.

Why does this happen? When too many stressful events take
place—a combination of job layoffs, serious illness, personal rejection, money problems, and the like—the stress can consume
us in such a way that our regular coping mechanisms are no
longer adequate. So we may turn to alcohol, or we may become
insomniac or engage in other self-destructive behavior. Gradually our outward behavior can change significantly. For example
a normally gregarious, effervescent, imaginative, somewhat absentminded, and spontaneous ENFP can turn into a pensive,
noncommunicative, detail-oriented, rigid individual—in other
words, the worst version of an ISTJ. And the normally contemplative, quiet, grounded, objective, accountable, and conservative ISTJ, when overly stressed, can become a boisterous,
disjointed, emotional, and fragmented person—in other words,
a very poor version of an ENFP.

The point here is to understand that such sudden wide swings
in behavior can have some underlying causes, are often quite
pronounced, and yet can be sporadic, coming and going over the
course of a day or week.

There's a tendency for many of us to rush in and try to play psychologist when we find someone we know who is so clearly in need of help. And that's fine. The problem is that we tend to go about it the wrong way. Being supportive is one thing, but if it is misunderstood by the person in need, it can be more destructive than constructive. Comments like, "What's wrong with you?" or even "What's going on?" can put the person on the defensive because, in their stress, they have deluded themselves into thinking they're coping just fine. By bursting their bubble, you're heading for trouble.

Sometimes it's more helpful to approach such individuals with your observations of their behavior. For example: "I couldn't help but notice that you seem especially quiet today." Or, "I've noticed that you're really into organizing things lately." Or, "You seem to be having a lot of trouble keeping to your schedule." All of these merely point out the individual's unusual behavior without suggesting that something is wrong. There's no guarantee that even this seemingly innocent comment won't evoke a defensive response, or even an outburst, but this is a much more delicate and unobtrusive way of breaking the ice. If it's appropriate, you might want to add, "If there's anything you'd like to talk about, let me know."

Having broken the ice, it is probably better to leave the person alone, letting him or her reflect on what you said. You've probably done all you can, and should, do. As a colleague, and not a psychology professional, your most important contribution is to be supportive.

Four Secrets of Coping with Stress

Because stress takes on so many different forms and comes in so many unpredictable ways, the more you are aware of yourself, the better equipped you will be to deal with stress. In examining a host of different stress issues encountered by all sixteen personality types, here are some specific tips we've found to be very helpful.

1. **Know your preference strengths.** This first secret may seem
   basic, but amid all those alligators it's easy to forget who you
   are typologically. What's key is not just to recall your four
   letters but to keep in mind the relative strengths of each
   preference. For example, if you have a very clear preference
   for Judging, then you know you have a high need for closure, control, and organization. You also know that your tolerance for spontaneity and open-endedness is relatively low.
   Therefore, stress will be resolved in direct proportion to the
   number of things about which you can make decisions and
   put behind you. You may want to make a plan, or at least a
   list, that can help you check off each stressor. You will want
   to avoid ambiguity at all costs.

   This assumes, of course, that you have a clear preference for Judging. That's not always the case. If you have
   only a slight preference for Judging—that is, if you have
   more than a little tolerance for ambiguity and open-endedness—then the stress will come from not knowing when to
   do which. This can show up in the form of frozen behavior:
   You are unable to choose which of several options you
   should take. It's a variation of "deciding not to decide," but
   in the process you appear as very wishy-washy and unable to
   move. Stress builds. You punish yourself for not deciding,
   those who looked to you for direction are frustrated, and
   everyone, including yourself, beats up on you.

   Now you may be saying to yourself, "The indecision of
   the slight Judger sounds an awful lot like that of the strong
   Perceiver." Not so. Strong Perceivers are not looked to for
   quick decisions, either by themselves or by others. Moreover, their strength is in generating options and variables.
   The slight Judger, by contrast, is simply stuck. The strong
   Perceiver enjoys the ambiguity, becoming stressed when
   forced to make or live by too many quick decisions or when
   seeing the options disappear simply for the sake of being
   checked off as "completed" on some Judger's list.

   The slight P, however, will behave much like the slight J,
   unable to move in any direction, sending mixed signals to

those who look to them for direction, and generally beating themselves up for their seeming immobility.

Each of the other six preferences creates much the same dynamic. A clear preference gives you satisfaction and direction but lowers your threshold for activities that call for your nonpreference. A slight preference gives you more options but tends to leave you more frozen about which way to go.

2. **Go for the rewards.** One of the best options available to those with slight preferences is to go with the flow of the workplace. There are four preferences who tend to find themselves in conflict with social norms: Introverts, female Thinkers, male Feelers, and Perceivers. There is an enormous amount of pressure on these preferences to be the opposite of what they are. Rewards—in school, at home, and at work—are bestowed upon their opposites. If you are among these types, you will find the going easier and the rewards more gratifying if you are able to play to your opposite preferences at work. Thus Introverts who are able to use their Extraverted skills during working hours will find themselves "fitting in" with greater ease; that may work over the short term, but over time it can cause serious stress. Thinking women who can emphasize their Feeling side, and Feeling men who can emphasize their Thinking component, will find much easier role acceptance. And Perceivers who have the capacity to play by J rules—being organized, meeting deadlines, and so forth—will find themselves being less self-critical and more accepted by just about everyone. Again, the more you know about yourself, the better able you'll be to manage yourself from a position of strength.

Not everyone will be able to pull off such transformations. Those with clear preferences—strong Introverts, for example—are much more defined in their behaviors and less in touch with their nonpreferences. So, too, with strong T women, F men, and Ps. The ability to call upon one's

IT'S MY PARTY AND I'LL CRY IF I WANT TO

When it comes to helping others in need, sometimes even the best of intentions can go awry if there's no awareness of type. Consider the case of Cheryl, the INTP news director of a big-city television station. She moved to town just after Thanksgiving to start her new job. She found herself immediately in over her head, both personally and professionally. Burdened with furnishing a condo and making friends, building a work team and establishing herself professionally, Cheryl quickly became impatient and curt with her colleagues and shied from them socially in her need to find even a few minutes for herself. Her largely Extraverted staff decided that what she needed was a raucous surprise Christmas party that would help her feel a welcome part of the group. When the surprise was sprung, it turned out to be the straw that broke Cheryl's back. Seeing the party as another unwanted social demand, she was torn between her need to be alone and her desire to be appreciative. The combined stress put her over the edge: She spent the evening crying, nearly out of control. This made both Cheryl and her colleagues feel guilty and somewhat blaming of the other party. It took weeks for everyone to get over this "good deed." Typewatching helped everyone to view the situation in a positive light and even to laugh at the absurdity of it all.

nonpreferences is best done by those whose preferences are less clear.

We're not suggesting that you should try to be something you're not. All we're suggesting is that if you have the flexibility to do so and prefer not to swim constantly against the tide, you may benefit from adapting to the predominant behavioral style of your workplace.

3. **Balance your preferences.** The third secret is to find a healthy balance between using your preference and allowing some tempering through your nonpreferences. For example,

while Extraverts naturally prefer to move the stressful situation or symptom to the external world—talking it through, getting others' input, generally using up a lot of air time—the Second Commandment would suggest that maximizing such behavior will become a stressful liability. Others will tune the Extravert out and not respond, perhaps even avoid the Extravert as he or she approaches. And the Extravert will stop listening to others' feedback.

Furthermore, the Extravert will suddenly realize the loneliness and rejection of the situation, further compounding the situation. In effect, the Extravert has been forced into Introversion, as opposed to choosing to exercise a healthy balance of Introversion and Extraversion. The Extravert would have been better off complementing his or her Extraversion with some internal reflection and contemplation of the event, its impact, and the feedback received from others. That allows the Extravert the chance to check perceptions and judgments against his or her own internal world before returning again to the preferred Extraverted behavior. Being able to Extravert and Introvert with some degree of ease is the beginning of successfully keeping stress in check.

4. **Accept the inevitability of conflict.** Conflict is a fact of life, and everyone gets stressed by it. There's no getting around that reality. Part of that reality is that different types, dealing differently with conflict, compound the stress. For example, the more an Extravert insists upon talking through a conflict, the more an Introvert clams up—until a strange thing happens. The Introvert, now overloaded, verbally dumps the entire load ("I'm so sick and tired of all this. And by the way, that reminds me. Three weeks ago you were . . . And while I'm at it, that wasn't the first time. Six months ago you said . . ."), at which point the Extravert, now stressed and aghast, slams the door and exits the scene. Any type, being true to type, can push a conflict past the boiling point. This can take the form of an extreme show of one's preference (an Extravert begins to talk faster and louder) to

a bizarre demonstration of one's nonpreference (an Introvert begins to babble endlessly). In either case such behavior is usually totally disproportionate to the issue at hand.

In a perfect world each of us would know our preferences well enough and enjoy enough personal security to say at some point in a conflict, "Here's where my stress level is going to make me say or do something I'll regret. I'm calling a truce until tomorrow so that I can sleep on it. We'll deal with it then." Sometimes it really is better to count to ten.

Stress Guide for the Eight Preferences

As the day unfolds and stress increases, you will note that one or more of your preferences will begin to move into its opposite. The guide on page 253 can serve as a quick reference for yourself or for those around you.

Note that "A Good Stretch" is a two-edged sword. Just as with physical activity, stretching can make one limber and toned, but too much stretching can cause severe pain and discomfort. Too much of a good stretch can be stressful. How much is too much? It differs with each individual and must be monitored accordingly.

Stress Guide for the Eight Preferences

	WHAT THEY NEED	A GOOD STRETCH
EXTRAVERTS	A chance to express, the opportunity to talk and share	Taking notes or writing in a journal; concentrated reflection time
INTROVERTS	A chance to write, reflect, and meditate	An extemporaneous discussion or sharing of something personal
SENSORS	The specifics spelled out carefully and a good experiential event	Fantasizing to music or imagining and discussing the unknown
INTUITIVES	A chance to add to the design with their own imagination and an opportunity to connect the learnings to their own experience	Experiencing the world of the senses; doing some detailed assignment, even things like proofreading or bookkeeping
THINKERS	An opportunity to analyze the situation, to confront things and challenge them; often they like a win/lose reward	Experiencing powerlessness or lack of control; exploring the world of nonverbal communication
FEELERS	Affirmations and positive rewards, a happy learning climate; seeing the value of what's being learned for themselves and others	Learning for the sake of the idea itself, with no other use or reward; doing some objective analysis and sticking to a conclusion, even if it is against their personal values
JUDGERS	An agenda, a schedule, a plan, handouts, and charts like this one	Having no agenda for some part of the course, just winging it and not following the schedule now and then to see if something positive can result
PERCEIVERS	Room to move, to know that there are rewards even if assignments aren't completed or deadlines are missed; the opportunity for self-pacing and self-determination	Contemplating some of the material on time and without changing it; not wandering down extraneous paths

15

Sales

"Let me tell you about our
Frequent Mower's Club."

Let's start with the basics: Any of the sixteen types is perfectly
capable of making a fine salesperson. For that matter, any of sixteen types can make a fine buyer.

We believe Typewatching makes an ideal lens through which
to view the art of selling. Since selling is an interpersonal transaction, self-knowledge as well as the ability to observe behavior
are the keys to success. Many of the communications skills
we've already covered can come into play in trying to make a
sale. Knowing when to talk and when to listen, or when to be
aggressive and when to back off, can make the difference between winning a customer's confidence and losing him or her altogether.

By the way, we're not simply talking here about selling goods
and services. Just about all of us "sell" something to someone
nearly every day: We sell ideas to our boss, we sell motivation to
employees, we sell enthusiasm to our children, and we sell ourselves in every new encounter. The ideas and suggestions in this
chapter apply to all such selling experiences.

The Seduction of Selling

In many ways the dynamics of salesmanship are not unlike the dynamics of seduction—not just the physical type but also intellectual and emotional seduction. In any seduction scenario the first person seduced is the seducer. That is to say, he or she must be convinced that what is being offered is something the other person needs or wants. In the marketplace, once the seducer (seller) acknowledges this, the seductee (buyer) is at a disadvantage. The sale is all but consummated.

To that end, there are some preferences that are natural seducers. ENFJs, for example, clearly have the biggest advantage as salespeople. Individually each of their four preferences is very effective in a seduction/sales situation. The synergy of the four letters combined consistently makes ENFJs the salespeople (seducers) of the month in any organization.

Why is this? Let's take a look at each of the four preferences:

- Feelers clearly have an advantage as salespeople—at least potentially. They bring their natural empathy and persuasiveness to selling. They tend to start with the customer and not with the product.

- Add iNtuition to Feeling (NF) and you've added an appreciation of possibilities, contagious enthusiasm, and a natural tendency to go beyond the obvious to find creative solutions to a problem.

- Adding Extraversion (ENF) brings gregariousness and aggressiveness, coupled with the reality that three fourths of the U.S. population has the same tendency to respond in the external world. An Extraverted sales pitch more often than not gets responded to in an Extraverted way, and the two parties are off and running.

- Finally, add Judging to the equation (ENFJ) and you bring the ability to stay focused on closing the deal with a certain amount of time consciousness and direction—all of which imply to the customer that he or she can have confidence in what the seller is saying.

When you examine the makeup of certain professions by type, you can see that ENFJs frequently do jobs that require some kind of selling. Take the clergy, for example. According to the Center for the Application of Psychological Type, which publishes a periodic *Atlas of Type Tables*, which includes career distributions by type, the clergy is a predominantly ENFJ profession. And if you think about those in the profession who have been the most effective sellers—such as Billy Graham, Jim Bakker, Jerry Falwell, Robert Schuller, and Martin Luther King, Jr.—all of them exhibit ENFJ sales prowess: All have used their awareness of the marketplace (human need) combined with tremendous packaging (charisma) to sell huge audiences on their sometimes radical ideals. In each case the packaging and sales pitches were carefully crafted to meet the "buyers'" different needs.

Another ENFJ career that reflects great selling abilities is teaching. And teachers are among the world's great sellers. They not only must sell their students on a given subject, they must

JUST SAY SOMETHING!

We once helped a company train its employees on how to conduct interviews over the phone. The goal was to help the interviewer become more responsive to the consumers' needs. To our amazement, we watched one strong Introvert on the phone nodding his head excitedly but not saying a word. The individual at the other end of the line became louder, more intense, even somewhat angry, shouting at one point, "Are you listening?" The interviewer continued to nod feverishly. We had to hold up a sign to the Introvert saying, "He can't see you." The Introvert saw the sign, smiled, and finally responded verbally.

also sell them on the need to show up for each class and to do their best. Indeed, in an unpublished dissertation at Claremont Graduate School in which teachers and administrators were asked to pick the most outstanding teacher they knew, ENFJs were consistently named. There was no close second.

What holds true for ENFJs probably works in reverse for their four-letter opposites, ISTPs. Each of the ISTP's four preferences tends to work against the sales process. For them to be successful at selling, they must spend a great deal more energy than other types.

We can't overemphasize what we said earlier: All sixteen types are perfectly capable of making sales. Being an ENFJ is no guarantee that you'll even like selling, let alone be good at it, and being an ISTP is no sure recipe for failure. The complex chemistries two people bring to any selling-buying encounter transcend mere personality preferences. That's the beauty—and the frustration—of salesmanship. But the understanding that Typewatching brings can provide valuable insight that can give anyone a leg up in the process.

How the Eight Preferences Approach Selling

As with any other activity, each of the eight preferences has its own strengths and weaknesses when it comes to selling:

Extraverts, being natural-born talkers, are likely to pursue any potential buyer with dogged aggressiveness. They are the bush beaters, constantly seeking out potential customers—at a party, in the supermarket, at the Kiwanis meeting. They rarely pass up an opportunity to hustle. As we've pointed out, three fourths of the population resonate on this wavelength, and the more others resonate, the more the E salesperson gets energized. Seller and buyer feed each other. Respond favorably and verbally (or even with a gesture) to an Extraverted salesperson's pitch and there's no end to the bull they'll feed you. The best of the lot engineer the process: They continually ask questions ("You can see the advantages, can't you?") that demand your response, thereby keeping you engaged—and them on top of the situation.

This strength maximized can also be the Extravert's downfall. Clearly, redundancy is a problem. (You can say that again.) If you don't respond to their pitch, they won't hesitate to repeat it—louder and faster—in a slightly modified way. The word "overkill" comes to mind. This might be eased somewhat if Extraverts would only listen, but that's not one of their strong suits. The worst situation for an E is when the customer (perhaps an Introvert) isn't responding as hoped. The Extravert may correctly read the situation ("I must not be reaching them") but, instead of giving the customer a chance to speak or reflect, simply keeps on talking. If the customer continues his or her nonresponse, the Extravert may quickly turn sour on the situation, sometimes lapsing into a personal funk or becoming angry or combative with the customer. This is not a way to win sales in any textbook.

Introverts bring good listening skills to selling, which can be effective with both Extraverted and Introverted customers. For example, Extraverted customers will tend to sell themselves on a product ("I really need one of these. Don't you think they're handy?"). A simple nod of the head by the salesperson will let the E customer consummate his or her own sale. And Introverted customers, of course, appreciate the space that the I salesperson offers, allowing them to reflect and come to their own conclusions. When they do speak, Introverted salespeople tell it like it is, picking a few choice words that reflect a great deal of confidence.

But Introverts can seem aloof and uninterested, especially to Extraverts. In their sparse conversation they may overlook some important information or key selling point about a product, perhaps wanting to avoid stating the obvious. Their apparent lack of enthusiasm can underwhelm a would-be buyer. They may have trouble showing that they believe in a product, even if they do. If Extraverts can be accused of overkill, Introverts are masters of the underkill.

Sensors can be easily gratified by the tangible, hands-on nature of selling. The results are often immediate: There is an exchange of goods or services for some consideration. A Sensor is likely to approach a potential customer armed to the teeth with facts and details and won't hesitate to share them freely, sometimes to the point of overwhelming the customer. A Sensing car salesperson, for example, will be equipped with every exciting—and even every not-so-exciting—detail, from its sticker price to its bells and whistles.

Of course, not all customers want or need such levels of detail, and this may result in some lost sales. The Sensor's obsession with detail can be blinding, obscuring the customer's real needs. Sometimes even short, simple, factual answers may be just as problematic. For example, a customer asks, "Does it come with a five-speed transmission?" and the Sensor simply responds, "No." For the Sensor that part of the conversation is over—a specific question got a specific answer. Actually the transmission question wasn't the customer's real concern; it was merely an opening to explore what options were available on that model car. For iNtuitive customers in particular, the Sensor salesperson's profusion of details may be confounding, with each opening a new range of possibilities that may leave the customer more confused than helped.

For **iNtuitives** in sales, a clear asset is their ability to generate possibilities and alternatives, increasing the chances that a customer will find something appealing. As a general rule iNtuitives are enthusiastic, and that enthusiasm is contagious. It is the nature of iNtuitives to see more than the obvious, which helps them find a use for just about anything by anyone. So, encountering a field full of used tires, the iNtuitive may dream up a score of ways to unload them—as bumpers on boat docks, swings, even flowerpots. They are the masters at turning lemons into lemonade.

Obviously such creativity can drive some buyers up the proverbial wall. Imagine walking into a store, money burning a hole in your pocket, hell-bent to buy a specific product at a specific

TAKING A BITE OUT OF SALES

We know a group of six dentists who went into business together. They were all ISTJs—Introverted-Sensing-Thinking-Judgers. Their explicit, agreed-upon mandate was to provide excellent dental care for the community. They hung out their shingle, and after two years they realized that business was not doing well.

What went wrong? They were all professionals, well trained, with the appropriate credentials. The community was in need of their services. How could they miss?

We found that the dentists were so type-alike—an inward-looking, structured, present-oriented, hands-on type—that no one had thought about the future, about the big picture, about communicating with the public, about the interpersonal aspects of their practice, and about how to be flexible and open-ended in their operation. In short, they had ignored the Extraverted, iNtuitive, Feeling, and Perceiving parts of their dental practice. None of them was speaking before the Rotary clubs and PTAs (Extraversion); they weren't forecasting the community's changing dental needs (iNtuition); they were ignoring some of the niceties of their profession, from giving toys to kids to sending out thank-you notes to grown-ups (Feeling); and their rigidity didn't allow them to explore how they got into this dilemma (Judging).

It was a classic case of the Second Commandment of Typewatching: Too much of a good thing became a liability.

price. Suddenly you're encountered by a bundle of enthusiasm pointing out a half-dozen other products you should be considering—some of them in place of, and others in addition to, your original quest. ("While you're considering the power-mower grass-catcher attachment, you should also consider the automatic trimmer and composter. And, now that you're going to have so much free time on your hands, how about a set of lawn furniture?") This can increase sales, to be sure, but it can also alienate and drive away customers. Sometimes in their enthusiasm iNtuitives overlook the specific thing the customer wanted. ("All I wanted was a grass catcher. A rake and some plastic bags will do just fine.") The N salesperson may be more caught up in designing an exciting sales program ("Let me tell you about our Frequent Mower's Club, in which you can earn valuable points toward your next purchase") than in completing the sale at hand. Even worse, the iNtuitive's enthusiasm can lead to exaggerating or misrepresenting a product ("You won't have to mow as often, and it's one hundred percent maintenance-free"). At best this habit will alienate customers; at worst it could result in a lawsuit.

Thinkers in a sales transaction remain analytical and logical, generating great rationales for any purchase. When you want a reason to buy something that you probably don't need, find a Thinker; you won't be disappointed. If the product has been rated or written about by some authoritative publication, you can be sure that the facts, if not the article itself, will be presented to you. T salespeople are likely to push quality. If you'll stand back and look at the product objectively, they'll say, you'll see it's a product that will serve you long and well. No matter that you're not crazy about the way it looks. Over the long haul its quality will win you over. Brand or national loyalty, while respected, is always secondary to a Thinker. ("I know we should encourage you to 'buy American,' but until the American-made product equals the quality of this one, I really must recommend the import.")

More than any other preference, the T salesperson may appear disinterested in, and perhaps even arrogant toward, the customer. After all, they've already figured it out, so why won't you agree with their recommendation? And if you're going to disagree, please don't use such a fluffy rationale as "It just doesn't feel right." Hard though it may be for a Thinker to understand, some people never learn to like a product, no matter how well it's made. (Indeed, some folks manage to find something of displeasure with any product.) At times it may seem like winning the argument is more important for the T than making the sale.

Feelers, as we've said, make fine salespeople. Prone to "get inside your moccasins," they often start with "How would I feel about buying this product?" Ideally they've already worked that dynamic through, enabling them to help the customer do the same. As we previously said, for the F salesperson the customer's needs come first. "The customer is always right" is a classic F slogan. The Feeler's natural empathy helps him or her identify with the customer from the beginning of the sales encounter to the very end. So, should a customer identify some different need, or even the desire to postpone making a purchase decision, the F has the ability to affirm him or her and to increase the chances of making the sale—whatever the customer ends up buying, whenever they decide to buy it. When Feeling salespeople are at their best, customers apologize for not buying from them.

But when a customer's needs drive the action, sales can take a backseat. With their hearts ruling their heads, F salespeople have been known to advance their own money toward a purchase if the customer is a little short ("I can see you really need this. Go ahead, pay me later"), throw in some freebies ("My boss would die if she knew I was doing this, but take these too"), or even buy it for them ("I knew you were looking for one of these, so I took the liberty"). Some of these may even increase sales, but that's not the point. The Feeler is in sales to help people; making money is the icing on the cake. One of the biggest drawbacks to an F salesperson's effectiveness is his or her tendency to overpersonalize everything. A lost sale is a personal rebuff that can cut into their enthusiasm and productivity.

Judgers, in every aspect of life, appear to have their act together and to be in charge, and sales is no exception. They tend to present themselves well and give clear answers (even when they don't know them), and they supply direction to a buyer who may be on the fence. Throughout the entire sales transaction, the J will be conscious of time, keeping himself and the buyer focused on closing the deal. If nothing else, such direction can make a customer feel secure. ("He certainly knows what he's talking about. I finally found someone I can trust.")

But Judgers, as we've said, are rigid, and as such can sometimes appear to be impatient with a customer's vacillation. Often convinced they're right, they can be quite argumentative,
even caustic, toward customers. Because they are not easily
open to alternatives, they may dismiss the customer's own suggestions—in effect talking a customer out of a sale. At worst a J
salesperson can be seen as pushy, obnoxious, and too eager to
make a sale.

Perceivers bring a plethora of possibilities to any sales transaction. No matter what you want, a Perceiver will find it—or
the next best thing. Through their natural tendency to ask questions and clarify, they can walk a customer through the decision-
making process with ease. Not needing to control the
transaction, they can adapt to the customer's pace. ("Hey, this is
a major purchase. Take as much time as you need. What can I do
to help you narrow down the field?") The P salesperson is, if
nothing else, flexible. Whenever it happens, it happens. And if it
doesn't happen this time, perhaps it will the next.

Certainly these same qualities can cut into productivity. A
salesperson not driven to closure will do little to meet sales quotas. The need to raise questions can also become very frustrating
to a customer looking for direction. Ps can appear not to have
their act together and as such can undermine customer confidence. Timeliness is another problem. At his or her worst, it is
the P salesperson who is late for an appointment or a callback,
losing the sale to a more heads-up competitor.

You can tell whether a salesperson is a J or a P through this
simple test: Just ask him or her for some direction or an opinion
about the purchase. Js will redefine your question, ask you a
question in return, and qualify their answer. Js will tell you what
they think. So, if you were to ask a waiter, "What's good today?"
the P would say something like, "Well, it all depends on what
you like. If you're into fish, there's two or three that are very,
very good. And we have a quiche today that's superb. Most people like the hamburgers. It depends on what you're in the mood
for." The J would say without hesitation, "The trout."

Sizzle or Steak?

If you've ever been in sales, you've no doubt learned the distinction between the "sizzle" and the "steak." The former are the things that get you into the store or showroom but that may have little to do with the actual purchase. The latter are the qualities of the product itself.

Consider cars. The "sizzle" part of the sale starts with whatever brings you into a particular dealer's showroom—hype, ads, recommendations, location, or whatever—and extends all the way to the car you end up considering. The things that first attract you about that car—whether a salesperson's recommendation, the literature you read before arriving, or the one you saw on the street that caught your eye—are all part of the sizzle. These are the things that provide the "hook." They are all rather upbeat and superficial. You've yet to make any form of commitment. At any moment your enthusiasm could burst, and you could be on you way out the door.

And then there's the "steak." In this case that's the car itself, the hands-on qualities that make you decide to buy or not buy: its engineering, craftsmanship, safety maintenance history, available options and colors, image, and the best price you can negotiate, among many other things.

The fact is you need both sizzle and steak to make a sale. You've got to draw people in and win them over—the sizzle—and then get them to buy something with which they will be satisfied—the steak. But the sizzle comes first. Without it there's little chance the customer will ever seriously consider the steak itself.

While all four letters of one's type are important in the selling process, they work in different ways. In typological terms, two letters are key to representing the sizzle, and two are key to representing the steak.

The Sizzle: E-I and J-P

The first and last letter of an individual's type—Extraversion or Introversion and Judging or Perceiving—are the more public sides of a person's personality, the first things customers see and the first things one sees about them. You can tell pretty quickly whether customers are Extraverts—if they have a high need to disclose a great deal of information early on—or if they're Introverts—if they're much more content to listen to the sales pitch without reacting and are generally more reserved throughout the process. For example, if you're an Extravert, you run the risk of either overpowering the customer or ending up in an unintended argument. You'd be surprised how quickly an Extravert can alienate a more Introverted customer or get drawn into verbal combat by another Extraverted customer. So it goes with the Introverted salesperson, who may need to take a deep breath and be ready to be more gregarious in the customer's presence. A Judger may need to give the customer a little leeway, backing off from yes-or-no-questions and allowing for some discussion that doesn't necessarily lead to closure. And a Perceiver may need to focus on just one or two options and keep the discussion moving toward resolution.

Because of their public nature, these preferences are the most potentially problematic in the sales encounter. These are the preferences that in the first few moments can almost effortlessly soothe or alienate a customer, drag the customer into an argument, invade his or her space, or make the salesperson appear to be either prematurely pushy and decisive or too laid-back and unhelpful. But with some simple self-awareness, recognizing these preferences can help you avoid the pitfalls and guide a customer directly from the front door to the cash register. In other words these preferences represent a key part of the sizzle—the information that will keep the customer there and interested. (The product itself will have some sizzle, too, but if the initial chemistry isn't right, the customer will never get that far.)

The Steak: S-N and T-F

The other two preferences come more into play when the customer considers the product itself. Handled effectively, they can be used by the salesperson to close the deal.

Unlike the E-I and J-P preferences in which sharing the same preferences with the buyer is usually an advantage, opposites do attract when it comes to considering the steak. Sensors can help iNtuitives focus on tangible specifics, and iNtuitives can provide Sensors with a range of possibilities. Thinkers can help Feelers deal with the objective costs and qualities of a potential purchase, while Feelers can help Thinkers consider the rewards and satisfactions a purchase can bring.

True, a Sensor can still overwhelm a customer with detail, and an iNtuitive can focus on a host of factors that may be unimportant to the customer. The Thinker can become hooked on a logical argument that may overlook the customer's personal needs, and the Feeler can become so gushy over the feel-good nature of a product that the customer's need for objectivity may be ignored. But these qualities are more easily controlled by a skilled salesperson than Extraversion, Introversion, Judging, and Perceiving.

The key, then, is to understand that it takes both sizzle and steak to make a sale. Your best efforts as a salesperson may have little to do with the product itself, at least at first, and more to do with gaining a quick "read" on a customer's first and last preference letters and using that information to maximize the moment.

Using Typewatching to Make a Sale

Sizzle and steak notwithstanding, the secret to successful sales has far less to do with "psyching out" the customer than with understanding yourself. True, that flies in the face of conventional wisdom, which emphasizes getting the upper hand in a transaction by "figuring out" the customer. We submit that while understanding the customer is important, it will have little effect unless you understand where you yourself are coming from.

That's how Typewatching can make a valuable contribution to sales effectiveness.

Here are some specific things to consider as you approach a sale:

IF YOU'RE AN EXTRAVERT

Some Extraverts can overwhelm even other Extraverts by yammering on about everything from the weather to what-have-you. That can make you ingratiating, to be sure, but it can also make you insufferable. If you feel the need to talk, at least do so in a way that allows the customer to say something occasionally. Be sure to listen when the customer speaks; try briefly repeating what's just been said before adding your own thoughts.

Listening is key. Even extremely Extraverted customers may want to be left alone, needing some time and space to explore the product. When that is stated—for example, "Thanks, I'm just looking. I'll let you know if I need help"—that is a request that needs to be honored. Often Es think they can help by wandering along with the customer and filling in the silences with seemingly useful information. But such "helpfulness" can quickly alienate an individual who has indicated that he or she needs to be left alone. This sentiment isn't always clearly or forcefully stated, which makes listening—and reading between the lines—so important.

IF YOU'RE AN INTROVERT

Customers want to feel important, so you may need an initial verbal expression of interest and even some seemingly trivial small talk. Not a lot, just enough to let the customer know that you're interested and that you want to be helpful. Even the customer who says, "Thanks, I'm just looking" may need to know that you're somewhere to be found when you're needed. Introverts too often hear the customer's request and vanish without a trace.

Introverts may need to go out of their way to state what to them seems obvious. That includes, for example, a simple welcome when they walk in the door. Many Introverts assume that a customer has come in because he or she is genuinely interested in buying something, is capable of looking on his or her own, and will speak up when in need of help or information. After all, that's what the Introvert would probably do in such a situation. Providing interest and guidance, even when it doesn't seem to be called for, can keep a customer around.

IF YOU'RE A SENSOR

Your tendency is to be well equipped with the facts—the practical, tangible aspects of the product. If the customer already seems to know these, then you can provide a great deal of help by supplying additional possibilities that may not be obvious from the facts. It's worth the stretch on your part because it provides added dimensions for the customer to consider. On the other hand, if the customer already seems loaded with possibilities but only has a broad, general idea of the product, your factual input can supply the missing link.

Again, listening is key. By listening carefully you can avoid overwhelming the customer with facts while being sensitive to providing whatever input the customer is seeking. It may be worthwhile to check from time to time, asking, "Would you like to know more about how this works?" Or, "What other kinds of information could I provide you that would be helpful?" The answers to such questions can serve as guidelines for your next move.

IF YOU'RE AN INTUITIVE

If you know your product, you know its potential but you may lack some of the specifics, relying on a printed spec sheet from the manufacturer for your data. That's good, but it may not be good enough for some customers, who need to understand the nuts and bolts of the situation. It's sometimes helpful to say, "Here are the printed specs, but let me highlight a few special features." This not only conveys that you are interested in specifics but that you've done your homework.

Of course, you can use your iNtuitive strength to help customers who are obsessed with the specs to look beyond the numbers to the far-reaching implications of the product. The product's reputation, history, resale potential, and company stability are all worth pointing out.

IF YOU'RE A THINKER

You are probably in touch with why this product is top notch. You've already thought through the logic as to why any customer would want to buy it. Often your reasoning is flawless, and your confidence will inevitably be conveyed to customers.

But not everything is logical. And the best reasoning in the world is for naught if it doesn't meet a customer's needs. If the customer agrees with your logic but interprets your confidence as arrogance, you will have trouble completing the sale. In fact, there's a risk that if you hold on too tightly to your logic, you could quickly find yourself in an argument with a customer over a product's merits. Clearly this won't inspire the customer to reach for his or her wallet.

While your logic is a valuable contribution, you must stay in tune with what the customer wants and needs to hear. Supplement customers' concerns by using your logical arguments sparingly. It's always helpful to elicit from them their needs and concerns. Ask some open-ended questions: "How do you feel about this item?" "What else do you need to know?" "Will this meet all of your expectations?" In doing so you can use your logic and analysis as needed, without wielding it in a heavy-handed fashion.

IF YOU'RE A FEELER

Your overriding concern is the customer's satisfaction. And your desire is to do whatever is necessary to make the sale while keeping the customer happy. But those two objectives aren't always in sync. If, for example, a customer falls in love with something that you don't think is right for him, you'll find yourself in a dilemma. Moreover, your and the customer's objectives may be at odds with those of your employer. "I know this guy really can't afford it," you might say to yourself, "but I'd like to see him have it, so I'll give him an extra discount." That may be good salesmanship and no doubt noble, but it may not be a smart business decision.

It's important at times to separate your personal concerns from what's good for the customer and for your employer. You're not there to rescue the customer or to save the world. Your mission is to make a sale and to make a customer feel important and essential, but within the bounds of company guidelines. Rather than overempathizing with the customer, you might want to step back and stay objective. As you listen to the customer's concerns, realize that they're not your problems and that you are not responsible for solving them. It's nice to give support, which you will do quite easily. But monitor yourself before you get in over your head—or your heart as the case may be.

IF YOU'RE A JUDGER

Your strength is in completing the sale, in getting the customer to make a decision and see it through to final payment and delivery. Your decisive nature conveys confidence, helps uncertain customers decide, and gives all buyers the sense that they've done the right thing. But "knowing" what is the right thing and imposing it prematurely or dogmatically can lose a customer in a hurry. If you sound too rigid or too much in a rush to make a sale, the customer may soon feel like a second-class citizen—"Don't I have anything to say about this?"—and may end up being on the defensive.

Because your tendency is to give answers, it might be helpful to deliberately refrain from doing so. Instead, try asking some of the same open-ended questions we recommended for Thinkers above. Remind yourself to be patient, flexible, and responsive to the customer's needs. Difficult as this may be to do, don't worry about making the sale; if you give the customer room to move, it will happen on its own.

IF YOU'RE A PERCEIVER

It's natural for you to follow the customer's lead, adding options where you feel it is appropriate. By doing so, you can convey enthusiasm and make the customer feel very important. You are adept at knowing whether the customer wants to buy or is "just looking," whether they understand what they want and what they are looking at or whether they need more information. But if you're not careful, the entire process can go nowhere. You can become so consumed with the process—providing information, suggesting alternatives, just letting things happen—that even a decisive customer can become uncertain, impressed but confused by all that you have presented. In being too flexible and open, you can lose the sale.

Try to focus on a few definite points you want to make about a product that you believe will move a sale to closure. If you'd like to offer options, limit yourself to one or two, no matter how many may be at your disposal. Avoid your tendency to run down "side streets," keeping the conversation focused on the potential purchase. Difficult though it may be, don't hesitate to push on occasion for a customer's decision— "So, shall I put this aside for you?" Or, "I think this is the one you should get." Or, even more boldly, "Great. Then it's all settled. I'll wrap it up."

Sales

IF YOU ARE AN . . .

	EXTRAVERT	INTROVERT
EXTRAVERT	• Be quiet and let your client talk; ask questions to facilitate disclosure. • Try not to interrupt clients while they sell themselves. • Edit yourself: Not everything you want to say needs to be said.	• Remember that the client's need to talk, connect, and disclose is more important than your need to have space and silence. • Don't be afraid to repeat yourself. • Smile, nod your head, and be physically expressive more than you think is necessary.
	EXTRAVERT	**INTROVERT**
INTROVERT	• Above all, don't crowd the client's space. • Remember that the client's need for silence is more important than your need to talk. • Be aware that silence with interest in the client breeds confidence in the salesperson.	• Bear in mind that while you both may be comfortable with silence, you may have to take the lead. • Don't assume something is happening during a silence—ask what is going on in the client's mind. • Think about what you would appreciate a salesperson's doing and then do it.
	SENSOR	**INTUITIVE**
SENSOR	• Remind yourself that the client knows what the product is. • Be prepared to talk about the product's practical aspects. • Keep in mind the fact that there is a high probability the client has checked out the product's facts and details.	• Be cautious with embellishment. • Be prepared to share three details or specifics about the product. • Remember that generalities will frustrate and puzzle the client.
	SENSOR	**INTUITIVE**
INTUITIVE	• Remember that too many facts will overwhelm the client. • Be prepared to talk about at least three of your product's big-picture possibilities. • Remember that your client wants to be inspired and thrilled about his or her purchase.	• Be prepared to talk about how useful and practical the product is. • Remember that the client might be more interested in exploring options than in finding out what the product actually is or does. • Be careful about being led down conceptual side streets. Stay focused.

LEADING AN . . . .

IF YOU ARE A . . .

	THINKER	FEELER
THINKER	• Avoid arguing the pros and cons of a product with the client. • Remember that it never hurts to massage your client's ego. • Keep in mind that it is logical to try to establish some personal, friendly relationship with your client—to facilitate this and future transactions.	• Remember that your client will close more readily when he or she feels confident. • Recognize that rejection of your product or pitch is not a rejection of you. • Tell the client why the product is the logical choice.

	THINKER	FEELER
FEELER	• Remember that your client may tend to personalize everything. • Explain how the client will benefit personally from the purchase. • Be aware that your client will close more readily when he or she likes and trusts you.	• Though schmoozing may be fun and easy, remember that selling is the central focus. • Don't avoid stating your point of view, even if it feels stressful to do so. • Remember that this is about your client's needs, values, and desires—not yours.

	JUDGER	PERCEIVER
JUDGER	• Allow clients to be right, even when you suspect they are wrong. • Bear in mind that you don't always need to give directions and suggestions. • Instruct your client: "Let's take ten minutes alone to make sure we're not overlooking any options or deciding too quickly."	• Suggest: "Let's take a few minutes alone to make sure we're not overlooking any options." • Your client will probably appreciate your flexibility, but will also welcome your direction and opinions. • Your client may be relieved when the sale comes to a close and could become anxious if you present additional data and options.

	JUDGER	PERCEIVER
PERCEIVER	• Suggest: "We've covered a lot of options—why don't you take a few minutes to reflect on everything we've talked about." • Be aware that while your client will probably appreciate direction, you should avoid being overbearing. • Remember that what seems to you like gentle direction may feel smothering to your client.	• Suggest: "We've covered a lot of options—why don't you take a few minutes to reflect on everything we've talked about." • As the client vacillates, it is okay to rule out certain things and to give suggestions and direction. • If the client is vacillating, create some quiet time and space for him or her to sort things out.

LEADING A . . .

Wrapping It Up

In the end the key to being a star salesperson—or for that matter a savvy consumer—is self-awareness. Knowing your strengths and limitations, and being able to monitor yourself in a sales transaction, allows you to be in command of the situation and to accomplish what everybody wants—a successful sale.

16

Typewatching from 9 to 5

Q: "What's the book about?"
A: "About two hundred fifty pages."

By now you've gotten a good taste of what Typewatching is all about at work. But we've barely scratched the surface of how helpful Typewatching can be in a wide range of situations. In our first book, *Type Talk*, we described in detail how Typewatching is useful in relationships—with friends, lovers, spouses, and so on—as well as in education, parent-child relationships, and other situations where it's necessary to "read" others effectively.

We've said throughout this book that "type begets type"—that where they can control the choices they make, people are drawn to others who share the same preferences. Whether hiring, socializing, or joining organizations, people tend to look for others like them. In our experience this is true in everything except marriage and childbearing.

The following type tables offer some hard data that show exactly how true this is throughout the workforce and how some types naturally gravitate to—or are pushed toward—the top rungs of the ladder.

The tables are culled from our own data base of more than twenty thousand individuals at hundreds of companies to whom we've administered the Myers-Briggs Type Indicator. They represent every level of organizational life, from entry-level positions to chief executive officers. They come from Fortune 500 multinationals to mom-and-pop start-ups. They also span many industry sectors—banking, food processing, insurance, accounting, law, manufacturing, communications, high-tech, and a very large sampling of government and military personnel, including every branch of the armed forces, from private to general, seaman to admiral.

One common myth among corporate, government, and military circles is that these entities are quite different from one another. Our data proves this myth false. Typologically four-star generals and senior executive service personnel are nearly identical to chief executives; majors and government managers closely resemble middle managers in the corporate world; and entry levels in all three systems look remarkably alike. Indeed, we had considered producing separate type tables for each group, but found that there was little difference among them.

If there was any difference at all, it had to do with gender. Women, it seems, get a little better break in government and the military than in the corporate world. We found a slightly higher percentage of women—and Feelers in general—in higher-ranking positions in those sectors. In general all three worlds are highly Thinking-Judging and therefore more statistically male than female.

Entry-Level Personnel

At the bottom of the organizational hierarchy is the broadest spread of the sixteen types. As you will see, as one climbs the ladder of success, this is no longer the case. Thinkers and Judgers will become the leaders, creating a production-oriented, accountable reward system in which goals, schedules, and deadlines are more important than creativity, innovation, and strategic planning.

Entry Level (Number = 1,320)			
ISTJ 19%	ISFJ 8%	INFJ 1%	INTJ 3%
ISTP 8%	ISFP 9%	INFP 5%	INTP 2%
ESTP 5%	ESFP 5%	ENFP 5%	ENTP 2%
ESTJ 16%	ESFJ 8%	ENFJ 2%	ENTJ 2%

Middle Managers

As one begins the climb up the ladder, self-selection starts to take over. Already we can see that Feelers and Perceivers have begun to disappear, either staying at the bottom or dropping out and opting for other vocations. Whereas the entry-level group was 58 percent Thinkers, the middle managers are 86 percent Thinkers. ISTJs as a group show up strongly here, as they will continue to do at higher levels.

Middle Managers (Number = 4,789)			
ISTJ 29.6%	ISFJ 2.6%	INFJ 1.5%	INTJ 10.1%
ISTP 4.2%	ISFP 1.0%	INFP 1.4%	INTP 3.2%
ESTP 3.3%	ESFP 1.1%	ENFP 1.3%	ENTP 6.0%
ESTJ 19.9%	ESFJ 2.8%	ENFJ 1.8%	ENTJ 9.9%

Senior Managers

The typological pyramid is getting less diverse at the top. These senior managers—branch and division chiefs and their principal deputies—are now 93 percent Thinkers. Extraverts and Sensors have taken a slight edge, making up about 56 percent of this population.

Upper Management (Number = 5,300)			
ISTJ 20.7%	ISFJ 1.7%	INFJ 0.6%	INTJ 11.2%
ISTP 3.9%	ISFP 0.1%	INFP 0.6%	INTP 5.5%
ESTP 2.8%	ESFP 0.2%	ENFP 1.3%	ENTP 8.1%
ESTJ 22.8%	ESFJ 1.6%	ENFJ 1.1%	ENTJ 17.7%

Executives

The very top of the organization is overwhelmingly TJ—95 percent Thinking and 87 percent Judging. Sensors mirror the overall U.S. population, comprising about two thirds of this group. Extraverts and Introverts are roughly equal, with a slight edge toward Introverts. It's also interesting to note that INTJs and ISTJs are represented in numbers way out of proportion to their representation in the overall population. What about the ISFP? They represented 9 percent of the entry-level workforce,

Executives (Number = 2,245)			
ISTJ 32.1%	ISFJ 0.5%	INFJ 0.2%	INTJ 15.8%
ISTP 2.5%	ISFP 0.1%	INFP 0.4%	INTP 1.3%
ESTP 1.0%	ESFP 1.0%	ENFP 0.8%	ENTP 5.3%
ESTJ 28.0%	ESFJ 0.9%	ENFJ 0.7%	ENTJ 9.4%

somewhat higher than in the overall population. At the top they are barely present. Where have they gone? If they're female, they have likely dropped out of the workforce altogether. Males will probably have carved out a trade for themselves, most likely in service-oriented jobs—beauticians, chefs, paramedics, and dental assistants, for example.

Training (Number = 2,951)			
ISTJ 6.0%	ISFJ 2.5%	INFJ 3.0%	INTJ 8.0%
ISTP 1.0%	ISFP 0.5%	INFP 4.0%	INTP 2.0%
ESTP 1.0%	ESFP 2.5%	ENFP 25.0%	ENTP 7.0%
ESTJ 8.0%	ESFJ 7.5%	ENFJ 8.0%	ENTJ 14.0%

Trainers and Educational Specialists

We've separated this to show how very different (indeed, nearly opposite) this group is from the people for whom they provide training services. Here is where the NFs and SFs have gone if they have stayed with the company; the group has eleven times more Feelers than are present at the executive level. Overall this group is heavily E (73 percent), N (71 percent), F (58 percent), and P (43 percent)—designing and implementing programs for a largely ISTJ workforce.

Career Guidance: Take This Job and Love It

Nowhere are the gifts insight Typewatching provides better demonstrated than in helping individuals seek and enhance career choices. The Myers-Briggs Type Indicator correlates highly with many respected career-guidance testing instruments, such as the Kuder Occupational Interest Survey/Strong Interest Inventory, suggesting that certain types do thrive in certain occupations.

It's important to keep in mind that the MBTI does not measure skills and abilities, only personality preferences. With a little effort any type potentially can perform any job. However, there are natural fits, and the more one knows about one's personality, the more one's career choices can be made from a position of self-confidence. We've used Typewatching to help hundreds of people sort out and make sense of their career paths, from high school students to those facing midlife crises to individuals who are seeking postretirement careers. We're constantly impressed with how increased understanding of one's natural preferences can open up a variety of job possibilities that would otherwise have been overlooked.

In choosing jobs and careers, most of us are influenced by a variety of individuals and circumstances; these influences can blind us to the range of possibilities to which we might otherwise be attracted. Young people in high school, for example, get a lot of direction from parents and career counselors. In midlife one may be getting in touch with natural skills and abilities that for years may have been kept under wraps. The tug-of-war created between what one "has always done" and what one "would like to do" is a crisis indeed. Retirees often want something different from what they've been doing—sometimes something completely opposite—but are often at a loss as to what that something could possibly be.

In all of these cases, and in many others, the key to success is heightening one's self-awareness. Enter Typewatching. There's no better way to get a fix on who you are, where you are, and where you'd like to be.

It's difficult to choose from the many career-counseling stories we've encountered as Typewatchers. Perhaps most notable is the tale of a young college student we'll call John, hell-bent on becoming an engineer. That, after all, was his father's career, and as his father's firstborn son, it was incumbent upon John to continue the legacy. The problem was that John, an ISTP who had demonstrated high intelligence and ability to work effectively to solve problems, while interested in the subject of engineering, had little interest in spending several years in college studying abstract introductory courses that seemed irrelevant to him. The esoteric nature of the courses did not appeal to his need for hands-on, immediate gratification. He had definite interests in practical aspects of engineering, but the first year in college did nothing to nurture those interests.

By the end of the first year of school John decided to drop out, to the dismay, frustration, and anger of his parents. This in turn put him into a tailspin of self-punishment. For this remarkably gifted young man, college just didn't have much to offer.

We used Typewatching to help both John and his parents see that there was nothing wrong with any of them; they just were very different types. John's parents, both Sensing-Judgers, believed in tradition, direction, and security, and believed strongly that college was the proper route to achieve that. John, as a Sensing-Perceiver, was more inclined to take life a day at a time, feeling that college would always be there if he felt the need for it. Right now he wanted to get his hands dirty, filling his days with hands-on projects and experiments. In acknowledging the differences, both sides were able to allow John to stay out of college yet maintain self-esteem and still feel supported by his family.

Another career-guidance case involved Beverly, a talented thirty-nine-year-old INTJ who had a lifelong career pattern of moving from job to job. In each case she rose rapidly but became impatient with what she perceived as the incompetency and rigidity of those around her. In each case she would leave in a huff, feeling she had not been appreciated for the good work she had done. Her former co-workers wrote the whole thing off as the product of one woman's arrogance. What followed for

Beverly was inevitably a deep depression about her own inadequacies and failures.

In discovering the intricacies of her preferences, it became apparent that Beverly was very true to her type: independent, a quick study, and an excellent systems designer. And true to type, she had little patience for details and implementing the very systems she designed and could not understand why others would not readily endorse her ideas. As she put it, "The company saw my brilliance; that's why they promoted me. I know my ideas are good and practical ones. I know where the company should be going. Why won't everyone else get on board?"

The problem was that in her own INTJ way she had little sense of other people's needs and little awareness of how to sell her good ideas to each of the disparate individuals, many of whom had been at the company much longer than she. We helped her to understand that such behaviors were very typical of her type and, while very frustrating, could be seen as assets instead of liabilities. The issue was to couple her vision and her management skills with an awareness of the human element. In doing so, Beverly became more patient and less arrogant, realizing that others could disagree and still be cooperative but that she had a responsibility to listen to and respect opposing points of view.

Five years later Beverly can still be volatile but has come to appreciate differing points of view. She knows that her initial resistance to them is just being true to type, but she has learned to communicate her resistance in a constructive way.

It's this whole notion of being "true to type" that seems to get many people unstuck in their careers. Whether you are switching jobs or just being more comfortable in a current one, the process begins with viewing the situation through a Typewatching lens. For example, in thinking about a particular job or position, you might consider:

- How much of the job is Extraverted—dealing with the public, handling phones, attending meetings, taking care of public relations—and how much of it is Introverted—working

HOW TO KEEP EXTRAVERTS FROM EXTERNALIZING EVERYTHING

- Suggest that they ask *themselves* a few more questions.
- Give a verbal signal that it's time to change roles, *from speaker to listener*.
- In meetings build in time for *interaction*.

alone without much interaction with co-workers or out-siders?

- How much of the job is Sensing—dealing with tangible and immediate issues and using practical hands-on skills—and how much of it is iNtuitive—requiring an overview of an entire project or system and making connections between and among several ideas, projects, and people?

- How much of the job is Thinking—involving objective and impersonal decision making, and careful, analytical handling of what needs to be done, regardless of what others think or feel—and how much of it is Feeling—involving interpersonal dynamics and making decisions that promote individual and group harmony?

- How much of the job is Judging—meeting deadlines, staying punctual and organized, and being accountable—and how much of it is Perceiving—dealing with the unplanned, tending to emergencies, and responding to whatever comes up?

It is likely that few jobs will fit your personality preferences perfectly. Lacking a perfect fit doesn't necessarily mean you aren't suited to a particular job, but the more preferences that fit for you, the less stress you'll be likely to encounter and the more satisfying each day's work will be.

HOW TO KEEP INTROVERTS FROM ISOLATING THEMSELVES

- Suggest that they ask *other* people a few more questions and add a few more lines to their explanations.
- Give a verbal signal that it's time to change roles, *from listener to speaker*.
- In meetings build in time for *reflection*.

We said it before but we cannot stress this too strongly: Type-watching aside, any individual is perfectly capable of succeeding at any job. But Typewatching can provide the insights that can increase the odds for success.

Professional Development: Keeping Round Pegs Out of Square Holes

Businesses spend billions each year on professional development—training, continuing education, career planning, and all the rest. And yet while professional development is a valuable experience for just about every employee, not all employees will be attracted to all types of programs. Take strategic planning, for example, or anything involving the mid- to long-term future. iNtuitive-Thinkers will thrive on such topics, while Sensing-Judgers would be more productive having the day off. The point is, different types need different projects to make them stretch and grow. If you try to stick a round individual into a square training program, metaphorically speaking, that individual is all but doomed to fail. That failure, in turn, may well set the individual up for a downward spiral within an organization. The bottom line is that a manager's good intentions may end up undermining an employee's motivation and commitment.

As professional trainers ourselves—we have trained over ten thousand individuals in administering the Myers-Briggs Type

Indicator—we have had much firsthand experience in this arena, particularly in the Sensing-Thinking-Judging corporate world. Our success can be attributed to at least two things: constant feedback from our audiences and continual refinement of the design of the training seminars. After fifteen years we're still perfecting it, fine-tuning our messages based on audience feedback. Although we are strong iNtuitive-Feelers—naturally drawn to interpersonal group learning models that emphasize self-awareness and theory—our largely Sensing audiences continue to respond that their training with us is practical, logical, and instantly applicable.

And that underscores the number-one Typewatching lesson around training programs: As a trainer don't assume that everyone is like you. In fact, the opposite is likely true. If you're a trainer and enjoy your job, there is a high probability that you are typologically very different from the bulk of the people attending your training.

Training experiences of most any kind are designed by iNtuitives, and though they use practical words throughout the event, the overall message often emphasizes strategies and visions over hands-on specifics and practical experiences. Training education departments are overwhelming NFPs and NTPs, who are designing the event for what we know to be largely Thinking-Judging audiences. If you take a look at the type tables in Part III, you'll see that trainers are overwhelmingly almost exactly the opposite types of middle- and upper-level managers—the trainees. Furthermore, when these training programs are designed, trainers (usually iNtuitives) seek feedback from colleagues rather than from participants (usually Sensors). As a result the field test is conducted on friendly turf, and the feedback is likely to be more positive than negative, however off the mark it may really be. To be sure, both sides need each other, but iNtuitives' arrogance often does not lend itself to feedback about the specific problems of the design, and Sensors' impatience with the abstract is not very conducive to fostering good communications that would produce a better training product.

So, how can these two different worlds come together?

We believe that the information-gathering preference—Sensing versus iNtuition—is the most important starting point when considering anyone's professional development. For starters, Sensors and iNtuitives learn very differently from each other. Sensors want to see the usefulness of training, cut through the theory, keeping it simple and practical, thereby reinforcing the bottom line, whereas iNtuitives want to see the big picture from the start. They want to challenge the presenters with questions that deal with the "whys" and "wherefores" of the training: "What are the implications?" "How can I use this?" "Why are (or aren't) we instituting this now?"

In her book *Gifts Differing*, Isabel Briggs Myers points out that Sensing students find theory dull and iNtuitive students find facts boring. So a program based half on a theory and half on facts is doomed to be both dull and boring.

In the best of all worlds one would know the type of every trainee from the start. With such information in hand one could allow for individual differences and design sufficient diversity into the training program to keep everyone interested. There would be opportunities for Extraverts to express themselves, Introverts to reflect, and so on.

However, given that we're rarely in the best of all worlds, here are some tips to keep in mind when planning a training program:

■ **Provide balance.** By doing so, you will cover the areas where each individual is most confident and naturally skilled. However, good training needs to explore areas that are new and challenging in such a way as to cause participants to grow in their individual paths. For example, a class in sales, while affirming Extraverted skills (cold calls, hyping, being gregarious), should allow the opportunity to develop Introverted skills as well (listening, reflecting on the customer's behavior, monitoring one's own behavior). A class on accounting, while needing to provide basic details about professional practices, would do well to include such intangible things as clients' needs or stress-reduction techniques. A class on leadership development, while concentrating on visioning and developing

awareness of the big picture, needs to heighten the importance of the immediacy of daily routines in order to point out
the interdependency of both in the leadership equation.

In each case there needs to be enough of the basics to meet
the primary objectives but also enough stretching in less-
popular but necessary areas related to the subject matter so
that trainees are pulled beyond the ordinary.

- **Consider both the majority and the minority.** Often courses
become tunnels of content, styles, and routines, with very little change occurring over the years. If you learn differently or
have different needs, you may not fit into the course structure. Any design for any training course needs to be field-
tested on various types of audiences before it is instituted.
We know, for example, that in any population of corporate
trainees there will be more Thinkers and Judgers. Moreover,
depending on the trainees' specific mission, there are likely to
be more Sensors than iNtuitives and, at least at midmanage-
ment, there are likely to be as many Extraverts as Introverts.

Given these probabilities, the things that will come naturally to most audiences are logic and analysis, presented in a
very organized, scheduled way. If the audience is more Sensing than iNtuitive, they will prefer to deal with specifics in a
very grounded and realistic fashion. Even if the audience is
largely Introverted, having come out of a system that has traditionally rewarded Extraversion ("One third of your grade in
this class is based on classroom participation"), they know
they will be expected to participate verbally. Balancing that
with their less-preferred styles—iNtuition (theory and visioning), Feeling (subjective and interpersonal aspects of
business), and Perceiving (not always being bounded by a
rigid plan or schedule)—is necessary and beneficial to
growth, but if not approached with Typewatching's principle
of respecting differences, it will only result in resistance and
negativism.

- **Remember Introversion.** Perhaps the greatest insight that
Typewatching can lend to professional development and

training is that Introversion is best accessed, achieved, and ultimately shared after the individual has first had time to reflect, contemplate, and meditate. Most training events ignore this altogether, or at least assign it to evening time rather than to class time. A genuine opportunity to jot notes, to be quiet and think, even to relate in small groups or one-on-one during the training event, not only legitimates the importance of the Introverted learning model, but says that the designer of the training event is interested in having the participation and contribution of all types.

Funny Business

Everyone loves a good joke, but true to personality type people differ widely in the way they relate to humor. Some types are natural joke tellers. Others love to hear them but can never remember them. Still others are excellent at puns and repartee but do not do well with a standard joke with a beginning, middle, and end. Even the practical joker is a particular type.

The eight personality preferences give us a frame of reference for adding a humorous touch to all of life:

- Extraversion legitimizes laughing at others.
- Introversion legitimizes laughing at ourselves.
- Sensing helps us to laugh at the absurdity of reality.
- iNtuition permits us to find humor in the unrelated aspects of life.
- Thinking helps us to laugh at life's less funny moments.
- Feeling facilitates laughing at the intimacies that sometimes scare us.
- Judging allows us to laugh at the confinement of schedules and routines.
- Perceiving lets us laugh at our absentmindedness and forgetfulness.

The eight preferences tend to be specialists when it comes to humor. Extraverts would rather tell a joke than listen to one.

SCALES OF JUSTICE

Thinking-Judger: I'd rather be assailing.
Extraverted-Feeler: I'd rather be fishing for compliments.

Introverts love hearing a good joke because it makes them laugh out loud. Puns and limericks are the domain of the iNtuitives, whereas literal humor belongs to Sensors. Thinkers can tend toward harsher humor, such as sexist and racist jokes; whereas Feelers, who laugh at (but are filled with guilt by) such humor, much prefer jokes that are warm, happy, and reflect life's good times. Judgers are the best storytellers because they are naturally organized, whereas Perceivers are marvelous with spontaneous one-liners. Perceivers, and especially Sensing-Perceivers, are the practical jokers, whether perpetrator or victim; they don't mind being "had" because it intensifies the challenge to "get you" the next time around.

In the spirit of leaving the reader laughing, here are eight jokes that we think illustrate the eight preferences.

An Extravert Joke

An E, working at a supermarket produce department, is approached by a customer who asks to buy half a head of lettuce. The E, disbelieving, responds, "I don't know. I'll have to ask the manager." He approaches the manager, unaware that the customer is following him. Shooting from the lips, he says, "Some idiot wants a half a head of lettuce. . . ." Suddenly realizing the customer is standing right behind him, he continues without missing a beat, adding, ". . . and this gracious gentleman has consented to buy the other half."

An Introvert Joke

It's a rainy day. The first-grade teacher is getting her kids dressed to go home. She struggles for five minutes with one child's boots and shoes, tugging them on and getting them laced up. Just as she's finished, the Introverted child says, "Those aren't my boots." The teacher sighs and spends another five minutes undoing everything—unlacing, unbuckling, tugging, and refitting. Just as she's finished, the child adds, "They're my brother's. My mommy said I had to wear them today."

A Sensor Joke

There's the true story of President Calvin Coolidge, the Introverted-Sensor of all time. At a dinner a guest sitting next to him said, "I have a bet with my husband that I can get you to speak three words to me." To which Coolidge coolly replied, "You lose."

An iNtuitive Joke

Two thieves are pulling off a breaking-and-entering job in a high-rise office building. Suddenly they hear someone approaching. The iNtuitive thief says to the Sensor, "Jump out the window, or we'll get caught!" The Sensor says, "You've got to be kidding. We're on the thirteenth floor!" To which the N replies, "This is no time to be superstitious. Jump!"

A Thinker Joke

Jim asks his brother, Sam, to dog-sit while he's out of town. The first night away Jim calls to check on his dog. Sam, a Thinker, tells him bluntly, "Your dumb dog died." Jim, clearly upset, scolds his brother for his insensitivity: "If you had a sensitive bone in your body, you would have broken it to me slowly. You would have told me, 'Your dog had an accident.' When I called tomorrow, you would have said, 'Well, the dog's condition has worsened.' And on the third night, I would have been ready for the bad news. By the way, while I've got you on the phone, how's Mother?" To which Sam replied, "Well, Mother's had an accident."

A Feeler Joke

A man with a glass eye accidentally swallows it one day. Two weeks later he visits his doctor and complains of stomach pain but doesn't mention anything about the glass eye. The doctor, examining the patient, asks him to bend over. When the doctor takes a look, only to find an eyeball looking back at him, he says, "Listen, if I'm going to help you, you've got to learn to trust me."

A Judger Joke

There's a flash flood carrying everything down Main Street. A young boy, watching it out the window, notices a red hat that floats by but turns at the corner of the house, only to reverse direction and float by again. Amazed at this phenomenon, the boy calls for his mother. She calmly replies, "Relax. That's your father. He said he was going to cut the grass today, come hell or high water."

A Perceiver Joke

A budding actor, a Perceiver, is finally hired to perform a one-line role in a play. The line is "Hark! Is that a cannon I hear?" For two weeks the actor practices feverishly, repeating the line over and over again. By opening night he has mastered every aspect of his role and in dress rehearsal has performed to everyone's satisfaction. The director, sending him out as the curtain goes up, gives the final instruction: "Remember, the whole play is riding on that line." The P walks out on stage, and there is immediately an enormous KABOOM! In surprise the actor blurts out, "What the *hell* was that?"

Okay, so maybe these jokes wouldn't bring down the house in Las Vegas. In fact, whether you found them funny—or even appropriate for this book—depends in part on your personality preferences. That's not the point. What's important is that each of us gets something different out of almost everything in life. It's valuing these differences that makes for a more satisfying workplace—and a more satisfying world.

17

Some Final Thoughts

We've just covered a tremendous amount of information and it may be overwhelming, to say the least. Yet Typewatching is, in its essence, a fairly simple concept. We've found that the four key points below represent the most important things you need to keep in mind. They are also a starting point for making Typewatching practical on a day-to-day basis.

1. **Learn your four letters.** Most important of all is to validate your type and commit it to memory. Once you determine your four-letter type, it is very important to be sure it's really you. The best way to validate it is to read your profile in Part III of this book and underline those parts with which you agree and disagree. (To get the fullest picture possible, we recommend that you refer to the set of profiles in our previous book, *Type Talk*, which covers attitudes and behaviors beyond the workplace.) If you find you disagree more than you agree, try another profile, altering just one letter. Soon one of the profiles will emerge with which you are most comfortable. There are other sources on Typewatching that may be helpful, including audiocassettes and videocassettes. (Contact us for information about many of these materials; our address can be found in the back of this book.)

Next, select a few people who know you well and ask them to read the profile you've chosen, asking them for feedback on it. Specifically you want to know from them how accurate it is in describing you and the ways it is most accurate and most inaccurate.

Keep monitoring your own behavior—through your own daily experiences and feedback from others—to give you an even sharper focus on your type.

If you do nothing else in Typewatching, do this. Use your four letters almost like you'd use your name—as a way of describing yourself to others.

2. **Mind your Ps and Js.** Having learned your four letters, the next key step is to understand two basic things about Perceivers and two basic things about Judgers that can greatly facilitate communication at work.

- If your last letter is P, no matter what the other letters are, it's your nature to generate alternatives. That is your contribution to the workplace—your creativity and your dynamism. When it's time for brainstorming, by all means be sure to have plenty of Ps on hand.

- Ps decide by the process of elimination. Often Ps know more clearly what they don't want than what they do want. So, in any decision-making situation, it's important to help the Ps sort things out.

- If your last letter is J, no matter what the other letters are, it's your nature to moan. Js moan about everything, even things they like and want to do. Don't interpret a J's complaining as disapproval. They may be reacting to other circumstances, such as the fact that your request interrupted whatever they were doing.

- When giving a J a new idea, use the "hit-and-run" technique: Drop the idea in his or her lap, get out of the way, and come back and discuss it later. That will give the J time to moan—if only internally—before he or she puts the item on a list so that it can be dealt with on its merits.

3. **Take some shortcuts.** The shortcuts in this case have to do with something called Temperaments. It is an attempt to make the complex system of Typewatching more manageable and allow you to become proficient more quickly. By combining certain letters you can simplify the number of preferences you are dealing with at any one time, facilitating your understanding of another's type. Granted, it's not as accurate as the full four-letter descriptions, but it is a way of getting a handle on some of the things that make the workplace work—or not.

There are four two-letter combinations that are particularly effective: NF, NT, SJ, and SP. Everyone falls into one of those four categories. Here are two potential strengths and weaknesses of each of these combinations:

- **NFs (iNtuitive-Feelers—INFP, INFJ, ENFP, ENFJ):** Their strengths include their ability to persuade and cooperate. These are the team builders. Their weaknesses include an overpersonalization of organizational problems and their tendency to carry grudges.

- **NTs (iNtuitive-Thinkers—INTP, INTJ, ENTP, ENTJ):** Their strengths include their ability to think systemically and strategically. These are the natural analysts. Their weaknesses include their tendency to make things more complex than necessary and their impatience with incompetency.

- **SJs (Sensing-Judgers—ISFJ, ISTJ, ESFJ, ESTJ):** Their strengths include their strong sense of responsibility and duty to the organization. These are the organization's backbone. Their weaknesses include their rigidity and narrow focus on meeting rules and regulations.

- SPs (Sensing-Perceivers—ISFP, ISTP, ESFP, ESTP): Their strengths include their ability to do a variety of tasks with ease and their sense of urgency when the situation demands it. These are the organizational troubleshooters. Their weaknesses include their disinterest in routine and their lack of a sense of the big picture.

4. **Think opposites.** True, it can be hard enough at times viewing the world through a Typewatching lens. But sometimes it's helpful to go one step farther, viewing a situation through the eyes of your opposite preference or type. For example, if you are an Introvert who has really come to enjoy and trust your inner reflections, every so often try to blurt out some verbal response. We'll guarantee it will throw just about everyone around you off their guard, but it can become a vehicle through which you can come to accept and develop your nonpreferences.

   Why would you want to do this? Let's go back to one of our original analogies—left- versus right-handedness. As a right-hander, you will add richness and versatility by being able to call upon your left hand with some level of confidence. As you probably know, this doesn't come easily, but with practice, age, and maturity, it can be done. Please understand: A right-hander will never, ever become a lefty— and an Introvert doesn't become an Extravert—but as Isabel Briggs Myers said, "One develops a capacity for one's nonpreference."

   Thinking opposite has another advantage: It allows you to be more aware of and sensitive to those of other preferences and types. It's like that old Native American adage, Never judge another person until you've walked in his moccasins. Having some familiarity with the way other preferences think and act will help you appreciate those differences and avoid making quick, negative judgments.

   Here are a few ideas to help you think opposite:

- **Extraverts:** Your tendency is to "shoot from the lip" and talk over others. Try counting to ten and maybe saying nothing. Trust someone else to say what you thought of saying. And if he or she doesn't, let the matter drop. Listen, listen, listen. Maybe even repeat what's been said before adding your own thoughts.

- **Introverts:** Your tendency is to reflect, contemplate, and stay aloof, keeping your thoughts to yourself. Try blurting out a response, saying something with no intent of measuring its worth or meaning. Deliberately waste some words and be a bit redundant. Repeat: Be a bit redundant. Say it again, Sam.

- **Sensors:** Your tendency is to stay grounded and keep your focus firmly on the issue at hand. Try to back off and let your imagination run wild. Generate ten positive possibilities about tomorrow or next week.

- **iNtuitives:** Your tendency is to revel in endless possibilities and enthusiastic visions of the future. Try to experience as many sensory events as you can crowd into five or ten minutes. Taste, touch, smell, see, and hear the world around you without trying to find any meanings in any of it. Experience the moment.

- **Thinkers:** Your tendency is to be objective and impersonal. Before making a decision, think about the other person's point of view. Actually use their words and ask yourself, "How do I feel about what's happening?"

- **Feelers:** Your tendency is to want everyone to be in agreement and harmony. When disagreement erupts, try not to rescue one side or another. Push against the situation—argue for the sake of arguing. If voices are raised, no matter what, do not become intimidated. Keep saying to yourself, "It's only an exchange of ideas, it's nothing personal."

- **Judgers:** Your tendency is to want closure, organization, and schedules. Try just to let things happen. At least once a day, try to let one thing that bothers you go unattended. Work on appreciating that it may never be taken care of. Ask yourself, "Will any of it make a difference a year from now?"

- **Perceivers:** Your tendency is to have many irons in the fire and pursue endless options. Try to finish at least one thing of some importance, even ahead of schedule, if possible. Cover the bases and promise yourself not to be distracted until you reach your goal of the moment.

Armed with just these four key points, as well as some of the insight you've learned from the previous chapters, the rest is up to you. Learning to be a proficient Typewatcher is much like learning any new skill, such as playing the piano or learning to speak French. At first you begin by copying others—practicing scales or learning dialogues, for example. As you gain confidence and experience, you will gradually be able to become more proficient—writing your own music or carrying on unrehearsed conversations. If you work at it hard enough, it will eventually become second nature.

We don't expect everyone to become hard-core Typewatchers, however. That's not the point of this book. If you've only picked up one new insight about yourself or someone with whom you work, it's all been worth it.

III

The Sixteen
Profiles at
Work

Introduction

In our first book, *Type Talk*, we offered comprehensive profiles of the sixteen personality types, detailing their behavior throughout their lives—as children, parents, mates, even as senior citizens. The profiles that follow focus primarily on the relationships and situations of the workplace.

Be careful: The danger in creating typological profiles is that they are usually viewed as rigid boxes encompassing an unvarying and static set of characteristics. That can make them more confining than liberating, ironically defeating the whole point of Typewatching, which is to allow room for you to be yourself and for others to be themselves. We do not intend these profiles to be the final statements; rather they are intended as points of reference for insight into yourself and others. Remember the Third Commandment of Typewatching (see page 47): It is only a theory; it takes real life to validate it.

There are several ways to validate your profile. First and foremost is to highlight those parts with which you agree and note the parts with which you disagree. Next, you might consider soliciting feedback about your profile from those who know you well—your mate, your staff, your co-workers, perhaps even your kids. These individuals will confirm or counter what you saw about yourself in the profile; where they disagree with you will provide the basis for a highly insightful discussion about others' perceptions of you. Furthermore, you might want to read the profile of your four-letter opposite—the ENFJ profile, for example, if you are an ISTP. Such a reading should provide a sharp contrast to your own preferences, helping to put your own profile into perspective.

Typological profiles have been accused from time to time of being like astrological horoscopes: general statements broad enough to encompass everyone. That's simply not true. These profiles are based on sound theory and empirical observation of human behavior.

Most typological profiles previously written have been more positive than negative. This concurred with the affirming nature of Typewatching in general: It is a psychological model based on health and wellness rather than on sickness. The workplace-oriented profiles on the following pages break that trend. Because the workplace, with its stresses and demands, often engenders a variety of behaviors that are not all positive, and because people often get tripped up by the negative side of a boss or a subordinate, we felt it was important to spend some time describing the various weaknesses that can plague each type. We believe it is important to know the potential stumbling points if you are to be well equipped to deal with the demands of the workplace.

Still, there are many strengths to be found in each profile. The more we can integrate those strengths and recognize the shortfalls, the more we can live with—and even prosper from—each other's differences.

How to Use the Profiles

The profiles below can be useful in several ways:

- First and most important, they can validate your own personality type. Whether you have taken the Myers-Briggs Type Indicator or simply tentatively identified your four preferences from reading this book, the profiles can substantiate your findings, showing how the four letters interact to create a unique personality type. In reading your profile, if you find yourself agreeing with most of the statements, you have likely reported yourself accurately. It may be helpful as you read the profile to underline and highlight those parts with which you strongly agree or disagree.

- Next consider sharing your profile with someone who knows you well, perhaps a co-worker, boss, or subordinate. Consider asking that person to highlight the parts of your profile with which he or she strongly agrees or disagrees. That will give you some powerful feedback about whether others perceive you as you perceive yourself.

- This exercise can also work in a group situation. Sharing profiles, and having them available at crucial moments—before meetings, on deadline, during crises—can help keep lines of communication open and allow each individual to use his or her strengths and be mindful of particular weaknesses.

- Another possible use of the profiles is in coping with individuals who may be giving you difficulty at work. If you know—or can at least guess—their four preferences, reading their profiles may provide some insight into the source of the problem. That can open the way to communication and resolution.

Life's Natural Organizers

This is the quintessential dependable, responsible type—hence the quintessential manager. Just like the work world itself, ISTJs are driven by accountability, productivity, and the bottom line. It is a natural and often happy fit.

ISTJs see the world in terms of facts and tangible realities (Sensing), which they prefer to deal with in an objective fashion (Thinking). Their day-to-day living is driven by structure, schedule, and order (Judging), and their Introversion makes them appear somewhat cool and aloof. Appearances can be deceiving, however, because ISTJs often excel when it comes to achievement, accomplishment, and social skills.

ISTJ is a no-frills, work-hard, play-hard type. They are seen as compulsive, hard-charging, capable, and true to their word. They live by the bottom line and can be very cost-conscious. They can be slow to change, but once they see the practical value in making a course correction, they can be quick to implement it and often become zealots of the new way of thinking.

While all Thinking females swim upstream in our society, this is particularly true for female ISTJs. The responsible, driven nature of this type, while admirable, flies in the face of traditionally "feminine" traits. Moreover, as traditionalists at heart, ISTJ females are inwardly conflicted about trying to balance the conventional feminine roles—mothering and nurturing—with their objective, organized (TJ) nature. A typical response to this dilemma is to work harder than ever, to the neglect of even some health issues. While ISTJ men are the least likely to have a weight problem, weight and bad eating habits can plague ISTJ women more than some other types.

Among the many strengths of the ISTJ is the ability to act quickly and, very often, correctly. They have a propensity for beginning projects and staying with them through completion. This drive is aided and abetted by their dogged determination for covering all details and staying specific. It is the ISTJ who has given the workplace so many of the "scripts" by which we operate: "An idle mind is the devil's playground." "Waste not, want not." "Work as hard as you can, save as much as you can." "Hard work never hurt anyone." "Anything worth doing is worth doing well." "A penny saved is a penny earned." Clearly ISTJs work to live and live to work.

For ISTJs work comes first, then family and community responsibility. When all of this is in order, then it is okay to schedule some play. These are the compulsive types who "bring the office home" at the end of the day. If it's a family-owned business, it is expected that the entire family *will* be involved. There is no choice in this matter; if everyone contributes, everyone will benefit.

The ISTJ is often very calm and cool, even somewhat unexpressive or undemonstrative. This can be a strength in some situations, particularly stressful ones, when ISTJs appear rock-solid. This makes them more effective in many of life's emergencies, from operating rooms to battlefields. Indeed, ISTJs predominate throughout the military, from enlisted personnel to general officers. While ISTJs themselves comprise only about 6 percent of the general population, they comprise about 30 percent of the U.S. armed forces. The ISTJ's four preferences are found overwhelmingly in the military: the combined army, navy, air force, and marines is 58 percent Introverted, 72 percent Sensing, 90 percent Thinking, and 80 percent Judging—ISTJ.

If anyone invented the chain of command, it would probably be an ISTJ. Throughout the business world, whether a megacorporation or a mom-and-pop shop, they establish a structure and work it most effectively, expecting others to do likewise. When they are lower on the organizational ladder, when given an order, being Judgers, they may first complain, then obey by delivering the goods. Farther up the ladder they give orders and expect obedience. If they don't get it, they are prone to take names and kick ass. They live by shoulds, and they impose them freely. They get the job done.

Unfortunately they sometimes get carried away. ISTJs can be the personification of compulsivity, driven by such things as deadlines and bottom lines without regard to employee motivation, satisfaction, or well-being. Striving for efficiency, they may instead produce a workforce full of hostility, stress, and absenteeism. In the process other types can get weeded out, resulting in an even more ISTJ-oriented organization. The result is compulsivity to the nth degree.

ISTJs not only drive others to the brink, they can also inflict severe damage on themselves. This comes partly from their combined control and compulsiveness, which can lead to an attitude of "If you want it done right, do it yourself." This sets them up for long, lonely hours of doing everything—or at least doing the same thing over until it's right. In fact, more than any other type, ISTJs are capable of literally working themselves to death.

ISTJs also can get tripped up by their high need for privacy and their low need to express themselves. As a result others have trouble "reading" the ISTJ, sometimes creating serious communication gaps in an organization. Without saying a word, they may give off an aura of being impatient and even disapproving when that isn't necessarily the case. As a result there's an unwitting "show me" or "prove it" stance to the ISTJ's demeanor: Show me how it will be cost-effective; prove to *me* that you're right. The ISTJ's inexpressiveness often results in others feeling frustrated, flustered, or on the defensive. It may come as no surprise that ISTJs frequently make good loan officers.

Their inexpressiveness extends to giving praise, something they do with difficulty. It is expected that work be done in a timely fashion, neatly, and correctly. Therefore, believes the ISTJ, why would one praise what should be done? Your paycheck is praise enough—and if you last twenty years, we'll throw in a gold watch.

The ISTJ's no-frills style can lead to a workplace that is plain, austere, and conservative. Other types may find that it's not much fun to be working or spending time in such an environment. (Someone once quipped that ISTJ stands for "I Seldom Tell Jokes.") Such "amenities" as a comfortable chair, office decor, and extracurricular activities can often be seen by an ISTJ as a waste of time and money. In the long haul their quest for efficiency can sap employee morale and motivation.

The good news is that given good direction, ISTJs can make outstanding employees, managers, and leaders. That "good direction" usually comes in the form of a strict set of rules and regulations. ISTJs approach life much as a pilot approaches takeoff: No matter the task, to be effective, it is imperative to have a kind of "preflight checklist" giving specific, tangible instructions about what to do in a given situation. So, if good managers say, "Good morning" and "How are you?" every day to employees (even though it may seem unnecessary for productivity's sake to do so), once they are on the checklist, such greetings become something that is done over and over until they are an integral part of the ISTJ's management style.

While many organizational activities can be scripted and included on an ISTJ's checklist, not everything can. Most critically, what cannot be scripted includes those things having to do with pondering the big picture (iNtuition) and coping with interpersonal dynamics (Feeling). The big picture represents the unknown to the ISTJ, and the unknown is often more bad than good. Hence, too much "strategic planning" becomes a waste of time and things that managers do to avoid what needs to be done today. There won't be any future—or even a plan to implement—if someone doesn't pay today's bills or stay on top of the current crises. As a result the ISTJ can get blindsided by the unexpected, because the focus on today means that there is no contingency plan when surprises arise. So, it is far more effective to be doing something constructive and useful today than to wonder about tomorrow.

Subjective, Feeling-type decisions are another area in which the ISTJ can be found wanting. The entire world of interpersonal dynamics is difficult for this type since it is not predictable and can't be controlled. It is the epitome of the "soft" sciences, which are abhorrent to the ISTJ because they cannot be researched and measured quantitatively. As a result ISTJs would rather avoid, or even deny, the existence of seemingly "touchy-feely" situations, even though these could include such innocuous encounters as saying "Thanks for your help," discussing as a team some work project, or having a beer with the troops after quitting time. These things can actually frighten an ISTJ because they can include so many unknowns and a high risk of losing control. Even more frightening are genuine interpersonal situations—an upset employee, for example, or someone expressing frustrations with his or her job. A quivering lip or the possibility of a tear being shed can paralyze an ISTJ, who is afraid of losing control and feels totally incapable of managing such situations. Furthermore, the ISTJ sees such behavior as inappropriate and unproductive, to say the least. Inevitably the ISTJ will react by tightening the control ("Stop that. Crying never solved anything") or simply denying the problem altogether ("Let's just forget this and get back to work").

Compounding all of this is the fact that it's inevitable that an ISTJ will end up managing and working with at least a few Feeling types. These individuals respond to a whole different array of motivations than the ISTJ—fun, harmony, happiness, personal fulfillment, and social responsibility, among others. The more ISTJs can understand and accept these differences, the more they can realize that they needn't control or deny such seemingly unacceptable behavior, the freer they will be to let others behave true to their own type, with greater productivity the inevitable result.

The same problems that confound ISTJs in the workplace can trip them up in the marketplace. Not understanding that half of the buying public is driven by such intangible things as appeal, looks, image, and just plain feeling good, ISTJs can create products that possess engineering perfection but lack marketability.

Historically, great innovators have been plagued by this very dilemma: Henry Ford's Model T, which worked great but failed to keep up with fashions, is a classic example. From carpets to car parts, ISTJs can often overlook the personal appeal that the Feeling side of preferences brings to a situation. Fortunately, true to their type, ISTJs who fully understand this potential blind spot have the capacity to equip themselves to overcome it, either through greater self-awareness or by surrounding themselves with other types who can fill in this missing dimension. To an ISTJ this can be just one more aspect of life for them to manage effectively.

The unknown, the future, and the unplanned are all stress inducers for the ISTJ. With their high need for accountability, they can become very edgy, if not angry, if deadlines are being ignored in favor of last-minute, seemingly harebrained aspects of a project. Even relatively simple things can trigger stress. For example, if a meeting is scheduled to end at 4:00 and someone raises a new concern at 3:57, the ISTJ will likely experience a rise in adrenaline, pulse, and anger. Anything that will help the ISTJ enjoy sensory awareness—touch, smell, taste, and so on—without seeming too irresponsible can provide spurts of refreshment and stress reduction. For them, stopping and smelling the roses (or watering the office plants), while extremely difficult for them to do, is absolutely necessary for their good health.

ISTJs' excellence in completing tasks and organizing life gives them a natural edge as leaders at all levels of an organization. The various accountability and productivity demands of all organizations, from meeting deadlines to staying within budgets to achieving production goals, are natural areas in which ISTJs excel. In addition to the basic management of equipment and personnel, they are well suited for a variety of positions, including certified public accountants (who require a focused and objective attention to details, must meet strict deadlines, and usually work alone), surgeons (who must be singularly focused, work by the book, and not get overly involved with their patients), and police and detectives (who must stick to "just the facts," stay objective, and work within the strictures of the law).

ISTJ

- **Workplace Contribution:** Establishes order dutifully and steadily and works within the system to manage and complete tasks on time and under budget.

- **Pathway to Professional Growth:** Must learn that both organizational change and people issues—ideas that may violate tradition—can play powerful and positive roles in organizational life.

- **Leadership Qualities:** Brings tasks to completion efficiently and dutifully while maintaining respect and order throughout the group or organization.

- **Team Spirit:** Teams, if well managed, are a good way to distribute tasks and complete projects, but the important work that is done is carried out by individuals when the team meetings are over.

Committed to Getting the Job Done

America. Motherhood. A Hot Lunch for Orphans. Each is interchangeable with *ISFJ*. Bound by fierce commitment, intense responsibility, and deep loyalty, the ISFJ is the embodiment of putting service above self in most aspects of their lives. Unless you've experienced this type, it's hard to believe that someone can be so dedicated and dutiful in so many aspects of his or her life. It is amazing how nobly they work behind the scenes, allowing many great things to happen and glory to be afforded to others. This is a direct result of the ISFJ's stringent personal sacrifice and their dependability.

Cautious, reserved, quiet, and inwardly oriented (Introversion), ISFJs are content to work quietly by themselves. Their perceptions of the world are realistic, grounded, and present-oriented (Sensing), and they use those facts and realities to make decisions that are interpersonally driven (Feeling). They prefer to live their daily lives in a structured, ordered, accountable manner (Judging).

ISFJs can become so wrapped up in serving others that they are soon taken for granted. It is such a noble pattern that many other types perceive them in disbelief, assuming there must be a catch somewhere. Or at least that the ISFJ is keeping score and will, some day or another, cash in his or her chips. But that's not the case. The ISFJs' mission and desire is to serve, and one of their great treats is to see someone they have helped succeed as a result of their benevolence.

The ISFJ female fits most of society's norms, including the martyristic suffering-servant image. While other types become protective of the ISFJ female or angry that she allows herself to be taken advantage of, very little actually happens in the workplace to change this situation. When gender issues surface at work—charges of inequitable salaries, for example, or inadequate maternity leave—they will most likely be raised by an iNtuitive-Feeler—male or female—or a Thinking female, much to the shock and amazement of the ISFJ female. She may even send signals that such provocative behavior by others is most inappropriate. As such the ISFJ female unwittingly serves as a pawn for the status quo. Though she may agree with certain dissenting points being voiced, she still believes that change should take place through the chain of command, not in opposition to it.

Such a commitment to duty and obedience can also be a problem for male ISFJs, especially if they have climbed the corporate ladder. They have probably done so by playing a more traditional male role during working hours, offering strength and tough-mindedness when needed. The ISFJ male must decide early on whether to give in to the Feeling-Judging side of his personality and exhibit a more nurturing demeanor, or play to more publicly accepted male expectations. Should he acquiesce to society's demands to be more Tarzan than Jane, given the ISFJ's natural caution about self-expression, the resulting turmoil can lead to ulcers, weight gain, or other stress-related problems.

Who would not want an ISFJ in the workplace? The qualities of being organized, pleasant, and a dependable team player is a manager's dream. One only needs to be around an ISFJ for a short while to realize how pleasant and quietly gracious they are. Like other Feeling types, ISFJs do not cope well with conflict, so when office strife arises, they prefer to take a blind eye or bury it deep within themselves in the hope that it will soon disappear.

Other types, especially Extraverted-iNtuitives, can become impatient with ISFJs in two areas. One is the somewhat slow, deliberate, methodical—some call it boring—way they approach specific tasks. Those types more prone to a seat-of-the-pants flamboyancy find the ISFJ's quiet, self-effacing dependability ir-ritating at best. Equally troublesome to others is the way that ISFJs let people take advantage of them—their cheerful readi-ness to be helpful to anyone at any time. Others view this as the ISFJ's low self-esteem, but in fact it is the ISFJ's high sense of duty that keeps them so committed. Interestingly, those who have a low tolerance for such blind loyalty don't necessarily stop taking advantage of the ISFJ's generosity; they only become im-patient that the ISFJ allows it to happen.

ISFJs can have high expectations of themselves and others re-garding rules, regulations, appropriate behavior, and a series of other *shoulds* and *oughts*. Breaking them or being disrespectful is a no-no, and if one reaps the ISFJ's scorn, then forgiveness can be very slow in coming. ISFJs are one of the backbones of the organization as well as a key part of its institutional memory. While other types may brainstorm the great ideas—from new products and programs to the next office party—little or any of it will happen without the deliberate, detailed follow-through of the ISFJ.

Once ISFJs befriend someone or become committed to a project, their patience is considerable. They will persevere to complete the task, notwithstanding overtime; setbacks in mate-rials, dates, or personnel; and personally performing at any level necessary, from sweeping the floors to hosting a reception. Like other Js they may moan about all the work, but unlike Ex-traverts they will keep it mostly to themselves. As good Fs they are always willing to pitch in and make a sacrifice for the good of the organization. While this feeds into their perception as mar-tyrs, for the ISFJ it is a self-fulfilling process.

Another strength of the ISFJ is their tolerance for detail and routine. They are motivated by established ways of accomplish-ing something and will work best when one expects them to do things "by the book." Likewise, when the ISFJ is in charge, he or she will expect subordinates to work within established rituals. If you follow the rules, says the ISFJ, you'll get it done and you'll reap rewards. If you break the rules, you'll be punished for the resulting failures. For the ISFJ this is a system that works.

The quiet support and affirmation generally associated with ISFJs are powerful assets in the workplace. It is a gift to be able to affirm others—at work or wherever—ahead of oneself. To give credit where credit is due is expected and reasonable, but it is purely ISFJ to let others get credit for work you have largely done. If everyone benefits from what has been accomplished, and the workplace is better for it, that is reward enough, thinks the ISFJ. The ISFJ is the ultimate team player. Moreover, for the ISFJ any activity can be part of a team endeavor. So, an ISFJ nurse is part of a "healing team" whose goal is everyone's good health. ISFJ teachers are part of a "community-family team" whose goal is to raise children. ISFJ clergy are part of a "spiritual team" whose goal is to offer moral guidance. ISFJ clerical-support staff are part of a "management team" whose goal is to deliver a good product.

Their sense of duty and obligation can also become a liability for ISFJs. They can become so hooked on commitment that they almost become doormats for the rest of the organization. There are times when ISFJs ought to be more assertive of their own personal needs, especially when others take advantage of them. If they are not careful, ISFJs can wear an invisible sign that says, "Here I am, take advantage of me." They would do themselves and others a service if they would work at being more vocal and direct about their own needs. However difficult, this is absolutely necessary.

Another weakness of ISFJs can be their inability to see the forest for the trees. They can get so caught up in the immediate service or need that they lose track of just about everything. Having attended to the crisis of the moment—whether an accounting problem or a person in need—they suddenly find themselves tired, drained, and quite irritable because there are still seven hours to go in the workday and they have spent all their energy. When ISFJs get overextended, they exhibit wide mood swings, becoming very disjointed and spacey, going quickly from fits of boisterousness to intense introspection.

Though it takes a great deal to strike the ire of an ISFJ, when that finally happens, it will come in the form of a stubborn, unforgiving, unbending way. Often this is followed with a flurry of anger that can include a laundry list of pent-up issues—about work, people, or anything else in range, regardless of whether it's related to this event or individual. Once that happens, there is little chance for recovery, and the response is totally disproportionate to the event at hand. Had the ISFJ tried to share some of these concerns all along, they would not have festered, allowing the ISFJ to deal directly with the problem at hand.

Notwithstanding these potential weaknesses, our institutions and organizations would simply not work so effectively were it not for ISFJs. They serve as role models and inspiration for so much of what society deems good and noble. That, coupled with their tenacity, is why life happens so beneficially for so many of us. Some ISFJ somewhere is working behind the scenes, putting things together that we can then have, use, and enjoy.

ISFJ

- **Workplace Contribution:** Offers quiet support, a sense of order, and attention to detail from behind the scenes.

- **Pathway to Professional Growth:** Must learn to be open to new possibilities and changing situations—this flexibility can often be the support someone most needs.

- **Leadership Qualities:** Produces results through one-on-one relationships and detail control and tends to perform tasks oneself rather than delegate.

- **Team Spirit:** Teams are worthwhile work units, vital and important structures that are yet another arena in which to provide quiet, unassuming support to the organization and its people.

INFJ

An Inspiring Leader and Follower

Wherever scholarly dependability is needed in the workplace, there's no better person to turn to than an INFJ. A popular human-services–oriented type, most of their energies, at work or at home, are directed toward bettering a condition, especially the human one. No one word does justice to the complexities of the human personality. However, the word "gentle" continues to come to mind when thinking of the INFJ.

The focus of the INFJ is inward, meditative, and reflective (Introversion), and their perception of life is to see it as filled with endless possibilities and meanings, usually in a big-picture context (iNtuition). These symbols and abstractions are translated through their subjective, interpersonal decision-making preference (Feeling), which in turn is acted out in a lifestyle that is structured, scheduled, and ordered (Judging). The INFJ's iNtuition is Introverted, and the Feeling-Judgments are more imposed on others. The combination is a rather rich and imaginative inner drive that reveals itself in the form of caring and concern for others—with just enough structure to be believable. They're not all talk; they deliver the goods.

Many of the INFJ's descriptors—gentle, caring, concerned, imaginative, interpersonal—are those typically seen as more female than male. As a result INFJ females fit most socially traditional female expectations; one exception might be the aura of mysticism that many INFJs possess. It is only as the INFJ female gets driven by her causes and concerns that she may be less than pliable and therefore more threatening to the male-dominated workplace. When this occurs, it can become compounded because as the male pushes for facts and objectivity (a typical Sensing-Thinking model), the INFJ female can appear less than grounded—but no less firmly committed. At such times the ST male pushes harder and harder, only to be stymied in the INFJ's rigid (Judging) but idealistic (iNtuitive-Feeling) issues. Still, INFJ women are respected for their intellectual acumen and are seen as generally soft, gentle, and caring at work.

In our society these same characteristics in males are problematic. INFJ males are confronted with a difficult situation: Their natural caring gentleness is threatening to others in the workplace, particularly other males. The INFJ's colleagues, superiors, and subordinates alike are prone to wonder, "Who is this person? Is he a man? A wimp? A guru? A flake?" The INFJ is aware of this paradox. He knows he is different from society's norm, and he feels society's pressure to be tough and macho. That leaves him with inner turmoil and with jammed circuits in his body.

All INFJs are more likely than most other types to suffer illnesses of the stomach and lower colon. It is almost as if they are punishing themselves for being unable to reconcile the public's expectation of their gender with their natural preferences. This can apply to women as well, but in our clinical observations, we have seen this much more in men.

In most cases the solution to this situation probably is not medical. It begins with an awareness of the dilemma and a recognition that INFJs are naturally adept at meditation—anything from a discipline such as yoga to the simple opportunity for a few minutes' quiet reflection. INFJ males would do well to take advantage of this for a few moments each day, even at company expense, for some sort of a meditative release. Such a break allows them to continue to be productive and allows others to benefit from their special contributions.

Outside of the clergy and perhaps private-practice psychology, it is not an easy lot to be an INFJ male at work. His intense concern internalized can become a heavy daily burden. It can also set them up for a martyr complex ("I'm so concerned about

Sam, but he doesn't even seem to hear, let alone appreciate, my concern. Poor me"), which serves no one effectively.

The INFJ's overall work style brings a good balance of schedule and accountability with an awareness of others' needs. INFJs are particularly reticent when it comes to conflict and often know ahead of anyone else when it is about to erupt. Their Introverted-iNtuitive-Feeling provides a radarlike perception that can serve as an early-warning system. Unfortunately, this ability flies in the face of their intense fear of conflict. The result leaves them debilitated. They bury the trauma in their Introversion and hope that it will simply go away.

INFJs like neatness and order at work and prefer a setting of quiet congeniality, a place where each person can be affirmed for his or her contribution, each feels a sense of accomplishment, and all work harmoniously toward some common good. Such qualities are extremely valued in the teaching profession, helping students to think for themselves and to appreciate learning; of course, in the faculty lounge between classes the process will continue. These same traits are equally valued in other professions, as INFJs share some friendly exchange, insight, or inspiration.

INFJs' strengths include their intellectual prowess, their personal idealism, and their general caring and concern for humanity. The combination of their four letters leads them to pursue the theoretical and accomplish most goals by which academic achievement is measured. Few people fully appreciate the rich inner life of the INFJ and how steeped it is in imaginative, creative, abstract ideas and concepts. The INFJ can easily spend an entire day just dreaming and envisioning. Such pursuit is its own reward, and to be allowed to do that—and to encourage others to do the same—is what life is all about for the INFJ. Consequently, any task or event will always be the richer if he or she can first place it in some conceptual frame of reference that includes thinking it through thoroughly. INFJs' nonstop search for learning, self-growth, and development—and wishing the same for everyone else—makes them very reassuring to others and people worth emulating. Their keen insights and generally strong character are an inspiration to all.

Feeling types as a rule are idealists, and INFJs (along with their cousins, the INFPs) lead the pack. This is interesting, because while they are not given to rocking the boat, when an INFJ's ideals are on the line, it seems that he or she can take on any odds and win. So, if the issue is better pay for teachers, it will be the INFJs who will present it to the public in a formidable fashion. They may be less likely to walk the picket lines or make speeches, but they will no doubt be a driving force nonetheless. Suddenly this pliable, gentle, concerned INFJ can become a strong-willed determinist who faces a cause equipped with the intellectual foundation that can render opponents defenseless. Whatever the cause, you won't do badly having an INFJ on your side.

It is not unlike an INFJ to wonder why everyone isn't affirming, honest, and productive with one another. There is no need for war, believes the INFJ, only improved understanding. INFJs are the embodiment of the Golden Rule and the notion "Let there be peace on earth, and let it begin with me." That is what INFJs give, that is how they live, that's what they want from everyone, and as much as possible, that's where they put their energies, at work and at home. Though their Introversion may make them somewhat slow to give strokes freely and easily, they can nevertheless be counted upon to stand by those to whom they feel loyal. Their interest in their fellow human beings is fierce, firm, and genuine. Life is generally a better place because INFJs have passed through it.

INFJs are not without their shortcomings. For example, they have a tendency to become severely depressed when their ideals go unfulfilled. It is amazing how quickly the strength of the INFJs' rich inner imagination can turn to discouragement when others don't readily join or support their cause. What was inspiration now spirals ever inward toward self-punishment and deep-seated feelings of failure. Guilt becomes overriding and depression abounds. In such cases the INFJ tends to distort reality and to bury himself or herself in a barrage of despair, ending in "No one gives a damn. How foolish of me to have thought otherwise."

Another INFJ weakness is their overpersonalization—almost

fanatically so—of events that may not even concern them. Once an INFJ has taken on the cares and concerns of a situation, even a simple office issue can escalate into a major disaster. Once an INFJ has accepted the burden of a problem, it is now his or her total responsibility to save everyone and to make things right. Anything from an unhappy colleague to the needs of a Third World country can be translated by the INFJ as a personal failure. If this eagerness to take on burdens is not checked, the feeling of failure only deepens, giving way to total self-deprecation and punishment. The INFJ's resulting sense of worthlessness can permeate an entire organization.

A third weakness is the INFJ's propensity for making the simple complex, then becoming quite extreme in response—in short, making mountains out of molehills. They

INFJ

- **Workplace Contribution:** Turns work into a cause and injects—with quiet, serious focus—inspiration and devotion throughout the organization.

- **Pathway to Professional Growth:** Must learn that his or her excitement about the future and the possibilities it holds for people is often overlooked, buried as it is beneath a serious exterior.

- **Leadership Qualities:** Provides inspirational and visionary direction with a moralistic or values-related spin, working with focus toward change and development.

- **Team Spirit:** Teams are complex human systems that need understanding and care and that, if well managed, can produce inspirational, valuable work.

can become fanatics, responding to a situation in a manner to-tally disproportionate to what's demanded. A disagreement over a company's new lunchroom policy can quickly move from a simple dispute over rules and regulations into a crusade for ending hunger worldwide. Others are baffled at how this occurs. Moreover, the INFJ will become rigid, with fits of anger followed by extreme withdrawal, making it almost impossible for others to reason with the INFJ.

When such behavior is minimized, the INFJ's contributions to the workplace can be significant. At their best they are imaginative and creative visionaries who are a source of inspiration to everyone. They are often the ones behind the scenes who make others look good, providing words, wit, and wisdom.

Life's Independent
Thinkers

When you consider how few INTJs there are in the U.S. population, it is astounding how much influence on corporate and academic life they have had. Their capacity for intellectual and conceptual clarity gives INTJs both vision and the will to see it through to completion—leadership qualities that are prized in our society. Perhaps more than any other type, the INTJ has played a dramatic role in shaping American corporate culture.

INTJs view the world in terms of endless possibilities (iNtuition), to be manipulated, conceptualized, systematized, and translated through objective decisions (Thinking). These decisions are readily implemented because of their daily lifestyle of structure, schedule, and order (Judging). Their Introversion is the arena for developing their many ideas, which are usually many more than will ever be realized. However, the four preferences combine to convey confidence, stability, competence, intellectual insight, and self-assurance.

These four preferences are things that most people naturally rely on for strength and confidence, especially in the upper echelons of business. INTJs won't embarrass us by Extraverting when we least expect it, but will instead convey confidence that everything is in good hands. Rather than getting locked into details and specifics as a Sensor might, they translate the facts to a bigger picture to provide perspective. While subjectivity may be comforting to most people, it is objectivity that we associate with business. And our society operates and gives rewards based on a J time- and goal-oriented model. The INTJ packages these four qualities in a way that is not only generally appealing but is indeed relied upon for leadership and direction.

There are few things that a well-integrated INTJ cannot conquer with ease and grace. As a result these people are frequently elevated quickly in corporate circles and are looked to for exceptional leadership, which they deliver with aplomb. (We believe that this is the predominant type among Japan's corporate leaders. Their ability to take existing ideas and improve each aspect of them, from design to production to marketing, has been a key factor in that nation's growing domination of world markets in the late twentieth century. One INTJ Japanese businessman even managed to adapt and improve upon the Myers-Briggs Type Indicator. Japan now has the second-largest population of Typewatchers in the world, after the United States.)

Though a single word cannot possibly describe any type, the word *independence* gives a thematic thrust to the overall drive of the INTJ. Clearly this is the force that motivates them. If they could, the INTJ would wish independence upon everyone. This drive for independence can conflict with the INTJ's need to control his or her immediate surroundings. So, colleagues and subordinates must recognize that while independence is the ultimate goal, it is to be meted out as the INTJ deems appropriate.

This apparent inconsistency can lead to some mixed messages. Verbal instructions that indicate flexibility and freedom— "Take as much time as you need and do it in whatever manner you think is best"—can have an underlying message of "Do it fast and do it right." The verbal message reflects the INTJ's Introverted-iNtuitive style, which is contemplative and open-ended. This can appear to conflict directly with their observable Thinking-Judging behavior, which seeks accountability and punctuality. But this is not inconsistent to the INTJ, whose real message is "Every time you do it fast and right, you'll earn more flexibility and freedom."

As a natural conceptualizer, the INTJ is the perfect "think-tank" specialist, intrigued by the future, stimulated with a rich imagination, and undergirded with good accountability. They are often looked to for solutions to complex problems. Consistent with their preferences, they provide direction and leadership with a creative flair. Someone once said that the most socially successful people are those who are independent (I), visionary (N), objective (T), and in control (J). Such individuals can be counted upon for anything; such a person is not always spraying you with his or her needs.

INTJ managers can be perpetual students. Always exploring and envisioning "what might be," their iNtuition is a reservoir of new techniques, programs, incentives, and directions for any system. Their propensity is to improve just about anything, even things that are working well; they'll fix it even if it ain't broke. It is an INTJ tendency to want to redesign IRS tax forms every April 15. This constant restlessness means that everything in the workplace is up for grabs. Constant evaluation and scrutiny— and perhaps revision—become driving forces on almost any project. Even if the mandate is to maintain the status quo, an INTJ won't be beyond trying to maintain the status quo with just a few improvements.

As with all Thinking types, female INTJs face special challenges at work. Many of the traits described above—independence, objectivity, and control—fly in the face of traditional feminine models. Moreover, the INTJ's need to challenge tradition and improve everything can cause friction in the male-dominated workplace. This conflict can lead to rejection by both genders: Males simply don't understand or know how to cope with the female INTJ's independence; other women see the INTJ female as arrogant, caring for no one but herself. Indeed INTJ women often have little patience for women who display traditional feminine characteristics.

Even more frustrating to some people is the INTJ female's tendency to be somewhat aloof: At work she is very carefully defined and extremely professional, guarding every word and action; private life is limited to a few chosen words and is kept quite separate from the office. Their guarded professionalism at work coupled with their seemingly asocial personal life wins them few allies among colleagues. Especially for INTJ females, it's lonely at the top.

The Typewatching maxim that one's strength maximized

becomes a liability is certainly true for INTJs, although they would likely argue to the contrary. The INTJ's rich inner imagination, when left unchecked, can set them up for every form of counterproductivity: suspicion, distrust, and even paranoia. While everyone, especially Introverts, is capable of carrying on internal conversations involving others—who says what to whom and what happens next—INTJs in particular can carry such conversations to an extreme. Their rich reflectiveness can trick them into thinking that an imagined conversation really took place and that subsequent actions were taken. When this occurs, an INTJ's behavior can be marked with self-righteousness, arrogance, and a certain refusal to admit that he or she could be wrong or that the whole episode occurred only in his or her mind. Defensiveness, coupled with TJ self-confidence, can lead an INTJ to assume that others are not only untrustworthy but indeed are out to get them.

Such misplaced projection on the part of the INTJ can be very undermining to others and can leave staff or colleagues permanently wounded. Even then INTJs can be blind to their own destructiveness. Their tendency is to blame others for these circumstances. "If I'm good enough to get this far, then others, not I, must be wrong in their perception or judgment," they'll likely conclude.

Another possible weakness of INTJs is their tendency to give only intellectual assent to various management concepts. Team building, goal setting, and time management are all marvelous concepts—for others. Generally they would much rather write about, think about, or even improve upon any of these ideas than engage in the actual processes.

Like other iNtuitives, the INTJ can become stressed from being bombarded by too many details. Their Introverted-iNtuitiveness would much rather imagine and speculate than put things into action. Consequently, when confronted with demands, especially those related to people's needs and seemingly trivial project details, the INTJ can become edgy, scattered, and even quite depressed. It's good for them to take a few moments out of each workday to allow time for reflection and contemplation. That will help to feed their inner inspirations and allow them to enjoy, even momentarily, the fantasy of "what could be" rather than "what is."

Such potential problems notwithstanding, INTJs can make a rich contribution to corporate culture. Their natural bent for achievement and excellence makes them successful in a variety of careers. Most anything to which an INTJ turns his or her energies can turn to success. They make excellent teachers, especially at the high school and college levels, because they bestow upon their students the gift of independent thinking. They are frequently good writers, administrators, researchers, and lawyers, especially managing partners.

INTJ

- **Workplace Contribution:** Provides organizations and groups with objective clarity, vision, and strategic thinking while driving toward change and improvement.

- **Pathway to Professional Growth:** Must learn that each idea for visionary change brings with it untold details to which someone will need to tend—the stresses brought on by visionary change are real and painful.

- **Leadership Qualities:** Draws energy from the complexity of future possibilities and shepherds individuals and groups through uncertainty and change with decisiveness and fairness.

- **Team Spirit:** Teams are powerful and complicated systems that, if well designed and managed, can play a pivotal role in bringing a group or organization's vision to fruition.

Just Do It

The ISTP is frequently misunderstood and often underestimated. Though very effective at most undertakings, his or her unorthodox way of accomplishing something, coupled with low visibility, can often lead to co-workers' wondering, to quote the people the Lone Ranger saved, "Who *was* that masked man?"

Indeed the Lone Ranger may be an appropriate symbol for ISTPs. They are frequently described with old clichés—"still water runs deep" or "a man of few words"—and they are difficult to read by others and slow to share in public. These qualities (Introversion), coupled with perceptions that are hands-on, tangible, grounded, and very much oriented in the present (Sensor), give the ISTP a somewhat cool demeanor. Decisions are typically objective, impersonal, and analytically driven (Thinking). The ISTP's daily lifestyle is spontaneous, flexible, and spur-of-the-moment (Perceiving), so that no matter what person or event comes along, the ISTP will be inclined to direct immediate attention, albeit privately, to the new set of circumstances.

Frequently ISTPs view the process of getting others involved as a waste of time. Participative management can be very difficult for this type. The ISTP is not opposed to it philosophically so much as psychically: Such a management style requires too much energy and effort to accomplish what to them is simple and obvious. It's not that they're lazy. Quite the contrary. It's just that they'd rather be doing than planning. They would rather be producing results than be bogged down in bureaucratic red tape. They would rather be putting out fires than designing fire drills. The tougher the problem and the quicker they can get to it, the better. ISTPs could probably embody the slogan of World War II's Seabees, a group of engineers that accomplished so much against so many odds: The difficult we do immediately. The impossible takes a little longer.

ISTP women, like other T women, have a particularly difficult problem with role identity and career fulfillment. Often when Introverted-Thinking is combined with Sensing-Perception, one finds a loner who loves the tactile world of craftsmanship. The very word, reflective of generations past, can hardly be said in the female ("craftswoman") or androgynous ("craftsperson") forms. Indeed there is little historically that lends itself to affirming the ISTP woman. At the turn of the century, for example, the ISTP was typified by the tool-and-die maker, the self-taught engineer, the tinkerers who played with the early automobiles—racing them, refining them, constantly handling each part until it was as finely tuned as possible. The grease monkeys, the athletic perfectionists, the oil barons and drillers, the early pilots who flew unpredictable crafts over uncharted courses—all these typify the ISTP spirit. It is for them that the institutes of technology were born a century ago to sharpen the skills of this craft-oriented type. Little of the above comes close to describing the nurturing, gentle traits often ascribed to females. And when it comes to job choices, there is little here that is readily perceived by the public as "woman's work."

And yet there are many ISTP women who are capable, competent, and willing to work at many of these highly technical jobs. Over the last two decades they have increasingly embraced traditionally male occupations, from forest ranger and fire fighter to emergency room surgeon and special police. But all of these roles can leave the ISTP woman questioning her own gender identity while simultaneously alienating the males, who may see her as a "turf invader." The ISTP's disdain for routine and flair for the untried are uncharacteristic of women in this society and are generally not well received in a workplace environment bent on structure and schedule. When the ISTP female appears in a male-dominated role—and proves herself to be as competent as her male counterparts—she sets herself up for endless scorn. Doing "man's work," and doing it better, is not the way to be popular on the job in today's sexist world. It can also raise doubts within the ISTP herself: "Am I normal to like such work? Is there something wrong with me?" She has a need for constant reassurance that her femininity is not measured by or wrapped up in any particular vocation. Both men and women must understand that one's femininity (or masculinity) is not defined by one's job or competence.

ISTP women are more likely to see a job as genderless and be drawn by its special thrills or tangible and immediate rewards. But by breaking from societal norms, they find themselves in direct competition with their male colleagues. It is sad that when an ISTP woman excels at work, so far removed from traditional roles, it becomes major news, whether it is a woman who gets a court order to become a municipal fire fighter or a sports reporter who finds herself in a men's locker-room dispute. Such overdramatization, while perhaps encouraging to other ISTP women, tends to make the individual the exception instead of the norm for a considered section of the population. Furthermore, with the media involved, sides tend to be taken immediately—men versus women—and the real occupational desire and the potential contribution of the ISTP gets lost in the process.

Much as they disdain management theories, ISTPs are uncomfortable with management practice too. The ISTP's overall management style can be abrupt, direct, and often unorthodox. It's a let's-do-it-and-not-talk-about-it approach to motivating others. The problem of course is that many other types need to talk about it before doing it. (Extraverts may want to talk about it *ad nauseam*.) As such, when ISTPs climb the management ladder, it is only done so long as it seems to be an exciting game. As the game wears thin, so do ISTPs' patience; they will be ready to move on at the slightest provocation. If they stick to it, they'll eventually find some way to upset the applecart, if only for the thrill of it.

In a society that throws out and replaces rather than repairs—possessions, people, ideas, whatever—it is difficult to appreciate what skill, exactness, and perfectionism the ISTP brings to life. For the ISTP the naked eye is a perfect plumb, the ear is

the instrument that tunes complex machinery into perfect harmony, the nose analyzes and interprets the various aromas for
the florist, the chef, or the gardener. These are accomplishments of the senses, and to rely on some technical machinery
for such expertise is to deny the special gifts of the ISTP.

A strength of the ISTP is the ability to self-start and to work
independently. As we've said, they're better independent workers than team players. Their perfectionism combined with their
personal integrity results in a job well done with minimal super-
vision. Generally projects that allow some flexibility of schedule
are readily accomplished. They'll get the job done on time, but
not necessarily on your schedule; they do not do well with
PERT charts.

The ISTP's flexibility allows them to adapt easily to unscheduled events that may unglue a more structured type. As long as
the ISTP can see the work progressing, interruptions are almost
welcome because they keep things from becoming too dull or
routine. Change Orders or Project Modification Sheets are frequently met with the response "No problem." This fits perfectly
the ISTP model: flexibility grounded in common sense.

Still another strength of ISTPs is their ability to amass technical data without being burdened by the need to create outcomes, schedules, predictions, or any of the other results often
demanded by the workplace. This makes them excellent research analysts, albeit somewhat slow to publish results. This is
not in conflict with what we earlier described as the ISTP's need
to do rather than to think or plan. In their endless gathering of
data it is the doing—the pursuit of information—that is what's
exciting; indeed the next steps—analyzing and processing the
data—are activities that leave the ISTP cold. We have a colleague who has collected thousands of completed Myers-Briggs
answer sheets. While he has scanned them and garnered some
fascinating insights from them, he has done practically nothing
with that information and finds little need to do so. (Other
types would find this anathema: Extraverts would want the
public recognition, iNtuitives would enjoy exploring the possibilities, Feelers would want to use the data to help others, and
Judgers would want to wrap the project up and move on.)

The bugaboos of the ISTP at work can be summed up in three words: routine, administration, and paperwork. Such statements as "We've always done it that way," "We've never done this before," or "This is the way it should be done" are invitations for an ISTP to break the rules or bend the routine just for the thrill of it. While any of the Perceiving types can become bored with administration, ISTPs in particular have trouble seeing the need for such boring work. For the ISTP, files are where you put things you'll never use again, ledgers are for figures you'll never need again, and Day-Timers™ are where you keep data you never really want. "Life is easy," says the ISTP. "Live it one day at a time, and don't sweat the small stuff. Use your time and energy wisely today, and tomorrow will take care of itself." And what kind of paperwork do you possibly need to keep the world in tune—technically, artistically, and functionally? Paperwork, the ISTP believes, was conceived by someone who wants to keep others from getting things done.

ISTP

- **Workplace Contribution:** Solves problems practically and immediately with a calm, clear-thinking resolve.

- **Pathway to Professional Growth:** Must learn that the complexity of people and relationships deserves consideration and offers no quick fix.

- **Leadership Qualities:** Sets an example to act independently and to attend to the needs of the short term, unencumbered by tradition, procedure, or the demands of others.

- **Team Spirit:** Teams are often an irritation and a diversion from effective, practical work, work that is best done alone.

Action Speaks Louder Than Words

The term "ISFP manager" is almost an oxymoron. Though a significant part of the workforce, they are rarely positioned in a leadership spot and would much prefer a service-related position. Indeed, they are not above passing up a promotion so that they can stay "where the action is." It's not that ISFPs aren't capable, although they do tend to be self-effacing. Indeed they possess some impressive natural skills for relating to all forms of life—plants, animals, and people.

Each of the four preferences feeds each other in helping the ISFP relate to others rather than invading their space. The ISFP begins by focusing internally rather than externally (Introversion) and strives to be sure that his or her own internal world is in order. Their principal goal is not to reshape others so much as to define their own needs and concerns. The world itself is very tactile, immediate, and grounded (Sensing), and this is translated through the ISFP's subjective decision-making process (Feeling). They have a low need to come to closure about any of these things—Introversion, Sensing, and Feeling—preferring to stay open and experience all of it (Perceiving).

As a result, it is this type more than any of the others whose style is to stand by another person (or plant or animal), with no intention to influence it, criticize it, or change it—perhaps not even to interact with it—only to be in its presence. Other types can hardly believe the ISFP's lack of intentions, let alone trust it. There must be some hidden motives, they believe.

Surprisingly enough, there aren't. Live and let live might be the motto of the ISFP.

ISFPs are generally very easygoing, low-key types with little need to influence those around them. They are so low key, in fact, that they can begin to question their own motivations, perhaps even wondering why they're not more given to controlling others and taking charge. Such questions can lead to large doses of self-doubt. Perceivers are generally prone to second-guessing their decisions, often wondering such things as, "If we waited just a bit longer, would things have turned out differently?" When you couple P with internal, here-and-now subjectivity (ISF), most of life becomes a series of what-if, let-it-alone, maybe-tomorrow-will-be-different experiences that leave the ISFP vulnerable to severe self-criticism. All of which is unfortunate because the natural, unobtrusive, accepting manner of the ISFP is not only a great strength—and much needed at all levels of organizational life—but it is also refreshing when encountered in the workplace.

Obviously, because of the preference for Feeling, there will naturally be more female than male ISFPs. ISFP males are rarely given to the macho, tough-guy compensation often found among other Feeling male types. As a result they are quite easygoing and laid back, pleasant to be around and skilled at helping others cope with—or make the most of—the moment, whatever that is. Whether it's helping someone relax, serving as someone's sounding board, or providing an alternative to a sticky problem, ISFPs of both genders are at their best when others are in need.

Like other Fs, the ISFP can get into guilt and self-punishment when a work situation goes awry. Even areas where they had no accountability whatsoever can become sources of overidentification, and undue energy can be spent in sympathizing with the underdog or the wronged or even the guilty party.

Leadership, as we said earlier, tends to elude the ISFP. They can be cajoled into accepting leadership positions, but it is really not the best use of their talents. They can be capable leaders for short periods, but over the long-term, being under the constant fire of deadlines and other pressures will be highly stressful to an ISFP, who would rather remain invisible and behind the scenes. If the position demands high accountability and high visibility, ISFPs will have to expend inordinate energy to rise to the task. Their natural talents lie in the service portion of a given job description. Service, in fact, is the cornerstone of ISFPs' motivation, and they are at their best when what they are doing has a significant service component to it.

Natural strengths of the ISFP in the workplace include supporting and helping others; finding alternatives to seemingly frozen projects or relationships; negotiating options to a problem in a way that everyone wins; troubleshooting difficult situations for more effective interpersonal communications; and, probably more than many other types, keeping people in touch with tangible, attainable goals. It's the ISFP who best helps us see the need to approach a project a bit at a time rather than being overwhelmed by the magnitude of the situation. Any dilemma can be conquered when subdivided into manageable parts.

People work best, believes the ISFP, when they are encouraged and helped rather than criticized. Consequently, when leading they do it by quietly supporting and working with their subordinates as well as their colleagues. Indeed, they may have trouble delineating between themselves and those below them, setting themselves up to be taken advantage of. But this unaggressive management style can also build fierce loyalty among those of their department who appreciate the freedom to work at their own pace and in their own style. Support and affirmation from an ISFP often come in the form of nonverbal self-expression. When you work for an ISFP, you are more likely to receive praise in the form of a deed or an unpredicted gift than a verbal pat on the back. A bouquet, an afternoon off, a special unexpected privilege are all signs of an ISPF's approval. For those who need more overt, direct, and regular affirmation, the ISFP's style can leave them wanting.

A happy work team is a productive work team, believes the ISFP, so energy is better spent in making the environment pleasant in the assumption that productivity will follow. Any excuse for a break in the action—a cup of coffee with a colleague or a moment to listen to someone else's problems—helps to keep things interesting and themselves motivated. Likewise if enough time is not spent in creating a spontaneous environment, then not only can the ISFP become critical and depressed, but this can also become an excuse for low productivity and absenteeism.

Even more than other Perceiving types, follow-through and routine plague the ISFP. It's far more exciting to be working on a new or nonroutine project than just doing the same old thing. It's much more stimulating to respond to some emergency than to be in an appointed place at an appointed time doing the stated assignment. It's significantly more important to rescue some person or animal in need than to be at one's desk, completing whatever was started yesterday. As a result both boredom and listlessness hover over ISFPs and can be their undoing if they are not actively pushing things to completion.

Because of the dichotomy between service to others and shortness of attention, the ISFP can lose interest in high productivity. That is not their interest nor their arena, and they need not punish themselves for not playing the accountability game. Above all it would be helpful for them to avoid the stresses that such high-performance demands can impose on an individual. For the ISFP those stresses can lead to ill health, frustration, even severe depression. It's better for them to focus their energy toward helping others and giving their best to a particular situation, meeting the needs of the moment and letting everything happen the way it will instead of beating themselves up for things they cannot control.

Often the more demanding types set the ISFP up to live or work on the wrong turf, then even join in helping the ISFP's self-flagellation. If an ISFP is a skilled bookkeeper, for example, others might encourage, even demand, that he or she strive for a CPA degree. But the ISFP may have little need for such ambitious achievements, being much more pleased to work responsibly where he or she is. In such a process the ISFP's contribution to the workplace can be lost, and the workplace becomes much less personal because of it. Because the ISFP is easygoing and harmonious, others are seemingly always "shaping them up" to be more like the mainstream or sending them somewhere—especially to therapy—to be "fixed." Even if the "fixing" is successful, what's lost in the process is the ISFP's unique contribution of support, encouragement, and self-enhancement, which most organizations so desperately need.

The ISFP is the type that can get things done, often unconventionally. And other types, especially Thinking-Judgers, find such unconventionality stressful. The ISFP is the type who quietly delivers the goods, knows the shortcuts through the complex bureaucracies, and can make others feel very affirmed and worthwhile in the process.

A severe dilemma in all of this, however, is that our system makes such demands for formal education and advanced degrees that the natural skills of the ISFP are rarely given a chance to be used. It is the ISFP at his or her best who embodies the humanistic ethic and who, when given the chance, quietly lives it. Deeds are always more fitting than words to the ISFP.

Professions such as teaching, especially grade school, clergy, any of the religious orders that involve service, nursing, paramedics, and clinical and educational psychology are all naturals for the ISFP. The bad news is that these careers frequently demand such prolonged academic training that few ISFPs can maintain interest long enough to succeed. In the nonprofessional workforce one finds the ISFP in the skilled crafts—butchers, bakers, and candlestick makers. Unfortunately, it is just these skilled, hands-on crafts that are increasingly outmoded in today's high-tech world. All of which helps to create a bigger "supply" of ISFPs for a work world that doesn't seem to "demand" them.

While Saint Francis of Assisi and Mother Teresa are probably perfect role models for an ISFP, a contemporary model might be Charlie Brown, the "Peanuts" character. He assumes the role of baseball team manager, only to his constant distress and undoing. His Introversion won't let him even say hello to the little red-headed girl, and his Sensing-Perceiving side will risk everything to try to kick the football, despite the high probability of failure. His Feeling side—indeed his whole type—is personified by his classic line "How could we lose when we were so sincere?"

ISFP

- **Workplace Contribution:** Supports people and their efforts with a gentle—almost anonymous—attention to detail and action in the moment.

- **Pathway to Professional Growth:** Must learn to focus on the patterns and problems beyond immediate concern—to look for and confront the systemic or root issues and not to get lost in the foreground, solving only the problems of today.

- **Leadership Qualities:** Leads by example—by tending to task details and providing gentle, unassuming support.

- **Team Spirit:** Teams are fine and can be fun, though they are personally draining and intrusive; quiet support and diligent work are what make teams effective.

Making Life Kinder and Gentler

Whether leading or following, INFPs work best and are more productive when the effort reflects some ideal or service. Work performed for the sake of work, or meaningless routine, can render this type listless and perhaps even rebellious.

Clearly INFPs are best when whatever they're doing serves their personal values. However, if they can at least translate the work into some sort of meaning or human service, it may make something they don't want to do somewhat worthwhile. For example, learning computer work for its own sake, while initially stimulating, will wear thin in no time. On the other hand, the same work, if it can lead to teaching or serving of others through computers, will be endlessly stimulating and satisfying.

For the INFP reflection and contemplation (Introversion) are coupled with a preference for abstract, futuristic, imaginative perception of the world (iNtuition). They make decisions subjectively, based upon personal values (Feeling), but such decisions are more directed toward keeping their own house in order than toward overtly controlling others. The INFP's day-to-day lifestyle is easygoing, flexible, and adaptive (Perceiving). All of which makes for a reserved but warm and gracious type who is frequently comfortable to let everyone "live and let live." It is only in the domain defined by their values that the INFP can become somewhat controlling. But that only happens when he or she feels something personally important has been invaded.

When INFPs are simply a part of the workforce—as opposed

to running it or being responsible for some part of it—it is only necessary that they find personal meaning in their work to be motivated. As their sphere of influence increases, so may accompanying controls. As a co-worker an INFP may stand by idly as you perform your job poorly. "It's none of my business, and you'll pay your own dues" is a typical INFP mind-set. But as a supervisor, or if your behavior has an impact on the INFP, he or she can indeed become quite (albeit somewhat subtly) controlling. Like other Perceiving types the INFP may not even be aware that you've stepped over that fuzzy boundary until it happens. Coupled with their Introversion, which impedes direct confrontation, it can make life a little frustrating for both parties: for you, because you were caught unaware of your misdeed; and for the INFP, who may have a reaction to the misdeed that is much more intense than is ever communicated and who may even be surprised by the suddenness and intensity of his or her own feelings. While it may seem out of character for this otherwise congenial and flexible type to become so rigid and unyielding, it's not out of character at all when one understands the unique nature of the INFP's four preferences.

In hard-charging executive positions the INFP is the exception rather than the rule: You'll find precious few INFPs as chief executive officers. However, when it happens, senior-ranking INFPs generally engender fierce loyalty among their subordinates. They usually do a good job of blending productivity with compassion for the workforce. While the genuine respect others feel for an INFP superior may get in the way of specific disagreements, and while open conflict may be dramatically eschewed, those who work for INFPs enjoy the freedom to develop personally, receive generous affirmation, and have a ready, willing, and supportive ear for almost any idea. Even if you try and fail, as long as you haven't offended the INFP's personal values, he or she will affirm and encourage you for your effort.

If you do manage to offend the INFP's value system—and remember, no one may know of the offense until well after the fact—then forgiveness may be very slow, if ever, in coming. The situation is compounded because the INFP's Introverted-

Feeling side may never forgive or forget. But their imaginative flexibility side—iNtuitive-Perceiving—will continue to give off accepting, easygoing "It's okay" indications. For example, if it's an Extraverted-Judger who goofed and said, "I'm sorry," and the INFP responds typically ("It's okay, it was nothing"), then the EJ would naturally assume that the apology has been accepted and the matter is settled. But that may not be the case at all.

Though INFPs are underrepresented in the general U.S. population, there will statistically be more females than males simply because more females share the F preference. Where one finds INFPs in positions of power and control is in the realm of movements or institutions centered around social causes. One only need think of some cause—such as Mothers Against Drunk Driving, Women's Lib, the Myers-Briggs Type Indicator itself—in which one person was the driving force behind a cause, promoting something better for some group—and an INFP will inevitably be that person.

The male version of the INFP usually assumes leadership positions in an effort to merge his vision with some sense of accomplishment. When that happens, the INFP male will be a highly inspirational leader, though routine details can be a bore and can lead to his undoing. He may also get hooked into some more macho behaviors in an effort to compensate for the congenial, tenderhearted, softer male image others may see and criticize. He may take an unyielding position or a tough stance just to prove his mettle.

A disagreement or an opposing point of view can be stressful to any INFP. It can also give way to the dynamic discussed above, where apparent surface-level tolerance of the disagreement belies a very sharp judgment. INFP males and females, in their desire to let others develop and be independent, can often be torn between direct influence (because the issue is important to the INFP) and gentle persuasion (so that the person involved can feel he or she has influenced the end result). If this process is not carefully executed, it can be read by others as manipulation and deviousness on the INFP's part. The INFP's four-letter opposite, the ESTJ, is most likely to be the one to interpret such behavior this way and the one who will be most offended by it.

An INFP manager once told us, "Once I have made up my mind to do something, my job as executive is to do it in such a way that the staff feels they have accomplished it."

When the workplace becomes too toxic or negative, the INFP can become restless or uneasy, falling into avoidance patterns typical of Feeling types. Tardiness, hypersensitivity, uncharacteristic mediocrity, and minimal effort are some of the behaviors that may begin to surface. All of this can grow into near-manic swings between sullenness and raging criticisms. The criticisms often carry previous baggage totally unrelated to the situation of the moment ("And that's not all. I've also had it up to here with . . .").

Such behavior is uncharacteristic for an INFP and indicates the presence of some stressor. If not checked early, the stress can fester, eventually escalating into bouts of ileitis and colitis, both of which are particularly prevalent in INFPs. Such problems can be minimized by offering INFPs a listening ear and encouraging them to talk through their issues. However, as Introverts they will find this difficult to do, however beneficial they may recognize it to be.

Because of their intellectual astuteness, competence, and idealism, INFPs do well in climbing the organizational ladder. In some ways it aids and abets their high need to provide service to others, but it can conflict with their equally high need for perfectionism. This can result in an overextension of self and tireless (often perceived as thankless by the INFP) efforts for the organization. This leads to severe self-criticism because, in the INFP's mind, there is never quite enough time or the job is never done quite right. As such they can become martyrs, cutting off meaningful dialogue with the very people who are attempting to help them—superiors, colleagues, and subordinates.

INFPs are probably at their best when they are enabling others and satisfying their own ideals. As their responsibilities increase, INFPs are inevitably promoted into positions that move them away from the matters of the heart at which they had been so successful. INFPs would be well advised to think twice about accepting a promotion that may offer ego gratification but may move them beyond those activities at which they excelled.

A good example is the INFP pediatrician who gives up private practice to run a state or federally funded program in pediatrics, thinking it will benefit more children in need; however, the job ends up involving much more politics and administration than helping, skills at which INFPs are not adept. In moving away from hands-on caring for children and into a world of bureaucracy, the pediatrician is likely to end up with self-doubt, self-criticism, and unhappiness. If INFPs are going to broaden their service base, they must swallow the bitter pill and recognize when to quit, when to live with a product that is less than perfect, and when to recognize that others are not going to live up to or work according to their expectations.

INFP

- **Workplace Contribution:** Holds and protects the values within which are rooted individual, group, and organizational identities—often serving as moral ballast for organizations and teams.

- **Pathway to Professional Growth:** Must learn to face conflict and confront it in the moment.

- **Leadership Qualities:** Appeals to values through personal relationships—controlling tasks and people in such a way that those concerned do not notice they are being controlled at all.

- **Team Spirit:** Though teamwork is difficult and draining, collaborating and working together to pool resources and ideas is valuable and motivating.

Life's Conceptualizers

INTPs are free-spirited idea mills and absentminded professors, which makes them fun to be around, easily diverted, and a plethora of unending creativity. Their love of the abstract is sufficiently deep that it can lead them in the course of the working day through a maze of inventive and challenging programs, policies, products, and processes.

The INTP's source of energy and favorite turf is inward, reflective, contemplative thoughts (Introversion). Their perception of the world is conceptual, abstract, and random, with endless possibilities (iNtuition), which is used as the basis for objective, impersonal decisions that weigh carefully the cause and effect (Thinking). All of this is translated into a flexible, spontaneous, adaptable, easygoing lifestyle (Perceiving).

The INTPs' iNtuitive-Perceiving nature frequently leads them astray in the pursuit of new adventure, which can interfere with their need for time to be alone and to think. For the INTP it's hard to stay removed and reflective in one's internal world when the outer world is so full of ideas and possibilities. The INTP is a very heady, conceptual type, whose ideas can be pure genius. Sometimes these ideas get lost because INTPs tend to rework them continually and don't always share their latest thinking.

Both male and female INTPs face gender issues, albeit very different ones. The female INTP often finds herself between the proverbial rock and a hard place, in which society's traditional demands are juxtaposed with her natural preferences. For example, at one extreme INTPs can be somewhat independent, antiauthoritarian, argumentative, sometimes shy and socially awkward (depending on the strength of their Introversion), and not particularly given to most of society's customs and traditions. They are not against any of those traditions; it's just that in their absentmindedness they can often appear disrespectful of some basic social gesture or observance. Coupled with the Introverted-iNtuitive-Thinker's propensity for intellectual arrogance and impatience, you can imagine the trouble in which the INTP woman can find herself.

Generally, before any INTPs seek to engage someone on a particular subject, they will likely have done their homework. They do it for at least three reasons. First, they would not want to appear incompetent. Second, "homework"—research, reading, getting one's ducks in a row—is something INTPs enjoy and do very well. Third, in such an engagement INTPs want to present an impressive point of view that reflects intellectual prowess. Though the INTP woman wants to excel at all of the above, none of this is perceived as "womanly" by others. The dilemma is compounded since the INTP woman appears intimidating and even condescending to others. In any intellectual engagement the INTP woman is likely to win her case, but may pay a price in the form of alienating others.

In a system that does not reward Introversion—and in fact is distrustful of it—the situation may be compounded when the Introvert is female. While it can be intimidating to encounter anyone who is intellectually astute, cool, and aloof, it is especially unnerving when the individual is female and appears more scientific and studied than soft and solicitous.

Male INTPs may have a somewhat easier go of it because being cool and aloof is more in line with expected male behavior. Yet being true to type can still cause problems. Their easygoingness and conceptual spaciness, for example, can put them at odds with the Thinking-Judging management style of most organizations. There's always some reprimand in order about the INTP being more grounded and less "out to lunch." "Stop daydreaming and get back to work!" and "I'd like to see you show a bit more respect for rules and regulations" are two common demands made of INTPs.

Other problems stem from their lack of social awareness. While all INTPs are uncomfortable socially, this is more pronounced among males; INTP women seem to get through social encounters somewhat more easily. INTPs may find themselves at odds with co-workers for their lack of enthusiasm for organizational parties and other social events. It's not that they don't want to attend these things—they may find them tolerable, maybe even enjoyable—but when the events continue for too long or, worse yet, don't include any deep or meaningful dialogue, the INTP sees them as a waste of time. So, INTPs would rather just keep on working, finding "meaningful dialogue" in their own inner thoughts. Both male and female INTPs may end up feeling guilty for having forsaken their social duty in favor of their own Introverted needs, perhaps not having satisfied either. While feeling true to themselves, they may be thinking, "I've screwed up again."

At work INTPs are sources of ideas and inspiration who often work most effectively on their own. They are generally creative and given both to high energy and to occasional bursts of fun. They are not beyond dropping everything to join in on some new project or brainstorming session. They can be somewhat frustrating if one expects too much detail or attention to the bottom line. Time constraints are not top priorities for INTPs, and they may find themselves stretching deadlines from time to time. All life—including work—is an intellectual challenge to the INTP. Things need to be thought through thoroughly before being undertaken, and then perhaps thought through one more time. INTPs prefer that words and arguments be formed with clarity and precision. They have little patience for those who talk out of both sides of their mouth, or who make small talk, or who reflect theoretical inconsistency—being both in favor of capital punishment and against war, for example. Such inconsistencies, when encountered in a dialogue, may bring forth an immediate—and very surprising—eruption from the INTP.

INTPs are easy to work for and with and enjoy banter, independent thinking, and especially self-directed projects. All life is learning for iNtuitive-Thinkers in general, and the INTP embodies this most completely. Therefore, anything that can develop one's intellectual awareness has some value. From hands-on mechanics to proposal writing, it's one opportunity after another to learn, improve, and grow. Such drive is behind most of the efforts an INTP directs toward anything.

One of the strengths of the INTP is a penchant for independent thinking, both in themselves and in others. To be able to develop something from scratch and think it through from beginning to end by oneself is a sign of real maturity. To command ideas logically and consistently is a work of art. The great theories of all time, from relativity to personality, evolution to thermodynamics, Parkinson's law to Murphy's law, probably had their incubation in the mind of an INTP. Even if your idea is harebrained, seemingly impossible, or even totally wrong, if in the process of developing it you have reflected good logic and verbal expression, then it is worthy of being listened to, according to the INTP. Moreover, in doing so you will gain the respect, perhaps even the friendship, of the INTP. However, the closer a friend you are, the greater the likelihood that your intellectual chain will be yanked by the INTP, because friendship will probably be defined as a mandate to challenge each other intellectually.

A second strength of INTPs is their clarity of thought and word, which accompanies most of what they do. INTPs are the natural writers and editors of life, who paint pictures with words. Their capacity to say exactly what's on their minds and to help others do so is a talent not readily matched by other types. The mind of an INTP is a steel trap, always tracking a conversation and restructuring it into perfect expressions. They can often repeat exactly what another person has said, even months later. Should one try to fend them off with an idle promise—"We'll talk about it later"—the INTP will undoubtedly be back "later," reminding the individual of his or her promise.

Still another strength of INTPs is their vision and enthusiasm for whatever is being undertaken. Sometimes their Introversion may block them from expressing all of what is going on inside them about a particular issue. However, they can usually take the general thoughts expressed by others and translate them into an inspiration and vision that motivates others. It is a real talent to see the ordinary for what it is. It is the gift of the INTP to add to the ordinary so that it becomes extraordinary. Day-to-day jobs become far more fulfilling when they are reframed by INTPs as integral parts of an organization's mission. If INTPs are given a moment to get their thoughts in order, their encapsulation may well be artfully stated. An INTP may view this process as natural; to others it's seen as "inner vision."

Perhaps the first and most serious shortcoming of INTPs is a direct result of their strength in the extreme: a failure to translate their rich inner concepts into meaningful action. It is not uncommon for an INTP to perform a job from beginning to end—but only in his or her mind. Whether assigned to write a request for a proposal or design a heater valve, the INTP will start by gathering all the data necessary to do the job—reading, listening, investigating, or questioning others. But the next step—translating this research into a report, drawing, or plan—may never actually happen. The INTP may well have thought it through thoroughly, and in the process even become excited about it, and then, having thought it through to completion, can safely lay the matter to rest. Moreover he or she will lose interest in any further pursuit of it, having likely moved on to some new project. Clearly this lack of follow-through can be extremely frustrating to those who were counting on the INTP's tangible results. For their part INTPs can get frustrated, too, knowing that the job is incomplete, but having little or no motivation to complete it.

Another INTP weakness is their social awkwardness. The INTP can exhibit wide swings, from genuine interest in a few special people to near-total disdain for just about everyone else; INTPs may even be aware that this is happening. At times their keen interest in intellectual pursuits may draw them to one or more individuals, but such bonds can be easily broken should the intellectual focus move on to others. When confronted about their apparent fickleness, the INTP will likely deny it, act surprised, and promise to make amends, but it is unlikely that anything different will happen. It's simply part of being an INTP to gravitate to where the intellectual action is.

A third weakness of INTPs can be their low grasp of reality. Like other iNtuitives, and especially iNtuitive-Perceivers, INTPs can become very removed from the practical and realistic side of life. As a result deadlines get stretched, half-truths get told, and they can appear variously rigid or flaky when it comes to dealing with specifics. Moreover, their behavior can become anything from loud and obnoxious to pensive and withdrawn. Such behavior will become more pronounced as the INTP is increasingly under the gun to translate his or her rich mental ideas into tangible results.

INTP

- **Workplace Contribution:** Uses cleverness and independent thinking to problem-solve and reinvent, and in an easygoing, unassuming manner prods organizational change and improvement.

- **Pathway to Professional Growth:** Must learn that connecting and communicating with other people is important—great solutions and ideas are adopted and enacted through personal relationships.

- **Leadership Qualities:** Creates and works toward a vision and a better solution and allows others to follow at their own pace and ability.

- **Team Spirit:** A team is okay if it allows members to enter on their own terms and to contribute in their own way—but the best visioning and problem solving is done in isolation.

The very intellectual basis of most of our life would not exist were it not for the INTP. Whether as teachers of higher education, scientists, editors, or computer programmers, they are the architects of our ideas. INTPs provide the conceptual framework by which manuals, organizational procedures, and even work assignments are translated and put into action.

Making the Most of the Moment

The ESTP is a somewhat risk-taking, entrepreneurial, give-it-a-go person, a type with a real flair for most things. The ESTP has a fly-by-the-seat-of-the-pants attitude and is pleased to have everyone know about it. With a basic built-in restlessness, these are the hyperactive "doers," who like to keep their hands in a variety of pots, churning as much as they can to keep everyone on their toes and to keep life exciting.

ESTPs prefer to scan the external world of people, things, and action (Extraversion). They perceive the world in a hands-on, grounded fashion (Sensing), which they use as the basis for objective and impersonal cause-and-effect–based decisions (Thinking). All of this is constantly and immediately translated through a lifestyle that is spontaneous, flexible, and responsive to whatever happens (Perceiving). As a result of being so grounded and so Extraverted, ESTPs tend to be up-front and "out there" about life, capitalizing on each moment—because that's all one can be sure of. You only go around once in life, the ESTP believes, and it is incumbent on each individual to make the most of it. For example, ESTPs can be so wrapped up in the moment that they can tell a story, overload it with exciting and colorful details, keep everyone in stitches, and have no point whatsoever. Clearly this can be extremely frustrating to those hanging on every word.

The nonconforming nature of ESTPs can make life especially difficult for females of this type. Like other Thinking women,

they can become caught in the tension between social expectations and demands (to be nurturing and interpersonally sensitive) and their natural preferences (to be objective and remain
detached from personal involvement). As a result, ESTP females can be quite rebellious, further exacerbating their gender
ambiguity in the eyes of most sexist workforces. The combination of Sensing and Thinking—hands-on, tangible objectivity—
is, by itself, somewhat at odds with expectations of what is
"feminine" in our society. It is a straightforward, direct, nonpersonal approach to life. If the ESTP female is capable and effective in living her preferences, then she is apt to work in isolation,
shunned by women who may be jealous of her ability to remain
objective or by those who simply don't understand her. Men, for
their part, find ESTP women's direct, pragmatic approach to
life totally incomprehensible. Being a direct, witty, competent,
and somewhat risk-taking female, no matter how refreshing, can
leave old-fashioned colleagues aghast.

Like other Thinking types, ESTPs separate work and home,
public and private, personal and impersonal, and everything else.
If the ESTP female can accept these separations, she will likely
affirm that she is no less feminine and that her contribution to
the workplace can be significant. Still, she will be faced with the
challenge of convincing others that her competency and her
femininity can coexist. But this convincing will be best accomplished when starting from a position of self-confidence.

Male ESTPs have a somewhat easier situation—but only
"somewhat," because their restlessness, love of the moment,
and "fly-now-pay-later" lifestyle can cause them trouble when
dealing with the structured, deadline-oriented, follow-through,
focused workplace. So, while it may be more acceptable for
males to be ESTP, it is still a type that will receive inordinate
pressure to conform to the overall organizational type. ESTP
males will resent such pressures and may react with disdain and
rebellion.

The nonconforming nature of both male and female ESTPs
often results in their prematurely tiring of the structured workplace, sticking around only long enough to master some skill.
Ultimately, in their impatience, if they have not yet reached

retirement, they will take their skill from job to job or engage in some form of independent work, either of which will offer the ESTP more immediate rewards.

The ESTP's overall work style is a potpourri of many things, largely driven by whatever works for the moment. Given the right incentives or deadlines, they may dig in and be both productive and dynamic. When the pace slows or the incentives disappear, it may be time to put up one's feet and shoot the breeze with colleagues. Rarely are they restrained by procedures or protocol. The sum total of this is unpredictability: When an ESTP is around, expect a spontaneous argument or a sudden burst of enthusiasm that leads the rest of the organization into some new adventure. Such apparent leadership notwithstanding, don't look to an ESTP for direction; they are less likely to take charge than to get wholeheartedly behind others' programs.

ESTPs are masters at getting to the heart of matters. Don't try to baffle an ESTP with flowery ideas and words; they not only see through it immediately, but your credibility will be lost with your own eloquence. Getting on with things—giving something a try, even a less-than-perfect idea—is better than debating it endlessly or studying it into submission. Doing something is always better than doing nothing—that's the Sensor's motto—and if you're a Perceiver, you can always change horses in midstream if things aren't going well. No matter that you didn't follow rules and regulations. If you get it done, the mere accomplishment will mend any people or policies that got bent out of shape along the way. For the ESTP tomorrow is a new day, and most of today's stuff will already be passé or irrelevant. As a result of this devil-may-care attitude, ESTPs are usually controversial leaders or workers.

One of the significant contributions of ESTPs to the workplace is their appreciation of the present moment. If we learn anything from SPs generally, and ESTPs most of all, it's that the only moment we can be sure of is the present one. Guilt over the past won't undo what has been done, and fear or even anticipation of the future is fruitless. ESTPs believe that focusing guilt, fear, or other such emotions upon the past or future only tends to make us less effective in the present. Get what you can and move on. For the ESTP, you work hard, and when it's time, you play hard. Don't bother with work that is intended to fulfill some long-range goal or requirement; that's all a waste. If the present is less than satisfying, don't avoid it or wish it away— change it now.

A second contribution of ESTPs is their ability to bring options to immediate situations and to move beyond the routines that might otherwise stifle productivity. For the ESTP all life is an option, and if your bent is to try almost anything once, something good is bound to come of it. Everything is negotiable, and there are alternatives to whatever is hindering a particular situation or action. So try, and try again. The trying not only gives you something to do, but it will inevitably create other options.

A third strength of ESTPs is the grounded pragmatism that surrounds them in the workplace. Working one project at a time is akin to living one day at a time, and that's where one focuses the energy of the organization. The ESTP has a sense of precision and attention to detail that is profound and can be very helpful when teamed up with another type whose absence of detail could stymie the project. ESTPs' social gregariousness makes them generally good team players and, as such, quite willing to be sure the specifics of a job are covered.

It's this same live-for-the-moment attitude that can engender ESTPs with a laissez-faire mind-set toward dependability and direction. Just when one is counting on them, they can be "somewhere else," either physically or mentally. It's a classic ESTP excuse to say, "I really intended to be here to help, but at the last minute . . ." As a last-minute type, "last minutes" become excuses for ESTPs to be anywhere other than where one expects them to be. Such apparent flakiness is not only frustrating to more structured types, but it can be downright disastrous to productivity.

Another weakness is the ESTP's proclivity for getting lost in the details of the moment. Their love of facts and figures can lead them to gather information for information's sake, ultimately inundating everyone with data for which there is no meaning or purpose. Thus, when a colleague or superior is seeking results, the ESTP's response could be, "I'm working on it" or "What's your hurry?"—both of which may be accurate, albeit unhelpful. At their worst ESTPs can get so wrapped up in details that it can become difficult for them to sort out what's necessary to complete a project.

A third weakness of ESTPs is their highly visible restlessness when it comes to routines and other mundane details of life. You can tell in a second whether ESTPs are bored with something; they wear their restlessness and impatience on their proverbial sleeves. One can see how such impulsive behavior carries with it a win-big-or-lose-big price tag, with very little in between. Feeling types are apt to personalize this impatience, assuming it's their own problem, not the ESTP's. Other Thinking types tend to dismiss ESTPs variously as hyperactive, imma-

---

ESTP

- **Workplace Contribution:** Goes with the flow, adapts to the unexpected, allows variables, and delivers what needs to be delivered.

- **Pathway to Professional Growth:** Must learn to be patient with routines and to be aware that others may find comfort in structure, rules, and contemplation of future possibilities.

- **Leadership Qualities:** Keeps oneself and others on their toes by being open and responsive to the unexpected and abandoning rules of hierarchy and tradition in the name of expediency.

- **Team Spirit:** Teams can be fun; however, without constant action and variation, or in dull meetings, they can run aground.

ture, or someone who needs their hindquarters kicked for their own good. Clearly the ESTP would be wise to attempt to lengthen his or her attention span. Similarly other types would be wise to try to help the ESTP see that routines, even at their worst, are necessary evils; at best they can become a challenging and productive way for the ESTP to move through the day.

ESFP

Let's Make Work Fun

ESFPs love a surprise and are a surprise. It takes little imagination to appreciate some of the challenges and opportunities this type encounters in the relatively rigid workplace. Effervescent and exciting, free-spirited and fun-loving, nervy and nonconforming, ESFPs bring a breath of fresh air to any situation. Unfortunately, their free spirit can also be a source of frustration to others and even themselves. Like most Perceiving types, for whom turning work into fun is an ongoing challenge, the ESFP is the embodiment of fun. That's what life is all about. So much a part of the ESFP is this fun dynamic that when something unpleasant cannot be converted to fun, or cannot be avoided completely, then it is time to simply drop the subject and move on to something different. For an ESFP, if you can't enjoy the fun, then you should at least enjoy the bliss of ignorance.

Each of the ESFP's preferences spells fun. These people are outgoing, socially gregarious, and interactive (Extraversion) and prefer to perceive the world very realistically, tangibly, and in the here and now (Sensing). These perceptions are all decided upon very subjectively, based upon the interpersonal impact each decision will have on others (Feeling). All of which is translated through a flexible, spontaneous, easygoing lifestyle (Perceiving).

Such a combination makes for a quick and ready wit, sometimes rather pointed and direct, but always out there for all to see, hear, and experience. Failure to understand this upbeat repartee can lead other types to misunderstand the ESFP and perceive them as either very superficial or coquettish or both. Such misunderstandings, when they occur, not only are harmful to the organization but also belie the real social breadth and inter-personal awareness that the ESFP contributes.

Gender issues for ESFPs affect both males and females. For males, it is the Feeling decision-making preference that can cause them to be seen as too soft-hearted to be a "man's man." But they can compensate easily by occasionally talking tough or dropping a little profanity into the conversation. However, they must still prove that they are capable of completing assignments and following through on whatever project is at hand. While all Perceivers can be plagued with this failure to follow through, for the ESFP male it can make others suspicious of his competen-cies. In general, ESFP males rise high within organizations and are frequently well liked by their peers, assuming their quick wits and blunt remarks don't alienate others along the way.

Female ESFPs are often subjected to a very negative stereo-type due to the combination of a flexible public appearance (Extraverted-Perception) and their tendency to be literal and obliging (Sensing-Feeling). The result is that they exhibit some of the characteristics of a Gracie Allen or an Edith Bunker: flighty, airheaded, dizzy, or bubbly. It's not that they're dingbats; indeed many are extremely intelligent. It's just that their un-daunted literalism can make them seem out of touch. (Gracie Allen, when asked "What kind of book are you reading?" would likely answer, "A paperback, silly. Anyone can see that.") Others often react to such responses with quick, personal judgments, missing the richness, capabilities, and keen social awareness that ESFPs bring to any situation.

The overall work style of the ESFP is marked with high en-ergy and jovial interaction. There really is never a dull moment whenever an ESFP is present. They may not always be around when needed, they may not always be as timely as others might like, they may be overextended with too many irons in the fire (at least by some other types' standards), but they do accomplish what needs to be done. They can be as effective as they are pleasant to have around. In addition they will keep the office social calendar in shape—birthday parties, hails and farewells, or any other recognitions are capably attended to, along with the other demands the job may entail. (But not necessarily all of them: Their scattered nature may lead them to miss something important, from forgetting to bring napkins to failing to turn on the coffee maker.)

As fast as they move and as hyperactive as they appear, one would think that the ESFP would stay skinny burning up all that energy. But like their first cousin, the ENFP, both ESFP males and females can have a lifelong struggle with weight control. The combination of their preferences leads them to eat when they are happy, when they are sad, when someone new walks into the room, and whenever.

One strength the ESFP brings to the workplace is the ability to keep many projects moving at once. They motivate others when necessary, they freely pitch in and work side by side with any level of the workforce, they have time to listen to others' personal needs—all the while keeping the overall goals and deadlines in perspective. All of this is accomplished in a very pleasant, flexible, and accepting atmosphere. Emergencies, however large or small, are viewed by ESFPs as welcome relief, not as intrusions. A busy day with a lot of variety—and maybe a few things left unfinished—is a great day and a real motivation to be back even earlier tomorrow. A spontaneous break, or a scheduled one, is an occasion to get caught up on office scuttlebutt, and all of this combines to make the time pass quickly and productively. Working with or for an ESFP is rarely dull—and usually a great deal of fun.

Another strength of ESFPs is their ability to let others be different and to work at an individual pace. Each of their four preferences—E, S, F, and P—lends itself to an optimal awareness of the present moment and how unique and significant each person is at that moment. Consequently, if someone needs structure, the ESFP can help that person bring order to chaos, and by means of their chameleonlike nature, even become structured, too, if appropriate. They can affirm each person's efforts and are usually aware of how much may be going on behind the scenes, without necessarily becoming embroiled in it.

In bureaucracies or large organizations, they are particularly capable of working the system for the good of the people involved. For example, we knew a government employee who needed travel money late one Friday afternoon. Getting money that quickly and late in the week was considered virtually hopeless. Yet an ESFP colleague came through with the cash. Any ESFP would much rather accept such a challenge than stay working at a desk. With their friends all through the organization, and their ability to see ways and means around the various rules and regulations, ESFPs can in no time deliver the goods, no matter what the odds. No questions asked, the job is completed. Only a simple "Thank you" is required.

A final strength of the ESFP is their tempering perspective when deadlines become stressful. While other types may see the ESFP as irresponsible about deadlines and demands, as pressures close in, it is the ESFP, like no other type, who can identify with the frustrations, and perhaps the feelings of failure, and can say the right word or do the right thing to relieve tension and keep impending doom at bay. Rarely does an ESFP sit around feeling sorry for what's happened. He or she will face it, have some appropriate amount of guilt, then move on. Auntie Mame's "We need a little Christmas" in the middle of total financial ruin is a classic illustration of how ESFPs move themselves and others from life's tragedies to life's triumphs.

Like the other types, ESFPs also have their downsides, and one of them is overextension. While they may work miracles in keeping so many balls in the air, it is easy for them to overcommit and run themselves into the ground. Once the process starts, the fatigue that accompanies such a situation can give way to despair, distrust, doom, and gloom. Such behaviors often grow out of ESFPs' failure to pace themselves, and with the inundation comes the misery.

Another shortcoming of ESFPs is their disdain for routine and their disrespect for structure and order. As a result they may never be where you want them to be, when you want them to be there. Though they may have a reasonable excuse for their absence or tardiness, it may have detrimental effects in the long run. Perceivers generally, and especially ESFPs, have trouble recognizing that routines are a fact of life. By simply ignoring them in favor of whatever is happening at the moment, the ESFP can be an irritant at best, an obstruction at worst.

Perhaps another downside is their weakness in grasping the long-term consequences of their actions. Because they are so grounded in the moment, ESFPs often do not see the impact their behavior, decisions, or actions may have on the big picture. As a result the consequences of something so simple as a whimsical flirtation or an offhand remark may be far more serious than the ESFP could ever have imagined. The off-putting was never intended, but it nonetheless remains an albatross to everyone involved.

A third drawback of ESFPs is that their never-ending quest for fun may not be welcomed in a workplace that sees profit and productivity as serious business. Indeed for many companies,

---

ESFP

- **Workplace Contribution:** Provides high-spirited energy that keeps a variety of people and actions moving in positive ways.

- **Pathway to Professional Growth:** Must learn to stretch to face the negative, stressful, and even hostile moments of work. Life is not always a barrel of fun.

- **Leadership Qualities:** Has a personal and often playful go-with-the-moment style that can be highly motivating to others.

- **Team Spirit:** Teamwork is the best way to approach any endeavor; all the world's a team, and only good can come from such joined efforts.

workplace fun is an oxymoron; fun is what you're supposed to have at home or at the company's annual picnic. As a result some colleagues and superiors can hardly cope with the notion that fun may be good for morale and productivity. They may simply ignore the ESFP's overtures. More often than not, however, they invoke scathing judgments about the ESFP's behavior. For the ESFP, good intentions can quickly turn sour.

Such stumbling blocks aside, ESFPs are naturals in the human services. They make excellent trainers, educators—especially elementary level—religious leaders, sellers of almost anything, and athletic players and coaches. In these and other endeavors co-workers appreciate how effectively ESFPs accomplish what they do and readily begin to rely upon ESFPs to bring a special dimension of play to work, giving the workplace a little extra zip.

People Are the Product

One doesn't typically consider the ENFP's characteristics—effervescence, enthusiasm, and spontaneity—to be those of top corporate managers, but the fact is ENFPs do very well in executive roles. At their best they bring a refreshing alternative style to top management and decision making.

A zest for life combined with social gregariousness (Extraversion) is linked with endless possibilities and alternatives (iNtuition) which ENFPs apply to a host of interpersonal encounters (Feeling) while always working their day-to-day events so as to maximize their options (Perceiving). Like their first cousins, the ENTPs, they can exhibit wide mood swings—almost within the same moment—and probably experience higher "highs" and lower "lows" in the process. Nevertheless, they tend to bring enthusiasm and energy to most activities, which can be highly contagious, especially to those they lead. As they do with most things, their tendency is to convert managerial tasks to some sort of a grand game plan, then play it to the max, relying on their persuasiveness and creativity to keep people motivated.

The problem is that ENFPs can be so skilled at "flying by the seat of their pants" and doing a host of different things fairly easily—sometimes all at the same time—that they can neglect to make advance preparations. As a result, on any given occasion an ENFP can be found saying, "This is exciting, but I wish I had been a little better prepared," or "With a little planning, it would have gone that much better."

Though there are more female ENFPs than males, when it comes to promotions, it is the males who tend to rise to higher positions. This is a reflection not so much on the females as on the male-dominated Sensing-Thinking-Judging leaders who are doing the promoting. This can create some special problems. For example, because all ENFPs tend to be caring, empathic souls, their warmth can be mistaken as flirting or even worse, when this is generally not intended. With male ENFPs in higher positions, it sets up a dynamic in which their female underlings may become anything from flattered to resentful. What starts out as a natural warmth or affirmation can, at a moment's notice, turn quickly into a misunderstood innuendo, perhaps even charges of sexism or harassment.

Ironically, in their attempt to circumvent such scenarios, and because they are so readily adaptable, male ENFPs sometimes adopt a pseudo-ISTJ persona in order to project an image of toughness and masculinity. In the process they lose twice: Not only is their attempt to be something they're not less than successful, they cover up or deny their natural skills.

The female ENFP, too, has her problems. If she gives in to her natural ENFP tendencies, she may quickly become labeled "fluffy" or an "airhead," which may be far from the truth, her spontaneous and gregarious behavior notwithstanding. While such workplace qualities as warmth and empathy may be acceptable in males, they may not be in females. Her attempts to compensate by behaving in a more abrasive, guarded way fare no better.

ENFPs' ability to empower others is one of their most impressive contributions to the workplace. Unlike the control-obsessed Thinking-Judgers, ENFPs more easily encourage freedom and independence. In their persuasiveness they can easily accomplish the basic manager's goal of "getting work done through others" and at the same time make those "others" feel vital and useful in the process. Certainly there are some areas of work where they have some need to feel in charge—the specific areas may be different for each person—but as a general rule they are a reasonably nontoxic presence that gets thrilled about and revels in others' accomplishments. In the process there will be no hesitation from the ENFP in giving credit where credit is due. This can be inspirational, to say the least. Inspiration, rather than control, is key to the ENFP's management style.

Another great asset of ENFPs is their ability to generate options. It's always more exciting to engage in several projects at a time and to have more than one way to accomplish any one of them. Like the other EPs, this is an idea person who loves to upset the proverbial applecart and come up with new ways of coping with boring routines and slow-moving projects. Indeed it's often more exciting to generate alternatives than to complete the task at hand.

Still another asset is the ENFP's people skills. As a rule ENFPs give strokes freely and are responsive to other people's needs. They can generally find time to pause and help, affirm, listen, or do whatever else is needed to get someone unstuck and back into the swing of things. They tend to feel loyal to those who are responsive to their own enthusiastic way of relating, which in turn engenders more loyalty throughout the system.

For the ENFP stress generally comes in the form of those areas of their lives, private and professional, that cannot be converted into play or fun. As a task or responsibility drags on and its mantle becomes increasingly routine, the ENFP can become more pensive, moody, and even rigid. The more rigidity is demanded of the ENFP, the more rigid he or she may become, giving way to behaviors quite removed from his or her normal enthusiasm and effervescence. Filling out income tax forms, paying bills, working too much alone, or being compelled to meet specific deadlines are the kinds of tasks that set the ENFP up for stress and, in doing so, make them quite stressful to be around. Interpersonal conflicts and other "people issues" can all be distorted when the ENFP is stressed and can lead to wide behavioral swings by the ENFP. Such behavior has a tendency to spread quickly among others.

Those who must confront such behavior would do well to check the sort of tasks or work that is problematic for the ENFP. It is important to help the ENFP see that it is okay to work in fits and starts rather than according to some schedule. It would be even better if the task could be done collaboratively. Talking through the tax form is better for the ENFP than doing it alone. Generally an ENFP's stress is reduced by engaging others, even competitively. It helps them to attack stressful situations by creating a grand scheme growing out of whatever inspiration strikes them. Physical exercise, mental activities, and any of the meditative experiences are especially helpful to ENFPs, particularly when couched in the context of meaningful relationships.

A happy work environment is very important to an ENFP, and without it he or she can waste a great deal of company time on the wrong issues. Their natural ability to identify with others can mire them in unconstructive bitching sessions. Alternatively they can respond to a stressful workplace through avoidance—avoiding issues, certain tasks or people, perhaps even avoiding coming to work. In whatever fashion, it is an ENFP trait to become absorbed, perhaps even obsessed, with others' personal problems.

Though quite productive when allowed to work by themselves, those dependent on an ENFP can become frustrated by the ENFP's poor ability to manage time, work flow, and quantity. This can create tremendous stress among those around them. Another constant plague is mixed signals: starting one thing and either getting redirected, misdirected, or losing interest altogether. Again, this can be quite frustrating to colleagues and subordinates. If the ENFP is the top dog in the organization, his or her tendency to generate ideas or alternatives constantly—few of which may represent more than thinking out loud—is yet another source of frustration, especially to Judgers.

Their hunger for the excitement of the new and different can lead ENFPs to respond to the brushfires of the moment, to the neglect of ongoing duties and responsibilities. This sometimes misplaced enthusiasm can lead to the wide mood swings already mentioned and may result in any of the three physical maladies common to both ENFPs and their first cousin, the ENTP: headaches, upper back and neck pain, and extreme fatigue. With each day a series of more starts than finishes, the ENFP ultimately becomes unstable, undependable, fickle, and easily discouraged. It is the ENFP of whom it was stated, "The road to hell is paved with good intentions."

When an ENFP successfully settles in on one of the many career choices that may be at his or her disposal, the ENFP's greatest reward will come from those careers that allow free and nonbureaucratic response in some sort of service to humanity. ENFPs excel especially in independent sales, public relations, pediatrics, psychiatry, general family medicine, and almost anything entrepreneurial.

ENFP

- **Workplace Contribution:** Motivates and invigorates through inspiration, enthusiasm, and unyielding attention to personal relationships.

- **Pathway to Professional Growth:** Must learn to follow projects and commitments through to completion and to be aware that one's wide mood swings can frustrate and confuse those with whom he or she works.

- **Leadership Qualities:** Motivates, inspires, and cajoles people to accomplish tasks and to develop both personally and professionally.

- **Team Spirit:** Teams are fun and energizing—especially when conflict, hierarchy, and tight time lines can be avoided.

Progress Is the Product

When there's an ENTP on the job, one truly does not know what to expect next. It seems like every moment can be up for grabs when this generally high-energy, dynamic, creative, resilient, argumentative type is around. They are the embodiment of "If at first you don't succeed, drop it or try something else." Upbeat, maybe even tiring to different types, ENTPs are the perfect punsters. They would much rather engage in intellectual banter than complete some meaningless task or be quiet by themselves.

For the ENTP the public world is an exciting one (Extraversion). If things aren't exciting, the ENTP will likely want to go out there and make it so, because the external world is full of endless possibilities, random abstractions, and theoretical connections (iNtuition). These perceptions are filtered through objective, impersonal decisions (Thinking), none of which is terribly binding because each day brings new options, openendedness, and spontaneity (Perception). Hence, while ENTPs can be exciting, they may not be terribly committed to a schedule or project if a better deal or a more exciting challenge comes along en route. It's the nature of the ENTP to be living on the edge of the future, and sometimes the present—always expecting, frequently achieving, and certainly changing each situation. Change for the sake of change will teach everyone involved something, even if it is only the reality that the change was a bad one. The experience of learning even that will have made it all worthwhile. Following a star that ultimately goes nowhere is often better than being bound by a routine or caught up in some form of dullness or doing something that involves no learning at all.

The ENTP female's lot can be a difficult one because she is frequently greatly removed from any stereotypical expectations. She is driven by all the argumentativeness and chutzpah that go with this type. Qualities that will not endear her to her colleagues in the workplace include intellectual arrogance, impatience when things aren't readily understood, arguing for the sake of provoking thought, and talking out of both sides of her mouth in the effort to stimulate conversation. The ENTP commits this "dual-speak" to make others think, but it can be frequently misperceived as flighty at best and downright obnoxious at worst. Whatever, it's certainly not "feminine." Actually it's very ENTP and generally great fun. It's just that traditional organizations do not expect females to behave in this way, so ENTP females must compromise their natural skills and abilities for some form of social acceptance—or let the chips fall where they may, alienating the traditionalists. Occasionally such direct behavior can be seen as heroic by those who befriend the ENTP female. When her attributes are appreciated, the ENTP female can provide a significant contribution to the workforce as well as an inspirational challenge to most projects to be done.

ENTP males generally have a great deal going for themselves and are appreciated for their enthusiasm and intellectual insights. Their argumentativeness is frequently accepted as part of a male role, and their visionary nature is considered an asset. Perhaps the most negative issue centers around their Perceiving lifestyle—particularly their spontaneity and disdain for routine. For a heavily structured organization, such behaviors can be disjointing, to say the least, and counterproductive when deadlines loom. However, though occasionally frowned upon for such behaviors, the ENTP male still receives much more acceptance in the workplace than his female counterpart.

Interestingly, when either male or female ENTPs come to terms with the organization, they are frequently promoted to the highest levels. Their inspirational vision outweighs any of the problems mentioned above.

The ENTP tends to see the workplace—indeed the entire world—as one large board upon which the daily game of life is played. The game is never over. There are some wins and losses, but mostly it is one exciting challenge after another. The important thing is the challenge, not the outcome. "Did you learn something in the process?" "Is life (the workplace) better off because of the process?" "Has there been some kind of movement, some genuine reevaluation in the process?" "How ready are you to take on tomorrow because of what you've learned today?" These are all semi-rhetorical questions that underlie most of the ENTP's energy for daily work.

As a rule ENTPs can be quite competitive and very free-wheeling. As such they are more architects—who draw rough plans so that people and things can be shaped and reshaped daily—than hands-on builders concerned about the details that turn such plans into action. They have a naturally inquisitive personality that, if not recognized, can drive others crazy. They will "Why?" or "Why not?" a situation, even a completed one, to death. As Extraverts they are prone to overkill; combined with their iNtuitive-Thinking-Perception, they sometimes lack good social timing and as a result end up beating dead horses, arguing subjects long ago resolved, or revisiting sore or sensitive subjects at inappropriate times.

While ENTPs would rather be the one to come out on top in any sort of argument or engagement (Who wouldn't? The Introverted-Sensing-Feeler, that's who), the exchange itself may be compensation enough. While losing may be frustrating, the ENTP's respect for the individual who engaged him or her will likely be enhanced.

ENTPs are idea people. Their single greatest contribution to life and work is the creation of ideas. These flow from the ENTP continuously. ENTPs are entrepreneurs who are always sharing or selling their next great idea and attempting to generate some enthusiastic support for it. The more the ENTP extraverts, the more life becomes visions and possibilities. ENTPs can have an

uncanny knack for predicting trends in the marketplace or products of the future or other designs for work, play, or home. No
sooner does the idea flash through an ENTP's mind than it is instantly added to or enhanced. It may then be dropped should a
new idea forge its way forward. To start the day with one or two
ideas, engage or be engaged by others, and end the day with five
or six ideas is exhilarating to the ENTP. Though frequently the
ideas may be within the expertise of the ENTP, they are not
necessarily limited to it. As a result ENTPs really do broad-
brush life, probably giving a whole lot more than they take, creating more than implementing, starting more than finishing. But
that is their excitement as well as their contribution.

Another ENTP strength is their visionary enthusiasm for
most of life. At their best they hear a drumbeat from the future.
ENTPs live the science fiction, that which the rest of the world
calls farfetched but that eventually catches up with us. The
future happens now, because ENTP visionaries stretch the commonplace and make it happen. Don't tell an ENTP that we can't
fly a rocket to Mars, build a 200-story skyscraper, or communicate over two-way wrist radios. That will be an invitation for the
ENTP to prove you wrong. And in the process a new invention
or some small step for humankind may result. Never content
with the ordinary, always restless with the mundane, ENTPs put
meat on the skeletons of society's ideas. Such visionary behavior
is not only infectious but readily becomes the core of growth for
the next generation. We change, grow, develop, and break
through to new frontiers because ENTPs are the ones that force
such ideas upon the rest of the world.

Still another strength of the ENTP is their zest for life. Everything is an excuse to engage others. Where ENTPs are concerned, even "reflective listening" can be a competitive sport.
Academically alert, ENTPs often have diverse interests. Fed by
their idea-generating nature, these ideas spill over into a constant drive for competency and capability in a wide range of interests. It's common for them to carry on many projects at once,
not always related to one another. Simultaneously they can have
a hobby that's very removed from their vocation. On top of all
this they can be engaged in one or more community or social

functions. To each of these they will bring high energy, imagination, and creativity that will reflect a great deal of competence. While others can tire of or be tired by the ENTPs' upbeat nature, they will still be inspired by their presence.

Perhaps another strength is their relentless drive for competency in themselves and others. To see life as a daily challenge; to compete, stretch, share, and learn; always to strive to improve oneself and others—these qualities can't help but have a positive impact. It's part of the mystique of the ENTP that they push onward and upward for better and better, never satisfied but always trying to make what's good even better. Such a spirit captivates every entrepreneur, and it's just such a drive for more and more competency that gives birth to zany ideas, brings them to fruition, and moves the world a little further. Of course not everyone wants to be—or needs to be—improved upon. And colleagues and subordinates can easily tire of the ENTP's restlessness and insatiable appetite for improvement. That can lead to frustration and low morale on the part of the rank and file— ironically the antithesis of what the ENTP was trying to do.

A marked weakness of the ENTP can be their inability to follow through on their exciting ideas. If anyone has ever had an ENTP boss, each day can start with a project, only to be interrupted by another, and still another, leading to frustration and a certain gun-shyness about never knowing what's coming next. At their worst ENTPs are a rage of ideas with little or no follow-through. It is this sort of ENTP that earns the label *under-achiever*. They have so much going for them but often deliver so little in terms of measurable results. When ENTPs continue in this pattern, they can even delude themselves into thinking they have implemented or completed a project when they haven't, only to the dismay and disillusionment of those around them.

Another significant downside is the extreme mood swings that can mark their day-to-day existence. ENTPs tend to be extremists at almost everything, and their moods are no exception. Hence, they have higher highs and lower lows than other types, and these swings can occur at a moment's notice. In one breath the ENTP can go from the entrepreneur par excellence to a fickle, depressed, discouraged, self-blaming ne'er-do-well for whom no good word could be spoken. When they hit bottom, they only "yes, but . . ." any encouraging words with lengthy lists of reasons that "prove" their failure and incompetency.

Still another serious flaw among ENTPs is their inability to cope effectively with facts and reality. When details and deadlines pile up, the ENTP can either run away to a new idea or deal with only part of the situation. They then use that part to seduce themselves into thinking that the entire project is completed. The result is at best a half-done job, at worst a total failure, either of which undermines the ENTP's sense of competency and leaves him or her seriously wanting. ENTPs have real trouble tackling only a piece of a problem; they'd rather solve the puzzle in one fell swoop. Failing that, they tend to take

---

ENTP

- **Workplace Contribution:** Regards the workplace as a system to be moved, challenged, and reconfigured so that learning is constant and worthwhile tasks are accomplished.

- **Pathway to Professional Growth:** Must learn to focus energy on follow-through and completion—even when one deems them boring—and to remember that wide mood swings can send mixed signals.

- **Leadership Qualities:** Empowers oneself and others by challenging, confronting, and even taking an opposing point of view to enhance each individual's contribution to the end result.

- **Team Spirit:** Teams are one more important vehicle for learning—an arena for testing ideas, discussing differences, and collaborating on results.

flight, neglecting the matter altogether. It's hard for them to see that tending to the little pieces will ultimately solve the whole puzzle.

As with other types, the ENTPs' contributions seriously outweigh their liabilities. However, liabilities cannot be denied, or they will become stumbling blocks, tripping them up or leading to ineffectiveness. Through heightened awareness, ENTPs and those with whom they interact will be more readily able to benefit from this type's contributions.

Life's Natural Administrators

More than most other types, the ESTJ is the proverbial jack-of-all-trades. Given to accountability, responsibility, productivity, and results, this type is remarkable at just about anything they do. You can find them in leadership positions in a cross-section of professions, from law and medicine to education and engineering.

Outgoing, gregarious, usually quite direct, and very upbeat to be around (Extraversion), ESTJs see the world in terms of hands-on, practical, realistic situations (Sensing). Those perceptions are translated into objective, nonpersonal, analytical decisions (Thinking) and freely imposed upon anyone within earshot (Judging)—always for someone else's good, of course.

This combination of preferences gives ESTJs a propensity for seeing a situation as it is and moving themselves and others to develop a series of procedures, rituals, or regulations that will not only take care of the situation at hand but will also provide a framework for any future similar situations. It is this special combination of hands-on perception and analytical judgment, focused outward and set in a lifestyle of structure, schedule, and order, that makes ESTJs the administrators of the world. If you want a job done, a regulation established, a system implemented, or an ongoing program evaluated, call on an ESTJ to manage it.

If anything gets them into trouble, it tends to be their EJ

attitude toward life, a type given to freely expressed opinions. They can be surprised when others see things differently, and that can lead to some hearty, even abrasive, arguments. From the ESTJ's perspective, it's an open-and-shut case. Having packaged the argument so neatly and precisely, how could anyone possibly disagree? Indeed, from an ESTJ's perspective, most intelligent people would want to get "on board" and take advantage of the ESTJ's homework.

As a general rule ESTJs will rise to the top of almost any organization. When this isn't the case, it's usually because their EJ orientation has alienated others or their argumentative nature has made enemies of someone higher up. If they manage to keep this behavior in check and can show their expertise without accompanying impatience toward those who do not readily see how capable they are, then they are a natural to achieve leadership roles. They often do well academically, which allows them to carry the proper credentials, and they use those credentials in a very authoritative way, demanding respect. If Joe or Jane Smith has earned a Ph.D., and you were to address him or her as Mr. or Ms. Smith, you would be instantly corrected: "That's Doctor Smith." (Similarly it's the ESTJ who will identify himself as "Capt. Joseph E. Smith III, USN, Ret.") ESTJs command—and demand—respect from others, and they give it to others when appropriate.

ESTJ women face particular and unique problems. We've said all along that T women swim upstream because life in general, and the workplace in particular, does not look kindly upon objective, hard-thinking females. In this case, as Extraverted-Thinking types, they are not only objective in their decision making, they are also up-front and outgoing about those decisions—often to the intimidation of many.

Complicating matters are the two conflicting roles suggested by the ESTJ's four preferences. On one hand, their Extraverted-Thinking management style is to "take names and kick ass." On the other hand, their Sensing-Judging preferences call upon them to be traditionalists. For women, "tradition" is for them to be caretaking, nurturing defenders of home and hearth. That they instead are top dog within some organizational structure flies in the face of that tradition. The result is an ongoing war raging within some ESTJ women between what they would like to do (be leaders at work) and what they "should" be doing (taking care of the kids at home). Some women compensate at work by dressing and behaving in a way that is ultrafeminine: wearing lots of lace and pink outfits, being soft-spoken, appearing petite, and using a flowing handwriting. However dressed, the female ESTJ's inner conflict can manifest itself in a variety of mixed signals. For example, she may proffer a direct and harsh command with a soft-spoken voice or dole out a compliment in a seemingly cold, offhand way. Such comments may be perfectly acceptable when coming from a male. When done by a female (especially one dressed in frilly pink), they not only raise eyebrows, they also tend to affirm self-doubt, insecurity, and ambivalence within the ESTJ herself.

Should an ESTJ overcome this internal tug-of-war, and should she find acceptance within the workplace, the ESTJ woman will demand the same respect as her male counterpart. If so, there's nothing to say that ESTJ women can't be just as effective at any of the professional areas to which they may gravitate.

Because they are more common than any other type—in the United States there are more Extraverts, Sensors, Thinking males, and Judgers—ESTJ males fit most of the corporate norms, even the statistical ones. They tend to be white, male, appropriate dressers, trustworthy, loyal, reverent, and to possess most of the other Boy Scout traits. To them such norms underscore their belief that "that's the way life should be," an attitude they freely impose on others.

Because ESTJs are a take-charge type with very high control needs and because of their severe sense of accountability, they do not cope well when things do not go as planned. They have no tolerance for disorganization, tardiness, sloppiness, or inappropriate behavior (as defined by the ESTJ). All are invitations for a barrage of criticism. ESTJs have a short fuse when anything suggests they are losing control. The ESTJ can become loud, rigid, domineering, and can induce a great deal of stress within anyone nearby. (As a rule ESTJs are ulcer givers, not ulcer get-ters.) Not that this is malevolent. Indeed it is intended to fur-ther what seems to be a self-ordained mission to keep the world running and to keep people doing what they should be doing.

Because of this, ESTJs can have real trouble listening to sub-ordinates, or anyone else whom they define as unqualified to render an opinion. This includes children and others outside the chain of command. ESTJs understand how the bureaucracy functions and work it to the max.

The ESTJ's chain-of-command mentality may produce be-havior that on the surface seems inconsistent with the ESTJ's everyday style. Hard-charging, take-charge, high-ranking ESTJs can appear almost milquetoast at home or in social gatherings. Once the ESTJ decrees that the home is the spouse's turf (or the party is the host's turf), that spouse (or host) is in charge. According to the chain of command, the spouse (host) should give the orders, and the ESTJ will follow quite obediently. Hours later, back at work, it is once again time to turn the tables

ESTJ

- **Workplace Contribution:** Drives to take charge, to see the practical facilitation of a task, and to complete it with dispatch and skill.

- **Pathway to Professional Growth:** Must learn to be less hard-charging by listening to and allowing alternative viewpoints.

- **Leadership Qualities:** Takes charge, demands loyalty, pushes hard to accomplish a task, and tells it like it is.

- **Team Spirit:** Teams are an effective tool for accomplishing tasks as long as they are well managed and people's roles and goals are defined.

and take over. What is important to realize is that neither of these seemingly contradictory behaviors is inconsistent with being an ESTJ.

Their innate compulsivity makes it difficult for ESTJs to relax. It's been said that they are capable of turning reading into a competitive sport. In later life this can manifest itself in a variety of stress-related health problems and make retirement difficult and intimidating.

As they progress through life—and up the organizational ladder—ESTJs would do well to mellow themselves by exploring areas contrary to their everyday styles and experiences—for example, the soft sciences, such as psychology and sociology, as well as literature, art, and music. All may provide insights and inspiration that can help ESTJs to respect others' points of view and to appreciate that there is more to life than compulsive deadlines.

Everyone's Trusted Friend

Graciousness describes the general lifestyle of the ESFJ, and it also sums up their management style. From separating conflicted workers to overseeing the company Christmas party, the ESFJ brings an appropriateness and graciousness to whatever is demanded. Such a quality is both an asset and a liability. It's an asset because ESFJs motivate and encourage workers to accomplish goals, and the work setting is a very pleasant one, albeit somewhat formal. The liability can result in the ESFJ's allowing himself or herself to be taken advantage of constantly.

ESFJs are socially gregarious (Extravert), which is manifested especially in the precious attention they pay to both organizational and personal details (Sensing). All of this happens in an interpersonal style given to praise and other affirmations (Feeling) against a backdrop of structure, schedule, and order (Judging). It is the ESFJ manager who will remember names and birthdays and do little niceties throughout the workday. When one works for an ESFJ, he or she is usually quite sure of what the ESFJ appreciates and what tasks have been performed well. However, one also knows when a mistake has been made. The ESFJ's parental judgment, even impatience, is apparent even if no words have been spoken.

It is a Santa Claus management style, in which the ESFJ keeps lists, even mental ones, and checks them twice, noting who's been naughty and who's been nice. Score is kept by an ESFJ manager; it's part of the turf. Rewards are forthcoming for good work and critical glances and guilt trips can accompany misplaced work assignments and energies.

Gender issues are a factor among ESFJs, but in very unexpected ways. For one thing it is almost impossible to find a female ESFJ beyond middle management. The ESFJ is very traditional and formal, and in keeping with those traditions upper management is considered "a man's job." These traditions are so strong that they are followed even by ESFJ females themselves, who may likely turn down a promotion, preferring a man to fill that role. In jobs where ESFJ females predominate—teaching, nursing, real estate, and sales—they still frequently refuse the promotion to top positions in favor of males. Such refusal, while frustrating to other non-ESFJ females, plays marvelously into all of the ESFJ's expectations, values, and traditions.

For the male ESFJ it's a very different story. Their traditionalism tells them they should compete and rise to top positions. As a result they may be found across all levels of management, and in higher positions their competitive drive can make them appear to be super-macho among other men. In women's presence, in contrast, they are prone to behave strictly "by the rules," with nary a misspoken word or other inappropriate behavior. All of this is done with ease and facility, which makes them quite acceptable to a broad spectrum of types.

Those who manage to catch the male ESFJ at both acts—one minute acting tough and drinking beer with the boys, the next minute appearing suave and gallant among the ladies—may well conclude that the ESFJ is two-faced, perhaps phony, and not to be trusted. This is a false assumption, and should the ESFJ get wind of it, he will likely feel severely wounded, having considered himself to be of extremely high integrity. It is very important for the ESFJ male to recognize this possibility and to do what is necessary to head off such perceptions. Others must understand that this behavior results from a dichotomy between the Sensing-Judging traditionalism and the Extraverted-Feeling need to affirm everyone according to his or her differences. Although these conflicting forces may seem irreconcilable, to the

ESFJ, they're not. In fact to the ESFJ, relating differently to each individual is part of the awesome responsibility of effective leadership.

The ESFJ's strengths are many and varied. They are punctual, neat, responsible, and highly productive, with a great concern for others. In no time they can become the institutional memory and can generally achieve a favorable balance between the people being managed (process) and the tasks to be accomplished (product). These things combined make them friendly motivators for whom to work. They know when to push the workforce, when to hold the line and be firm, and when to back off and socialize. A sense of duty, loyalty, and ethical commitment to the organization are embedded deeply in the ESFJ's management style. They live and work that way—and expect others to do the same. Such commitment can at times make them seem like slaves to the organization. The ESFJ would see no problem with that description and would wonder why everyone isn't similarly inclined.

All of these qualities, while certainly admirable, can also set ESFJs up for some serious problems. For example, their good nature seems to be constantly tested by others. And when pushed to the limit, ESFJs are more likely to acquiesce than to hold fast. That's doubly problematic for the ESFJ: Not only are they taken advantage of in the workplace, but the residual anger may be carried home and directed to friends or family members. In either case it is an issue that ought to have been dealt with at work. Moreover ESFJs' sense of appropriateness can, when pushed to the limit, make them appear rigid and closed to new ideas. When backed into such a corner, it is the ESFJ more than other types who is prone to induce guilt and shame as a way of making colleagues or subordinates respond. They can unwittingly pour on the guilt—"After all I've done for you . . ."—which is neither becoming nor appropriate, especially at work.

Perhaps even more serious is the ESFJ's proclivity to avoid conflict. They would rather deny something's wrong than confront it. When a disagreement occurs, it is particularly ESFJ to sweep it under the rug. Failing this, an ESFJ will be inclined to buy everyone a cup of coffee (or chicken soup or beer), sit around a table, and say, "There, there. We're all friends. Everything's okay. What's the big deal?" A simple raising of the voice in a hearty argument or simple disagreements can be interpreted by an ESFJ as extreme hostility and ultimately destructive to relationships and productivity. Such a reaction generally renders the ESFJ somewhere between traumatic ineptitude and total frozen incompetency. What may seem to be a harmless yet necessary process—simple day-to-day discussions that move the organization toward its goals—can result in the ESFJ losing control and can leave them feeling very incapable. It may be nothing short of a terrifying experience.

ESFJs need to realize that conflict and disagreement are a part of everyday activity. They must understand that they will be respected far more for sticking to their guns than by caving in to other points of view in the name of harmony. They need to remind themselves constantly that conflict and disharmony can ultimately lead a group to increased creativity and productivity. Most of all, ESFJs must continually remind themselves in such situations that the disharmony is generally not a reflection on them and that seeing it through to a solution is better for all involved.

Given such responsibility and nurturing tendencies, the ESFJ can become stressed when people do not live up to what the ESFJ defines as appropriate and responsible. For someone in authority to tell the ESFJ not to worry about such things only adds to the ESFJ's tension; "not worrying" becomes another thing to worry about. Instead ESFJs need to talk things through with others. They especially need support, encouragement, and social connections during stressful situations, even though their own tendency would be to deny such support or to feel unworthy of it. Hard work, even busywork, is better than sitting around alone imagining the worst. Diverting the stress energy into some meaningful activity with measurable results and positive social reinforcement is probably as effective as any stress-reducing technique for this type.

Careers in which ESFJs excel include the social services—public health and social welfare agencies, for example—sales (especially real estate), school administration, and clergy. All of these areas allow ESFJs to maximize their natural talents to be gregarious, interpersonally skilled, organized, and focused upon others' needs. In addition, because ESFJs, more than other types, often find themselves in careers that result from emulating childhood role models, they can and do work well in many other fields for which they would not normally seem appropriate, including accounting, law, and engineering.

ESFJ

- **Workplace Contribution:** Builds a harmonious environment that supports personal achievement and task accomplishment.

- **Pathway to Professional Growth:** Must learn to accept differences, allow them to be expressed, and recognize that conflict is not always destructive.

- **Leadership Qualities:** Projects inspiration and graciousness with a constant yet gentle nudge toward task completion.

- **Team Spirit:** Teams are good and can be productive; however, arguments and disagreements should not be tolerated.

Smooth-Talking Persuaders

If you need to sell the impossible to a reluctant buyer and make the buyer like it, then you'll do no better than to call upon an ENFJ. These smooth-talking persuaders are life's salespeople, and once an ENFJ is convinced that you need the product in question, you will become putty in the ENFJ's hands. He or she will combine the perfect combination of words and rapport to clinch the deal.

Each of the ENFJ's preferences compound to make them a natural convincer. Their energy comes from the outwardly directed, socially oriented, gregarious external world (Extraversion). They prefer to perceive the world as having endless possibilities and meanings (iNtuition), which they use to make subjective, interpersonally based decisions (Feeling). They prefer to live their daily lives in a structured, scheduled, and orderly fashion (Judging).

When the ENFJ scans a situation, he or she is often aware of the many interpersonal dynamics that may be taking place. From the start, their iNtuitive preference interprets each party's actions and reactions—who seems stressed, who may need to be motivated, who should be reprimanded, who needs a listening ear—with their Judging preference providing direction or suggestions as appropriate, at least in the ENFJ's mind. Frequently their advice is apt, which engenders both gratitude and dependence on the ENFJ. When an individual or group doesn't pick up on the ENFJ's advice, the ENFJ can, in a moment, become bruised and angry at such ingratitude.

ENFJ females tend to fit in well at work. They possess a good sense of propriety, fulfilling a great deal of socially expected shoulds and oughts, not necessarily because they want to but because, as Extraverted-Feelers, they have a high need to please others. Generally they present a pleasant and acceptable image, acting out their natural caring and concern for others. Often they will be perceived as popular female role models, something they enjoy and espouse. If the ENFJ female has a failing, it may be when her idealism leads her to take a rigid stand on some issue, alienating others in the process. While her male counterparts are equally likely to do this, such behavior seems out of character for women at work.

ENFJ men, on the other hand, face more serious problems at work. They are confronted with the struggles of all Feeling-type males in the workplace: being perceived as tenderhearted, nurturing, and even wimpy. Consequently ENFJ males are torn between imitating a more traditional male role model (an imitation they can do very well) or giving in to their more natural preferences and risking being labeled as effeminate. If they opt for the macho role, their behavior may be accompanied by guilt and ambiguity about their identity. If they choose the more natural route, their masculinity may be called into question, leading to a variety of sexually seductive games intended to prove their manhood. In either case it's a serious struggle for the ENFJ male. One way they resolve the struggle is to be drawn toward careers involving psychology, theology, and other "people-oriented" issues. These professions are largely male-dominated, with a female aura to them: nurturing, caring, self-extension, martyrdom, sacrifice—all noble, but largely traditionally feminine attributes.

The overall work style of the ENFJ is upbeat, affirming, and usually marked with an above-average social awareness. Their iNtuition tends to keep them enthusiastic, even when the task may be somewhat dull or routine. ENFJs can seem like cheerleaders in such situations, calling forth others' loyalty, perseverance, humor, or whatever else may be needed when the chips are down. This is done by maintaining a positive outlook and generously affirming others. In fact, if they are not careful, ENFJs can be dubbed superficial by others, who see the affirmations as nothing but cheap talk. When this happens, ENFJs are cut to the quick, because they felt they were doing their best for the good of the cause, only to be shot down. Work should be a team effort, says the ENFJ, no matter what it is. And people need to be happy with one another, caring well beyond their individual job descriptions. It's "Go, team, go" from nine to five, followed by a beer or two together and anything else that will affirm the group and its capabilities. ENFJs have a listening ear for others' troubles and may even be offended if one isn't willing to bare all. That's what friends are for.

While all Feeling types prefer a happy, harmonious work environment, the ENFJ has an unusually strong need to be the one who leads the workforce to this goal. However, for all their good intentions, they can run afoul of others, particularly other Extraverted-Judgers, who may also be vying to take charge.

As a Judging type, the ENFJ usually has enough natural need for closure that deadlines get met and production requirements get fulfilled, though some immediate interpersonal need or human need may momentarily sidetrack them. This makes ENFJs very promotable within the organizational hierarchy. What usually motivates the ENFJ to climb the ladder, however, is not mere good behavior so much as having a vision that organizations exist to serve people. Inevitably, as they accept promotions, they find themselves at odds with corporate realities: profits, productions, cutbacks, and the like. The more ENFJs rise to the loftier positions within the organization, the more they may be setting themselves up for a struggle between their personal demands and organizational demands. At the higher levels such issues won't go away by themselves, nor can they be swept under the rug, as the ENFJ would prefer to do. For everyone involved, it will be much more productive if an ENFJ could be more in touch with his or her real drives and motivations and could consider whether they are realistic in terms of the organization's mission. This could save personal—and even organizational—heartburn.

One of the strengths of ENFJs is their capacity to inspire others. ENFJs have been called life's teachers. To the degree that teaching, leading, and working with others to accomplish something involves understanding others' needs, finding the exact words to inspire, and the appropriate affirmations along the way, ENFJs are naturals: Their Extraversion focuses the attention on others; their iNtuition can prove inspirational and encouraging, especially when things may be going badly; their Feeling serves as a constant barometer, sensitive to the people and the situation; and their Judging keeps the entire process task-oriented so that upon completion, everyone will have a sense of accomplishment. Generally people can face difficult moments with an ENFJ as a support and end up not only reaching a goal handily but coming to enjoy the process of getting there.

Another strength of ENFJs is their interpersonal skills. At their best they can keep any number of people, issues, and events moving toward happy conclusions. ENFJs are good psychologists, with or without training, and generally listen well to others' problems. They can also conciliate stressful situations that may be blocking productivity. (They are usually better at this conciliation when they are not personally involved.) All of this serves to make ENFJs natural sounding boards for just about everyone in the organization, a position that most ENFJs readily enjoy.

Still another strength of ENFJs is their ability to present organizational values for both the workforce and the public in such a way that all parties benefit. ENFJs are political animals whose mission it is to define life's values and provide leadership in shaping those values. More often than not, those values will be centered around interpersonal issues: making the world a safer place to live, making the workplace more congenial, having the organization do well by doing good. Hence, when an ENFJ is present, no matter what the product or mission, the people involved will be important and the human dynamic will be made a central part of the process. ENFJs often become the organizational conscience.

One of the drawbacks of ENFJs is the facility with which they can overpersonalize negative reactions to their ideas and ideals. "If people are not motivated by me or not open with me, then somehow I have failed," the ENFJ believes. The ENFJ can then become filled with a sense of inadequacy and can be almost incapable of proceeding. An individual who shares a personal problem or experience with a group could lead an ENFJ to wonder, "Why didn't she share it with just me? Doesn't she like me?" In the ENFJ's mind, because the individual in question had previously shared other personal issues, her failure to do it this time reflects the ENFJ's personal failure. This can lead the ENFJ to distrust her, perhaps even projecting that distrust onto others.

Another ENFJ weakness is the almost demonic character they can assume when their values are questioned—or worse, assailed. Should one question or challenge the validity of an ENFJ's motivations, the ENFJ will likely see that as a questioning of their integrity and trustworthiness. And it's downhill from there. It's almost as if the values had been formed by some force greater than the ENFJ, and to go against them is to go against the universe, in the ENFJ's mind. For example, should a group of co-workers reject the ENFJ's promotion of teamwork as a necessary part of the workplace—"We don't have to like each other to get the job done" might be their rationale—the ENFJ would probably feel personally attacked and may redouble his or her efforts. These people can become unbelievably rigid, admonishing others, "You are not only going against me on this. You're undermining the moral fiber of the whole organization." It is this overreaction that can lead others to consider the ENFJ fanatic, extremist, or simply overemotional.

A third ENFJ weakness can be a sense of guilt, inadequacy, or failure that can plague them for no apparent reason. ENFJs can be loved and revered by colleagues and staff and yet feel undeserving of such accolades or guilty over unreached goals. When this behavior gets in the way, ENFJs distort issues badly and can move through mood swings that range from "People are no damn good, and no one can be trusted" to "I've got to try harder and harder to get them to love me and my cause."

When such weaknesses can be kept in check, ENFJs can be infectious and inspirational at any level and in almost any job. As long as there is a need for teaching, promoting interpersonal skills, and exploring morality, there will be a need for ENFJs—and they will rise to the occasion.

ENFJ

- **Workplace Contribution:** Personally inspires and motivates all to work harmoniously for the common good.

- **Pathway to Professional Growth:** Must learn that not all situations need rescue and that disagreements are not personal attacks.

- **Leadership Qualities:** Empowers others to accomplish what needs to be done by nurturing relationships and making personal appeals.

- **Team Spirit:** Teams are good, people are good, and work is good when the theme of togetherness drives the task.

ENTJ

Life's Natural Leaders

The ENTJ has been called life's natural leader, and that's not by accident. The special combination of preferences gives this type the right mixture of basic leadership qualities: enthusiasm, vision, objectivity, and accountability. So natural are these qualities that it is almost difficult for an ENTJ not to step in and take charge. And they do it with such finesse that others tend to appreciate it and begin to depend upon them in any variety of situations. More often than not, the ENTJ is pleased to respond with facility and competence.

Their outer-directed, people-oriented energy (Extraversion) gives them a basic social alertness. They prefer to translate that alertness into possibilities, meanings, and connections (iNtuition) as they deal with their perceptions of events. Those perceptions are then dealt with objectively (Thinking), helping to create a vision, a strategy, or a complex system that will move the organization toward its goal. Their need for closure, structure, and accountability (Judging) makes sure that these visions, strategies, and systems are not left on the drawing board or lost to some abstract inspiration. With ENTJs, they are more likely to become finished products. As a result, it's an onward-and-upward, over-and-over-again kind of existence for all within the ENTJ's sphere of influence.

While all of the aforementioned qualities are indeed marks of a good leader, and while they are universally appreciated and respected, they are most commonly attributed to males. Thus the ENTJ female has a particularly rough course in life, if she has any savvy and gumption. Most of the words used to describe leadership can, with no effort, be interpreted as pushy and over-bearing when referring to females. Consider: *take charge, commanding, objective, confrontative, gregarious*. These are just a few of the descriptors that men are lauded for, but for which women can be scorned. The combination of Extraversion, iNtuition, Thinking, and Judging offers all the same behaviors in females as it does in males—strategies, visions, big-picture thinking, and impatience with those who see things differently. But an ENTJ woman is in a special bind. If she gives in to her enthusiasms of the moment, she can become downright intimidating to those present. On the other hand, if she denies these impulses to take charge, she can become impatient and irritable in relegating herself as a quiet, supportive bystander. ENTJ women can overcome this seemingly lose/lose proposition by staying objective in a difficult situation and by recognizing that though things may seem personal, that is probably not the case. They can also thrive by balancing their natural femininity with their natural leadership skills, recognizing that it's okay to exhibit both characteristics in the workplace and that these are in fact synergistic; and by recognizing that many of the problems they encounter are common to all ENTJs, regardless of gender. While these may not be panaceas for all ENTJ problems, they are good starting points.

As Extraverted-Judgers, ENTJs are robust, direct, and hearty strategists. Quickly and keenly ENTJs can see possibilities in almost everything and can act upon those possibilities instantly. They share their directions and opinions quite freely and easily, assuming that anyone who disagrees does so fully ready to engage in meaningful, albeit somewhat confrontative and direct, dialogue. For ENTJs that's how growth happens and mountains are moved. Because the ENTJ is something of a political animal, the communication process is one in which differing points of view are placed squarely on the table and opposing forces go head to head until a resolution is reached. This is a very exciting process to ENTJs. They see daily life as a kind of chessboard, upon which people, things, and entities are moved, removed, altered, and engaged—constantly for the organizational good.

Such objective, removed behavior allows ENTJs to become highly involved in many things and at the same time never really become personally invested in any of them. They can argue— they call it "discuss"—any subject with zeal and not be personally hurt by what's said, annoyed even that someone else may have become bruised in the process. ENTJs are often accused of sounding angry, a reflection of the enthusiasm and directness with which they freely express their opinions, all in the spirit of a healthy exchange. But the ENTJ may be neither angry nor uncaring and may find such an accusation surprising and infuriating. Similarly they can become deeply involved in another's personal trauma yet let it have almost no impact on themselves, a trait not always appreciated by others. An ENTJ might listen to another's tale of woe with genuine empathy, then moments later say something totally unrelated and seemingly uncaring; it's not that the ENTJ doesn't care, it's just that having gotten the problem out and "solved," it is time to move on.

The strengths of the ENTJ include their penchant for handling complexities. While they may go overboard and make even simple things complicated, their uncanny ability to arrange people and things in configurations that motivate and inspire is a rare and unique trait. ENTJs understand that success is measured in terms of what is accomplished, not in terms of how much one is liked by others. As a result they readily accept the hard reality that they may make enemies in making decisions for the good of the organization; like all TJs they would rather be right than liked.

Another strength of ENTJs is their ability to balance a vision of the future with an ability to take risks. Because they are structure oriented, they make better intrapreneurs (working innovatively within an organization) than entrepreneurs (working on one's own). In any case their risk taking is buffered by their need to produce bottom-line results. Unlike their ENTP cousins, who are prone to take more extreme risks—with bigger wins and bigger losses—ENTJs' risks, and rewards, are more moderate. This makes for an acceptable level of instability for the conservative corporate culture of most larger companies.

For the ENTJ all of life is learning, so one is forever a student. Any event that will increase one's mental capabilities—even something as mundane as a freewheeling office discussion—should never be taken lightly and must include intense involvement. Even when the event is over, the ENTJ will likely revisit it, restating what was learned, conceptualizing it, integrating it into the system—in short, beating it to death, at least in others' minds.

ENTJs pride themselves on their independence, and it is a legacy they would give to their subordinates. They want staff to be independent and freethinking and to disdain the "yes man" mentality. It is better to have challenged and lost than never to have challenged at all. The problem is that not everyone wants to be independent and freethinking; some simply want to be told what to do. This frustrates ENTJs to no end. For those who do not meet the challenge, ENTJs can become quite impatient and intimidating. This dynamic carries on day in and day out, even to those who meet the challenge. Those working with or for an ENTJ inevitably tire of this stress and wonder if there's anything they can do right in the ENTJ's eyes.

ENTJs' biggest drawbacks are their arrogance, their impatience, and their insensitivity. Their objectivity and love for the abstract provides them with a healthy amount of intellectual competence; they usually do well in academic pursuits. But they tend to look down upon those who don't learn or make connections as readily as they do. Because they are Extraverted-Judgers, they are not shy about informing others of their opinions of them. Such arrogance is demeaning to underlings and can cut into morale and productivity.

Similarly, because they have quick minds and readily see what needs to be done to move an organization or system toward progress, they can become abrasive when others aren't equally perceptive. They often have a short fuse for those who want to delay action in favor of more careful review of a proposed plan.

Their special combination of preferences often provides them with a good working plan of action. They are often right, and they know it. They view the process of getting others on board as a waste of precious time.

Another waste of time, in the ENTJ's mind, is having to beat around the bush in communicating with others. Their motto: Say what needs to be said, and let the chips fall where they may. Clearly such directness, combined with their arrogance and impatience, can at best bruise egos, at worst cause insurrection. Moreover, having placed themselves as the vocal arbiters of just about everything, they leave little room for their own shortcomings. When they do make mistakes, they tend to admit them with the same directness and arrogance with which they criticize others. Still, the rest of the organization takes great joy in seeing that this paragon of competence is only human.

In short, ENTJs are natural architects, and this in fact is one

ENTJ

- **Workplace Contribution:** Through hard-charging arguments and action, intellectually inspires and challenges everyone to experience a vision and to move toward its fulfillment with dispatch.

- **Pathway to Professional Growth:** Must learn to allow time for others to develop at their own pace and level of commitment.

- **Leadership Qualities:** Is task-driven and demanding, with a motivational spin for everyone to get on board and move toward achieving the goal.

- **Team Spirit:** Teams can be good and do provide opportunities for more involvement—as long as the task is completed and the group's process does not slow or water down the vision.

of the careers in which they abound. But they are not limited to designing buildings. They are equally capable in careers that allow them to design institutions, programs, even people's lives. They make excellent teachers, CEOs, and strategists, whether in the military or in government. Their inquisitiveness makes them natural scientists, lawyers, and journalists.

Afterword

Twenty-three years ago, Otto Kroeger and Janet M. Thuesen started a Myers-Briggs Type Indicator® training firm around their dining room table. Otto was a longtime psychologist and organization development consultant, and Janet was an education consultant in the White House during President Jimmy Carter's administration.

Over the years that followed, Otto and Janet developed a reputation for teaching type with such skill, relevance, and humor that they attracted students by the thousands, as well as other consultants. They were instrumental in bringing type theory to leadership development training in the military and in a number of private organizations. This was during the infancy of both the MBTI® assessment and organization development as a focused field. What began as a mom-and-pop operation soon grew to include nearly a dozen first-rate trainers and consultants and a sharp support staff.

We have since increased our number of consulting and training Associates to more than twenty-five, opening offices in Australia to keep up with demand. In addition to our two best-selling books on type and communication, OKA has produced an invaluable software package for consultants and trainers, and started cutting-edge research that looks at the connection between psychological type and college students' performance, and at how information technology work teams can benefit from type theory.

As you can see, while we are still the authority in the field of MBTI® qualification training and application, our expertise has expanded to reach far beyond the MBTI® assessment alone. Let us know if OKA can contribute to your future success.

We hope you have enjoyed the tenth anniversary edition of *Type Talk at Work*.

—Hile Rutledge
                CEO, Otto Kroeger Associates

For more information, please visit: www.typetalk.com.